GIRONIMO!

GIRONIMO!

Riding the Very Terrible
⚡ 1914 ⚡
TOUR OF ITALY

TIM MOORE

PEGASUS BOOKS
NEW YORK LONDON

GIRONIMO!

Pegasus Books LLC
80 Broad Street, 5th Floor
New York, NY 10004

Copyright © 2014 by Tim Moore

First Pegasus Books hardcover edition May 2015

5652   7418   06/15

ISBN: 978-1-60598-778-1

10 9 8 7 8 6 5 4 3 2 1

Printed in the United States of America
Distributed by W. W. Norton & Company, Inc.

Thanks to Paolo Facchinetti, Jim Kent, Matthew Lantos, Lance McCormack, Suneil Basu, Thierry, Emile and the other tontons, Fabio at Free-Bike, Paul Ruddle, Matt, Fran and Bethan at Yellow Jersey, C.D. Conelrad and many others at AS, my arse, and my mummy and my daddy.

The sun has just slipped behind the lonely Campanian Alps, taking summer with it and surrendering a dishevelled mountain-top lay-by to shadowy, misted silence. Briefly, at least, for an ugly noise now builds from beneath Monte Licinici's final hairpin, the desperate gasps and creaks of aged toil. At length, inching waywardly out of the gloom, comes the ghost of a bike, and hunched over it the ghost of a man. Even in this light the pair are visibly past their ride-by date. The man could, theoretically at least, be a great-grandfather; the bike could have belonged to his. Their geriatric struggle demands sombre respect, but doesn't get it, because the man is wearing a giant Rubettes cap and blue-glassed leather goggles, and when he comes to a squeaky halt in the lay-by his woollen-pouched nuts slam stoutly down onto the crossbar.

As formerly round objects, the man's reproductive organs are not alone in this scene. You now note that his bicycle's wheels are rather less circular than is considered traditional, and 100 per cent more wooden. The rear is unencumbered by gears, and keen eyes may spot the words 'VINI DI CHIANTI' printed on the crudely hand-crafted brake blocks. A wise observer – he's just behind you – might take account of all this, and the rust-mottled frame's heft and geometry, to date the machine to the very dawn of competitive endurance racing. That bicycle, he will tell you, is one hundred years old. And that man, you will tell him, has just burst into tears.

Set into the lay-by's rocky retaining wall are two weather-beaten plaques, each honouring a long-gone local cyclist. His unbecoming tears are a tribute to their lives and times, the glorious, brutal age of Fausto Coppi and a generation either side, when those who gave their all in the saddle stood alone as towering national heroes. He's weeping for them, and for anyone who's ever ridden a bike up a hill too far. Which, predictably enough, means he's really weeping for himself, because it is getting dark and he's a spent force in the unpeopled middle of a mountainous nowhere; because he has never felt so far from home; because he and his ancient steed have both aged twenty years since the distant foot of this mountain; because a largely decorative braking system means he should put his name down for a plaque on that wall of death before the forth-coming descent.

This is a man on the cusp of surrender: he has just emptied himself once too often, and is barely halfway through a ride that a century before decimated a field of braver, better and much, much younger men. All things considered, it's just as well that his nuts have by this stage long since been pummelled and battered into a pain-resistant coma, or he'd probably still be crying up there now.

CHAPTER 1

'You have some, uh, *expérience mécanique* with the bicycles?'

My questioner smiled at me across a stained garage floor bestrewn with dead and dismembered machines.

'A little,' I said. 'You know: *un peu.*'

This was a hard, straight fact, delivered in a deceitful tone of manly understatement. I had driven to a village in Brittany's damp, green fundament to meet this man, whose name was Max, and purchase the mountain of ancient bike bits he had advertised for sale. The trip had involved a dawn ferry and several hours of wet autoroute. I gazed across the jumble of corroded spokes, sprockets, rims and tubing and felt my mind clog with misgivings.

'*Voilà,*' said Max, picking up a dented tin full of hollow, square-ended brass bolts and handing it to me. '*Très importants!*'

I weighed it with a knowing smile, thinking: What in the name of crap are these? More generally, why have I gone to all this trouble for the privilege of filling my car – and then my family home – with rusty artefacts of largely unknown purpose? Above all, how had I come so far without considering, even once, the ludicrous enormity of the task I had set myself?

The hands that held this tin had not attempted such an overwhelming technical challenge since the Airfix age. The legs beginning to tremble on Max's oil-blotted concrete had last been put to sustained athletic use twelve years previously. Yet somehow I expected to employ these appendages first to assemble a functioning bicycle from the century-old components piled up before me, then ride it around the 3,162km route of the toughest race in history.

I passed the tin back to Max and asked him where his toilet was.

The journey that led me to this Breton garage had started sixty mornings earlier, when I opened the inside back page of my paper and read that US federal prosecutors were dropping a two-year investigation into allegations of systematic doping by Lance Armstrong and his former team, US Postal. The article ended with a quote from the world's best known and my least favourite cyclist, muted by his usual pugnacious standards but still enough to pepper the insides of my cheeks with angrily shattered fragments of Bran Flake. 'It is the right decision, and I commend them for reaching it.'

In June 2000, I rode the route of the Tour de France, a race that Armstrong was about to win for the second time. His first victory had seemed like the ultimate feel-good comeback: from the ravages of cancer to triumph in sport's most fearsome physical challenge. But when I watched his second – on telly and, for a couple of stages, from the roadside – something was beginning to trouble me. Not simply Armstrong himself, who although uniquely disagreeable, certainly wasn't alone in unearthing a previously well-hidden command of the core Tour-winning skill, that of riding extremely fast up mountains. It was a more general unease, a sense that even average riders seemed to be breezing through an undertaking that had reduced their predecessors to vacant, mumbling wrecks of men. As a physical challenge, it seemed much less fearsome.

Disquiet crystallised as I stood amongst the flag-faced young drunkards on Mont Ventoux's most brutal section, a pine-lined stretch so steep we should have all been roped together. Armstrong had already sped past us, in an elite group whose combined career accomplishments are now absent from the records or served generously salted. When two of his US Postal deputies presently trundled by – irrelevant *domestiques* whose work for the day was done – no one else paid much attention. I alone tracked their progress with wide, unblinking eyes. These two men had just cycled 140km at an average speed in excess of 35kmh, pacing their leader up three substantial climbs and the relentless lower slopes of Ventoux. I knew what they'd just done – a month before, I'd done it myself, albeit rather more slowly and without Lance Armstrong up my arse. The memory of that terrible, hollowing day was still fresh and raw, and here were these two blokes rolling up an especially tender 11 per cent slice of it, nattering to each other. Sharing a joke with one hand on the bars and the other scratching an earlobe.

This probably isn't the place to hold forth at righteous length about the curse of EPO and all the other forms of blood doping that have blighted professional cycling over recent decades (for a full overview, I would direct you to Jeremy Whittle's *Bad Blood*, and *The Secret Race*, by Armstrong's former teammate Tyler Hamilton). Suffice to say that all the bad thoughts came rushing back when I read that Armstrong, the cheatingest cheat in Cheatsville, had once again somehow cajoled and bullied and lawyered his way out of trouble.

The basely gladiatorial incident that hooked me on cycling was Stephen Roche collapsing just past the line at La Plagne in the 1987 Tour, oxygen mask clamped to his waxen face, eyes a million miles away, too far gone to grasp that his extraordinary, soul-flaying effort had all but won him the race. That, with apologies to Roche's mother, was what Grand Tours were supposed to be about. As if to emphasise the extent to which they no longer were, during the 2001 Tour I had to put up with Armstrong feigning exhaustion, gasping theatrically for the cameras before slipping away to victory up Alpe d'Huez without breaking sweat.

In the years that followed, improved drug-testing and public opprobrium at least reined in the blood-doping free-for-all. But something had changed, and for good. Riders, in the preferred argot of endurance sport, just didn't seem to bury themselves any more. Legs seemed fresher and so did minds. Races became ever more predictable, more calculated, more professional in the worst sense of the word. When the camera closed in on a rider's face, you rarely saw suffering. You saw concentration.

Sport, of course, was the real loser in all this. Sport, and me. I had pushed myself to the vomity edge of my capabilities riding the Tour route, and now people would look at these focused cyclo-bots pedalling calmly around it and think: Meh. Every race that finished without some shattered Rochian collapse seemed to erode my accomplishment. The age of blood, sweat and tears – my age – was fading into sepia-toned history.

Three months after my Tour ride, I went up to Manchester to watch Chris Boardman take on Eddy Merckx's twenty-eight-year-old hour record. Boardman had, in fact, already beaten the mark on several occasions, and by gigantic margins: four years previously, he had cycled almost seven kilometres further than the 49.5 that Eddy had managed in sixty minutes. The intensity of Merckx's 1972 effort – he called it the hardest ride of his life – took something out of the great man that he would never recover. Boardman, though an indubitably talented athlete, was no Merckx: his Eddy-battering achievements were a tribute to the technology and wind-tunnel ergonomics of a new era. Chris Boardman piloted a disc-wheeled carbon-fibre space-racer with his arms out like Superman and a big plastic teardrop on his head. Eddy had just stuck on his old leather-sausage track helmet and ridden a bike.

Shortly after Boardman rode 56km in an hour, the cycling authorities drew up new rules to defend the integrity of the sport's blue-riband record. Merckx's distance was reinstated as the official mark; any future attempt to better it would have to be undertaken in comparable fashion. Old-school bike, equipment, riding position. When Boardman accepted the challenge, it seemed almost foolhardy. I remember looking at him as he sat on the start line astride his stock, steel-framed track bike, thinking: Fair play for giving this a go, Chris, but you're not going to make it. He very nearly didn't. As the velodrome roof loudly rose, a superlative, bankrupting effort in the final seconds hauled him past Eddy's mark, by a mere 10 metres.

Spooning up the last Bran Flakes, I thought of Boardman, and how he had struck a blow for old-fashioned grit and old-fashioned kit. He had shown it was possible, after all, to reclaim cycling from the high-tech, low-sweat Generation Armstrong, clicking impassively through its electronic gears, taking orders from the cardiac monitor on its handlebars and the *directeur sportif* in its earpiece.

I noisily turned the newspaper page, feeling a quiver of righteous, flinty determination run up my spine. On another day, this neurological tremor would have fizzed swiftly through my synapses and been forgotten. Instead, and in impressively unanticipated fashion, the words of survival expert Ray Mears now caused it to splatter my brain with raw, claggy hunks of earnest resolve.

The interview laid out two compelling facts: Ray was precisely my age, and he was hanging up his bush hat. Announcing that he would henceforth focus on reviewing past adventures rather than planning new ones, Ray said: 'You get to a point where you can look back and enjoy the view, because you're not having to climb the ladder so hard.' Jesus. An ex-adventurer at forty-seven. Was I at that point? Was I shit. Speak for yourself, Mears. I've got a few rungs left in me.

I set my jaw, and scratched the grizzled stubble that lined it. OK, so maybe at my age I wouldn't be Raying it up in the woods, living off bark and making a tent out of cuckoos. But surely I still had some big bike miles in my legs, enough for a proper ride. Something epic, a challenge from the old school. Keeping it real, Boardman style, two fingers up at Lance and a salute in tribute to cycling's whey-faced, lion-hearted heroes of old.

The hour record was, I reflected, something riders generally attempted as a finale to their sporting careers. This would be the crowning achievement for what passed as mine. I was going to bury myself one last time, before someone else did it for me.

Obviously, had I known that Lance Armstrong would end the year thrashing himself ever deeper into the quicksands of disgrace, I could have spared myself – and more importantly spared you – everything that now follows. Blame him. These days everyone does.

*

How very rewarding it would have been to have homed in on my quest in appropriate fashion, perhaps through a series of encounters in derelict velodromes that led to a rasped first-hand account of suffering and glory from some leathery veteran, ideally on his deathbed. However, for an impatient man in the age of Google, that was never going to happen.

'Hardest ever grand tour'

Click.

About 3,900,000 results (0.38 seconds)

www.bikeraceinfo.com/giro/giro1914.html

'The 1914 Giro was without a doubt the hardest-ever Grand Tour. Only eight riders were able to finish this staggeringly difficult race.'

Confirmation of this stark verdict was delivered a week later, in the pages of a slim account of the event, embellished with some evocative photographs. It was written by a veteran Italian sports journalist in his native language, which presented certain difficulties: in 1985 I signed up to a course in Business Italian in order to gaze at an extremely beautiful young woman, then noticed she had really hairy forearms and quit halfway through. Astonishingly, this dried-up puddle of knowledge proved sufficient to translate Paolo Facchinetti's title, though online assistance was required with the subtitle and the rear-cover blurb.

THE 1914 TOUR OF ITALY: TOUGHEST OF ALL TIME
Those Magnificent Men on their Pedalling Machines
[translator's note: may sound better in Italian]
Eighty-one riders set off, and just eight finished. Terrible
weather conditions, appalling roads and 400km stages
proved too much for even the greatest champions of
'il ciclismo eroica' . . .

Il ciclismo eroica, as I was to discover, succinctly embodied the spirit I hoped to recapture. In recent years, Italians have developed a powerful affection for their 'heroic age of cycling', when the sport ruled supreme in Italy, and Italian riders led the world. Between the 1920s and early Fifties, Italians won almost as many Tours de France as did the French, while maintaining a monopoly of their own national tour, the Giro, which had cemented itself as cycling's second-most prestigious race, and first-most gruelling.

That the toughest race in history should have been a Giro seemed inevitable now that I considered the event's fearsome reputation. A few recent verdicts:

'The Giro d'Italia: Why Grown Men Will Cry', *Peloton* magazine, on the 2011 edition.
'A massive, brutal physical overload,' Dan Hunt, Team GB's cycling endurance coach, 2012.
'There's so much more carnage than at the Tour. You keep thinking: "Why on earth did I choose to do this bloody race?"' Sir Bradley Wiggins.

Of *course* my challenge would wind up being a Giro. The race that Lance Armstrong – hah! – dared enter only once, and then finished eleventh. The race that raised the curtain on Eddy Merckx's Grand Tour reign in 1968, and brought it down in 1974. And the race that introduced the world to Fausto Coppi, a template for tragic heroism and one of the most exquisitely flawed sporting geniuses of all time: a five-time winner in the Forties and Fifties who received a two-month prison sentence for adultery, gaily blew the lid off the sport's endemic amphetamine habit and died of malaria at forty.

As an unassuming specimen with ideas above his sporting

station, I'd always held a candle for Fausto, a beaky, pigeon-chested rake of a man whose physique made no sense until you put him on a bike. That silky, tireless pedalling action bagged him his first Giro at twenty, and an hour record that stood for twelve years. At thirty-two, riding towards his second Tour de France win, he set a time up Alpe d'Huez that no one bettered for three full decades.

As a mark of Coppi's extraordinary, transcendental achievements, my father – a man with absolutely no interest in sport of any kind – recently identified him alone in a photographic quiz of athletic legends that included Pele, Björn Borg and Muhammad Ali. (In the interests of full disclosure, my father spent part of his childhood in Rome, and was living there when Fausto passed through the city en route to his debut Giro win: '*Viva Coppi* was painted on half the walls in town,' he told me. 'Though to be honest, I only recognise his face from the adultery trial.')

So the Giro d'Italia was exactly the sort of epic challenge I was after: a hard race for proper heroes, which you could win on guts alone without looking the part, which was everything Lance Armstrong wasn't. I'd just begun to warm to my task when I made the mistake of opening Paolo Facchinetti's account of its uniquely onerous eighth edition.

The 1914 'Giro of records' in numbers:
- *Longest ever average stage length: 396.25km*
- *Smallest number of finishers: 8*
- *Highest percentage of retirements: 90%*
- *Longest individual stage by distance: 430km, Lucca–Rome*
- *Longest individual stage by time: 19h 34' 47", Bari–L'Aquila*

The Bullet Points of Doom in Paolo's foreword abruptly put my planned endeavour into perspective – on the *Spinal Tap* scale, too much fucking perspective. An *average* stage length of nearly 400km? On my Tour ride, 100 a day had almost done for me. And back then I was nearer thirty than forty. Younger than the oldest Tour winner. Younger, much younger, than David Beckham when he signed up for a swansong at Paris St Germain. Now I was the wrong side of forty, the extremely wrong side, the one hard up against fifty. At thirty-five you can still cut it. At forty-seven you've forgotten where you put the scissors.

The best I could manage for inspiration was Bernard 'The Executioner' Hopkins, who at the age of forty-six had just won the IBO and WBC light-heavyweight titles. But though Bernard made a great case for the physical feats one could still achieve in late middle age, he made a very poor one for their cost. Here he is addressing journalists before a subsequent title defence: 'I just found out a month ago, the doctor will be here before the press conference hopefully to explain this, but I must confess that I am not human. I am an alien. No, seriously. I'm from Mars.'

Try as I might to suppress it, the memory of my one significant two-wheeled undertaking of the previous decade now reared its putrid head. In 2007, the year the Tour de France started in London, I rode to Canterbury along the route of the first stage. My preparatory training programme reprised the schedule that had done me proud seven years earlier: do absolutely nothing, and get through on will-power alone, the 'suitcase of courage' that veteran cycling commentator Paul Sherwen so memorably references a rider digging into as he toils through adversity. In sedentary middle age, as I discovered to my cost, this metaphorical receptacle was more a 'handbag of sick'. With that emptied out onto an Ashford lay-by, I had nothing left in the tank. Many unspeakable hours later I crawled onto a train home, fumbling chips into my slack and pallid gob and vacantly submitting to a new reality: I had now passed the age where determination could stand in for preparation.

Possibly I was even too old to prepare. A couple of years after that game-changing debacle I went mountain-boarding with my teenage son, rolling down a Surrey hillside on knobbly-wheeled skateboards. As we never got up above a trundle it didn't seem like I was asking for trouble, but I got it anyway. An innocuous rollover on our final run somehow severed an important shoulder muscle – the one that lets you go about your daily business without imitating a 498-year-old Chelsea pensioner. It took four months to heal, ample time to contemplate a looming future of age-related infirmity. 'There's Mr Moore over by the telly: poor chap had a bit of a tumble last week. No, Mr Moore, that's *Countdown* – the Tour de France doesn't start for six months. No, *months*. MONTHS. Just give him a nod, he likes that.'

Every physical undertaking emphasised that these days I should be taking it easy, rather than contemplating the polar opposite. A year of weekly badminton sessions brought on tennis elbow and a dicky knee, while doing nothing to deflate my horrid first-stage man-boobs, those pert little cherry-topped David Cameroons. I turned our mattress over, as I do every spring, then couldn't get off it for two days.

That should have been the end of the whole daft business. Retracing the 1914 Giro was, quite plainly, no contest for old men. But there was a counterbalancing aspect to my planned endeavour, one that played very much to the strengths of a male's middle years.

CHAPTER 2

Ever since Paolo's book arrived, I'd been captivated by its illustration of the Stucchi road bike that won the epic race. Humble didn't begin to describe this rhombus of slender tubing, not so much low-tech as no tech: a gearless machine with chunky drop handlebars and a stout saddle, clearly plucked at random from the company's Milan production line. I smiled every time I looked at it: pure, simple, honest, the graceful antithesis of today's six-grand pro bikes, with their stubby, artless geometry dictated by drag coefficients, material science and biomechanics. After a while that smile hardened into a frown of covetous determination. With a bike like that I could pay proper tribute to Eddy and Chris's finest hours, to *il ciclismo eroica*. I could stick it to Generation Armstrong: out with energy gels and titanium, in with heavy steel and sarnies. Spending months trying to get in shape for this monstrous enterprise would be witheringly dull, and probably pointless. No, I would for now focus on doing what people of my age and gender do best – stockpiling rusty old shite.

Initial enquiries mixed good news with bad. Hundred-year-old racing bicycles were more common than I had anticipated, but also more expensive. eBays on either side of the Atlantic offered restored examples at a grand and a half upwards. A complete but very distressed 'barn find' wouldn't cost me less than £700. Italians, as I was simultaneously excited and disappointed to discover, nurtured an unrivalled attachment to bicycles from their golden age. Excited because I could already picture myself riding a wave of warm nostalgia through cobbled hill towns, and disappointed because this wouldn't be happening with a period Italian machine between my knees. Stucchi was a now-defunct marque whose survivors all seemed to be on public or private display. It was the same with the Mainos, Gannas, Globos and Atalas that had lined up alongside them on the 1914 start line. The closest I found for sale was a 1913 Bianchi, Stucchi's bitterest rival and the only firm still in business today. The pedals didn't match and it was priced at €3,400.

At length, ignorance and creeping dismay had compelled me to broach the final frontier of male desperation: I asked for help. One website kept cropping up when I Googled period manufacturers, a Gallic forum of old-bike enthusiasts that styled itself TontonVelo ('Uncle Pushbike' – in French it probably sounds less like the nickname of a wanted paedophile). These *tontons* knew their stuff but were refreshingly relaxed about its application. For every fanatically authentic, nut-and-bolt collector's rebuild there was a tale of some knackered old crock unearthed in a neighbour's shed, doused in WD40 and ridden to the shops until it broke in half.

As the nation that invented the bicycle, held the first ever bicycle race and still hosts the globally pre-eminent bicycling contest, I had imagined that France would venerate its related relics with the loftiest respect and price tags to match. I had imagined wrong. As the sheer number of barn-find stories on TontonVelo suggested, and as the incorporated discussion of comparatively modest euro-sums confirmed, there was nowhere better on earth to buy an extremely old bike. I registered on the forum, fired up Google Translate and posted a request for assistance in the 'pre-1945 racing bicycles' section.

Almost at once a private message arrived from a poster who called himself Roger Rivière. I rather wished he hadn't: Rivière was a rider who famously came to grief in the 1960 Tour de France, plunging through the barriers and down a mountainside while off his face on pills, and spending the rest of his days in a wheelchair. Anyway, this new Roger kindly alerted me to a forthcoming vintage bike festival in northern France, where he said I might be able to source a period machine. He also, more arrestingly, provided a link to a classified advert on leboncoin, his nation's leading online craporium. It was Max's, and offered the aforementioned mountain of aged parts for €400.

Having already spoken to Max, Roger reckoned this to be quite the bargain. Along with a great assortment of random spares, the collection included the full component pieces of two venerable machines. One was a 1940s racing bike, in which I had no interest beyond its appealing bonus inclusion. The other, though, was a La Française-Diamant. Having inspected an emailed photo, Roger could date this frame no more precisely than 1910–20, but that would do for me. I didn't know much about the marque, but I knew enough: Maurice Garin, winner of the inaugural Tour de France, had ridden to victory on a La Française-Diamant.

My heart leapt, then distended several neighbouring organs when I Googled up the stirring image of a grandly moustachioed

Garin astride his garlanded LFD at the 1903 winner's pageant. I'd wanted an Italian bike, but surely nothing could trump the daddy-champion's chosen steed. In my excitement I immediately booked a ferry ticket, then went straight outside and removed the passenger seat from my car to make space for all that wonderful booty. This took me four hours, which seemed a poor omen for the rather more complex engineering that lay ahead.

Anticipation and supermarket energy drink had fuelled me all the way to the end of Brittany, and over-proof trepidation kept my synapses a-tingle as I took stock of Max's stack. Most of it, I'm pretty sure he told me – all his English seemed to have been used up in that welcoming salvo – had come from the back room of a local bike shop that closed when its elderly owner retired. Wrestling my mind away from the appalling mechanical challenge it presented, I could see in this pile beauty and fascination aplenty. There was a brown paper sack full of winsomely engraved brass bells; a magnificent pair of ancient handlebars, splayed and sinuous like a detail from some old Parisian Metro entrance; a couple of hundred spokes in their original inter-war packaging; a tin bucket groaning with oxidised sprockets. Half a dozen wooden wheel rims, a crate full of brake bits and a shoebox of pedal parts, a mummified assortment of leather saddles and toolbags . . . tip into the mix those square brass bolts and a thousand more mysteries and this much was plain: I had myself a big load of really old bike stuff. Max, a compact chap of middle years with a trim grey 'tache, raised his eyebrows at me and smiled again. '*Il y a beaucoup*,' I said.

In French as rusty as the bits piled up before us I asked Max how he'd acquired this motley collection, and why he was now selling it. To introduce his explanation he led me through the garage and into a side cellar dominated by a gleamingly immaculate vintage motorbike.

'*Ma Velocette*,' sighed Max, gesturing fondly at this symphony of gloss black and chrome. I gathered that the La Française-Diamant was to have been the follow-up to this frankly overbearing achievement. '*Mais, uh, ma femme . . .*' With the shrug perfected by shed-centric tinkering husbands worldwide, Max indicated why Project Vélo had been reluctantly shelved.

In truth, he hadn't got very far. A single brake caliper had been nickel plated, and he'd crudely slathered the ancient frame with white primer-undercoat. This made for a fairly dismaying spectacle, though at least Max had wisely first removed the La Française-Diamant frame badge. Like a religious relic this was now housed in its own tiny glass jar, a miniature brass escutcheon emblazoned with the marque's name, its city of origin, Paris, and five 'diamonds' that stood proud of a glorious starburst. The shield that broke the finish-line tape at the inaugural Tour de France. I gazed at it with the portentous rapture of that Nazi as he opened the Lost Ark, then plunged it into my pocket before my face melted.

It was almost dark when I left, supervising a ginger three-point turn through the €400 scrapheap that entirely filled the car. As I slowly reeled Britanny back in, rusty tubes grazing my neck and my nose wrinkled against the scent of sour iron and stale oil, I began to consider again just how and why I expected to succeed in a task that had already defeated – or anyway been abandoned by – an inestimably better equipped man. Over many delicious crêpes prepared and more or less folded into my helpless mouth by Madame Max, I had been brought up to speed with the many relevant things that her husband was and I wasn't. Max was a plumber by trade and a ninja-grade DIYer by inclination, a restorer not just of vintage motorcycles but of nineteenth-century Japanese architectural models. Max had built the furniture we were sitting on and eating at, and was also a landscape gardener and a communist. There was some common ground between us, though, as it later transpired that Max was a thunderous bullshitter.

Riffling through the newspaper a few mornings after my return, I came across a large picture of a dismantled bicycle, part of a Canadian photographer's project to capture everyday objects reduced to their individual components. I'd always thought of the bike as a triumph of utilitarian engineering, an invention whose global success was dependent on its pared-down mechanical simplicity. The deconstructed bicycle in the Canadian's photograph was a low-end, low-tech 1980s Raleigh, yet this humble machine had, I learned, been assembled from no fewer than 893 bits, an overwhelming profusion arranged in neat geometrical groupings around the frame. Beside it were a similarly dismembered digital camera and a chainsaw, which together mustered forty-eight parts fewer.

I stared at this appalling image and felt my appetite ebb nauseously away. Unbidden, my career in bicycle maintenance now spooled through my mind. It didn't take long. At the age of twelve I could repair a puncture, as long as it didn't involve taking the back wheel off, a daddy-grade skill. At the age of thirty-four I could change a set of brake blocks. Between these landmark triumphs, failure outweighed success. Mechanical prowess was not my friend. Mechanical prowess didn't call or write. Despite hours of filthy-fingered, filthy-mouthed tinkering, I never even vaguely understood how to index the Sturmey-Archer three-speed hub gears that graced most of my early steeds. Sturmey-Archers had a knack of letting you down *in extremis*, when you stood up on the pedals to tackle the lower slopes of Hanger Hill, or to effect a blistering getaway from the gathered ranks of the 577 Crew. And when they did let you down, you knew about it. If you were lucky, the sudden loss of mechanical resistance introduced your groin to the saddle with great violence. If you weren't, it was the crossbar.

My passion for bicycles, rather than learning how they worked and what to do if they didn't, was their fantasised embellishment. A hefty chunk of my Ealing childhood was spent at the window of B & L Accessories on St Mary's Road, gazing wistfully at rubber-bulb horns and checkerboard go-faster decals, and with humbled unworthiness at the showpiece Huret speedometers. It was my dearest wish to grace my handlebars with one of these chromed French beauties. What a thrill to imagine that red needle wobbling past those art deco digits, clocking it right off its 40mph scale down Hanger Hill with the wind behind me. Then with a thwarted sigh I'd look again at the price tag – some forgotten but exorbitant sum – and accept I was stuck with my little fork-mounted mileometer, the one that reckoned Gunnersbury Park was the size of Belgium.

Over the years that followed, giant strides in reliability meant that ten-thumbed, half-witted incompetence became less and less of a handicap to bicycle ownership. As the twentieth century wound down, I was commuting across southwest London on a crap-arse Chinese-built mountain bike that thrived on neglect. Nothing wore out or broke off, and any other issues that arose seemed within my mechanical remit, unless they involved taking the back wheel off, a brother-grade skill. The brand-new, fairly flash bike I did my 2000 Tour de France on took even better care of itself. In a ride of over 3,000km, I suffered a single puncture. Occasionally one of the twenty-seven gears would slip vaguely out of alignment, but whenever the resultant *drrrrr-thwick* grew sufficiently irksome to make me wonder what on earth I might do to stop it, it stopped. I took enough tools and spare parts to, I dunno, make a robot scarecrow or something, and never once used any of them. Some bloke even sorted that flat tyre for me.

That was now, this is then: my La Française-Diamant scrapyard challenge represented a rude and rusty return to the era of needy tinkering. It was a week since I'd come back from Max's, and I squatted down on the patio with a slow puncture of enthusiasm. The pile of things I knew I definitely wouldn't need – principally that 1940s bike and three shattered wooden wheels – was dwarfed by those I definitely would and possibly might. I'd bundled the first of these piles into the shed, and heaped the last under a huge blue-plastic tarpaulin that was to prove an irresistible piss-magnet for the local cat fraternity. It had taken me four hours to bodge and bully the remainder into something you might see painted on a bike lane, and to suspend this assemblage from my newly purchased workshop stand.

From the shed-end of the garden it hadn't looked too bad at all: saddle, two wheels, handlebars, away you go. A few paces towards the house and things began to unravel. The wooden rims, resistant to my untutored fumblings with wrench and nipple, were semi-attached to their hubs with three spokes each and a cable tie. The handlebars, so becomingly profiled, were deeply and dangerously pitted with the rust that would be staining my palms burnt ochre for the next few months. The only saddle I could fit onto the seat post might recently have been dug up in the Somme.

Everything else was conspicuous by its absence. I'd failed to make any sense of Max's cats' cradle of brake stuff – perhaps two dozen sets, rust-fused together in a wooden beer crate. I similarly hadn't troubled myself with the cups, rods, washers and dusted, oily *confiture* jars full of ball bearings, some or all of them relevant to the bottom bracket, the bike's engine room, the stuff that goes in that round hole in the frame between the pedals. Hence no affixed pedals (from a choice of eight), cranks (six), chainring (three) or chain (eek – just the one).

I looked at the thing with my eyes half closed, then very widely open. It was true that bicycles hadn't changed much in one hundred years. It was even truer that this particular one would have to change enormously, and soon, if I entertained any hope of riding it up the Alps before it started snowing. To the optimist, that bike-alike crucifixion on the workshop stand was a start. To the pessimist – let's call him Tim – it had the ominous look of an end, some over-ambitious 'abandoned project' put up on eBay by a clueless tit belatedly trying to cut his losses.

Clearly I needed help, and those estimable *tontons* were able to supply at least some of it at the grubby-fingered click of a mouse. Many of their restoration tips proved encouragingly straight-forward. Corrosion, it transpired, could be magically lifted away by a long bath in a purgative solution of citric acid. I came to love everything about this technique: the faintly illicit purchase and delivery of bulk chemicals, the goggles-on dilution and immersion process in a dozen roasting tins on the patio, the mutant dande-lions that still grow up through the paving-slab gaps where I spilt a load. And how wondrous to behold the slow-mo rebirth of heavy metal, from corroded thing to smoothly machined, functional component, the chamfered edges and serial numbers that would ghost forth in the acid bath, then take hard and exciting form in the frenzied, patio-ravaging wire-brush assault that followed. My chosen pair of cranks were a particular source of post-citric pleasure, carbon steel re-endowed with the dour lustre of durable purpose, like something from a Victorian steam locomotive.

I couldn't decide what was more extraordinary: the time-rewinding effect of the acid, or the fact that these century-old bits could be so simply returned to foundry-fresh, full working order. The wear and corrosion on the pedals spoke of several decades of intensive use, followed by several more of damp abandonment.

After nothing but a citric bath they were good to go. We just don't make things that last like that any more. Why bother when machinery must now interact with flimsy electronics that are expected to fail in a few years, and in ways that no one is expected to fix? Who repairs a DVD player or a hard drive, when replacement is always cheaper? Nothing is built for the long haul. Once a modern car is ten years old, any breakdown more serious than a flat battery is likely to see it packed off to the scrapyard. Everything is under-engineered. Even spoons don't last more than a decade these days. Especially if you keep stirring citric acid with them.

It turned out I had quite a talent for soaking or smearing things in stuff, then rinsing or rubbing it off. I degreased axles, hubs and ball bearings in white spirit. The crusted saddle was laboriously revived with the entire contents of a very expensive jar of horse-tackle renovator acquired many years previously (at Cruft's, while hungover – you know how it is). I picked the best of the bells (its gilded dome advertised F. Pellen Cycles de Saint Renan – just up the road from Max's Breton gaff – in florid, *belle époque* splendour) and the most presentable old pump, and went at them hard with a toothbrush and Brasso. Then noticed I had scrubbed half the plating off, and went at them a little softer. These were happy days, filled with unchallenging, moderately purposeful pottering that seemed like excellent preparation, if not for this trip then for senile dementia. I think I could have strung out this gently satisfying phase indefinitely. Indeed, I did so for the best part of a month, until one sunny evening I found myself polishing up a second-reserve bell, and accepted it was time to move on.

Doing so meant requesting the input of my friend Matthew, who had helped set up my Tour de France bike all those years before. In addition to establishing himself as the headmaster of a petrifyingly vast school in Wembley, Matthew has devoted the time since elapsed to acquiring, maintaining and upgrading increasingly impressive bicycles, and riding each of them for several thousand miles. Leading him out onto my patio I expected gasps or even howls of dismay and disbelief, but Matthew appraised the rusty skeleton, warped wood and roasting tins full of fizzing scrap with measured insouciance. He squatted down to pick through Max's jars and boxes, and watching him nod and squint and tinker I recalled turning up on his doorstep the week before my Tour ride. I particularly recalled the uncertain laughter – *you're joking, right?* – that was his stock response to my last-minute technical enquiries.

Matthew had quite logically presumed, back then, that as a well-educated father of three I would have responsibly pre-equipped myself with at least the basic principles of maintenance before setting off on a 3,630km bicycle ride. Being twelve years older, I should, by traditional extension, be twelve years wiser. The procedures Matthew now ran through, tipping out jars of threaded rings and slotted washers into my stupid hands, were evidently second nature to any sensible middle-aged cyclist: he wouldn't insult me by detailing the tools required to strip down a headset, or appropriate headset lubricants, or what in fact a headset precisely was. For me to demand such answers at this stage would be like Neil Armstrong interrupting the Houston countdown to ask what all these buttons did.

Every spring I'd been round to Matthew's house to watch a stage or two of the Giro, and a stage or two of the Tour every summer. My passion for both events remained uninformed by technicalities; all the same, whenever Matthew took exception to some Eurosport pundit's critique of gear ratios or riding positions, I shamelessly echoed his tuts and snorts. When, during those endless ad breaks, he led me to the shed to show off his latest bike or its most recent titanium enhancement, I felt obliged to disguise my ignorance with some cringingly generic blokeism: 'That's a beauty' or 'Heard those cost a few quid'. It was much the same when the conversation branched out into vehicle maintenance, guttering or the best ways to avoid Hanger Lane in the rush hour. I had disgracefully passed myself off, to a friend I had known for thirty years, as a competent grown-up man.

Matthew left me with several useful-looking tools, a slow-burning sense of panicked inadequacy and the number of Jim Kent, a former teaching colleague. Jim was very much the right man – kind, know-ledgeable, breezily can-do – in the right place: a bike shop. Three days later I drove over to There Cycling in Hanwell with a boot full of extremely clean but still largely mysterious bike parts, and spent the first of many afternoons in Jim's little back-room workshop, drinking tea, bitching about Lance Armstrong, and toiling pain-fully away at his wheel-trueing jig like some village idiot trying to spin flax in oven gloves. 'Well, a bike's a bike,' he breezed when I'd rather forlornly emptied Max's beercrates and shoeboxes onto the workshop floor for his perusal. 'Anything's doable, everything's fixable.'

Jim didn't even dismiss my best set of original wooden rims, which after a good scrub had offered up the stirring legend 'SUPER CHAMPION' and the neat perforations left by several dozen Breton woodworms. 'Might be all right once you've got some more spokes in them,' he said, eyeing the lonely, cock-eyed trio inserted in each by my efforts to date. 'Have you fixed up old bikes before?'

'Not many,' I said drily, in tribute to a Scotsman I'd once over-heard being asked how often his nation had won the World Cup. 'But I'm learning fast. You could say I'm bike-curious!'

Leaving Jim with a smile of encouragement frozen to his face, I backed smartly out of the workshop and took a while to appreciate his front-of-house showroom. There Cycling specialised in retro-look machines, all wicker baskets and polished chrome. I found myself drawn to one that paid strident homage to the age of Maurice Garin: glossy black frame, tan-leather handlebar grips, bulbous buff-coloured tyres. Being called a Pashley Guv'nor, it was targeted squarely at the 'hipster bell-end' market, but running my eyes and fingers over its magnificent, funereal coachwork I felt a galvanising surge of hope and want. Whatever I had to do, or whoever I had to get to do it for me, my La Française-Diamant was going to look like that. I wouldn't just get the LFD on the road, I'd get it on the Corso Sempione in Milan on 24 May 1914, gleaming in the gaslight, Giro-ready, thronged on the start line by top-hatted sponsors and flat-capped fans.

This ambition – by rights a moment of delusional madness – matured into expectation with the infectious input of Lance McCormack, a friend of Jim who kindly dropped by to assess my project on my second afternoon in There Cycling's back room. Lance was immediately impressive, a silver-quiffed medley of mechanical omniscience, expensive tailoring and twinkly-eyed profanity. Our introductions revealed a stirring bond: we'd both been brought up in Ealing in the Seventies, and had both idled away large chunks of that decade with our faces pressed longingly to the window of B & L Accessories. 'Could have been there together,' said Lance, 'nose by fucking nose.'

Lance had, not quite like me, parlayed this youthful enthusiasm into a career in bespoke engineering. When he wasn't restoring vintage cars to the very highest standard for loaded enthusiasts, he did the same to vintage bicycles for himself. This was a man who had named his son Merlin not after the beardy, made-up wizard, but in honour of a trailblazing manufacturer of titanium bike frames.

'That's a fancy fucker,' he said, stooping to retrieve a chainring from one of my boxes. It was: a delicate encirclement of steel hearts that I hoped to marry to the LFD's bottom bracket.

'Forty-eight, right?'

'Not for another three weeks,' I replied, before Lance's expression – and then voice – advised me to be less stupid. He was referring to the number of teeth on the ring, and a count affirmed his estimate.

'Oh dear. You know the Eroica?'

I did now: it was an annual vintage-bike race on Chianti's *strade bianche*, rare survivors of the white gravel roads that formed the national network back in 1914. 'I did that with a forty-eight a couple of years back. Old chap came up to me on the start line: "*Quarant'otto?* Crazy English!"' Lance reprised the agonised thigh-rubbing that had accompanied this verdict. 'He was bang on. I suffered like a fucking dog. Mind you, two other blokes died.' Lance left this seductive precedent hanging in the air, and continued blithely rooting through Max's stuff.

'Looks like you've pretty much got everything,' he announced when he was done. 'Just depends how far you want to go. I like to get a bike looking just like it did when its first owner wheeled it out the shop.' He paused to show me a phone picture of the current pride of his fleet, a 1947 Hetchins, in precisely such a state. 'If that's what you want to do, I can help you do it.'

I found that I very much did, and a few days later drove up to an ancient light-industrial estate by the Grand Union Canal in Uxbridge, with Max's scabby white frame in the boot (that'll teach him to rip me off). The estate may well have been the most male place on earth, a ramshackle warren of gloomy corrugated sheds, each exuding its own furious mechanical din and bespoke waft of solvents. The dimmest and most distant was home to Lance's recommended shotblasters: in slightly deflating reality, my first serious step forward with this project was a step back, the removal of Max's horrid undercoat. I checked the unit number on the bit of paper Lance had given me, and refreshed myself with the instruction scribbled alongside: 'MUST NOT GO IN TOO HEAVY!'

Inside the shed, three men were gathered around a shuddering blast cabinet, inside which something metal was being viciously relieved of paint and rust. 'IF IN DOUBT, DON'T' read a notice beside this infernal machine, and while waiting for one of its operators to notice my presence I wondered how often I would fail to heed this prudent warning in the months ahead. At length, a man with an unlit roll-up wedged in his yellowing beard noticed me, and gestured that we converse outside.

Someone called Elliot Percival should by rights have been out spying on Napoleon or deflowering milkmaids, but this example had turned to shotblasting after several decades as a software engineer. 'I just wanted to get dirty,' he said, scratching a cheek that bore witness to this objective's very successful realisation. 'These days I don't even know how to turn a computer on.' My frame, and the detached front forks, were assessed with brisk efficiency. 'Looks old. Lance's stuff always is.'

I essayed an understated shrug. 'Hundred years, give or take.' A manly sniff; a pause for effect. 'Don't go in too heavy.'

I didn't really know what I was talking about, but how good it felt to say it, standing out there in the dusty, turps-scented sunlight, shooting the shit with smoking blokes in overalls. Places like this were now my realm; men like Elliot were now my people.

Newly enthused, I barely took my boiler suit off for the next fortnight. It wasn't always a focused operation. Having steeped almost everything Max had sold me in citric acid, I went around looking for yuck-encrusted household objects to submit to its savage rejuvenating powers: can openers, secateurs, the base of our electric toothbrush. I took my first tentative steps into proper stuff-fixing with the pump, which looked lovely in a piebald brass/chrome manner, but didn't work. There was a small eureka thrill when I found that the little hose I'd kept from some long-lost pump threaded neatly into the airhole at the end, and another when a leather disc in my drawer of old washers proved a perfect replacement for the perished scrap inside. Never has a loud hiss been so celebrated.

This was the stuff. I felt myself tapping into an indigenous tradition of DIY engineering that had run from the industrial revolution to my early adulthood, when taking broken things to pieces and fixing them with bits salvaged from other broken things was a core skill of the British male. My father had excelled at this, being particularly strong on the last part of the equation. Large zones of my parents' house are still set aside for the storage of old crap that Might Be Useful One Day. My mother's sisters used to swap stories about my father's adventures in hardware retrieval: he once pitched an aunt face-first into the Zephyr dashboard after an emergency stop, throwing the door open and rushing back down the road to retrieve a single screw he'd spotted in the gutter. ('Come on,' he told me thirty years after the event, 'it was a three-inch Phillips.')

Nature had short-changed his son on the inheritance of mechanical talents, but courtesy of nurture the cupboard under our stairs is dominated by a plastic cabinet filled with surplus IKEA fixings, dismembered washing-machine motors and three dozen other drawers of reclaimed ironmongery, most notoriously the one labelled 'Shit Nails'. For twenty years I have repulsed my wife's efforts to rationalise this ever-expanding collection, insisting, with ever-shrinking credibility, that one day its time would come. And now it had.

Quite suddenly, significant things were beginning to happen. I retrieved my blasted frame and forks from Elliot – stripped back to smooth, old gunmetal – and delivered them to Lance's recommended bodyshop nearby. Along with two litres of period-correct black cellulose paint, which I'd sourced with great difficulty: the substance is so exciting to work with that the EU banned it in 2007. Three days later I was back out on my patio, peeling away several yards of bubblewrap to expose the deep and timeless lustre of my freshly ebonised frame. I felt excited by how excited I felt. Who was this new Tim, thrilled to speechlessness by a diamond of metal tubing that some bloke in Uxbridge had just sprayed black? Who felt something close to shame in the contrast between this diamond's glossed magnificence and the merely presentable components he planned to attach to it? Who not only vowed to eradicate this contrast, but actually kind of did?

Courtesy of the *tonton* archive, this same new Tim discovered and slowly mastered *la méthode Piotr*, which sounded like a practice that would see you cold-shouldered by a disgusted community, but was in fact a potent burnishing regime named after the Polish-born *tonton* who devised it. Saturate extremely fine-grade wire wool with renovating car polish, gently rub in, gently rub off, repeat, repeat, repeat. Tim 2.0 acquired a number of microfibre cloths, and several delicate buffing attachments for his electric drill. He sent off to France for a large tin of rust-proof metal varnish, a gaggingly malodorous substance that took a fortnight to dry and endowed his patio with many of the most complicated stains that still besmirch it. He was, in all, quite a fellow, a tirelessly dedicated restoro-lord who only came to grief, as so many have before him, in the Great Roundening of the Wheels.

Matthew had already flagged up my severest challenge when he described wheelbuilding – the task of connecting a central hub to a rim with a load of spokes, then making the whole thing roll straight and true – as 'a dark art'. I put it off for weeks, then one sunny morning found myself with nothing else to do, nothing except arts that to me seemed even darker, like making sense of the brakes and bottom bracket. Now for it: when the last child had left for school, I squatted down on the patio with a wooden Super Champion between my knees. Arranged about me on the soiled paving slabs lay many packets of Max's new-old spokes, in assorted lengths and gauges, a big *petits pois* can full of oily brass spoke nipples – the former tin of mysteries whose significance Max had emphasised – and a step-by-step guide printed out from the fabled website of Sheldon Brown, late lamented Bikefixer General. Arranging the spokes of one wheel in Sheldon's recommended '36 cross 3' lattice was the work of minutes – 240 of them in all, after two false starts and one particularly enjoyable false ending. By the time I'd laced the second, the last child had returned from school, and indeed eaten supper and gone to sleep.

The next day it was raining. 'Don't even think about doing that filthy stuff in here,' said my wife when she left for work. This screamed out for a riposte involving nipples and rims, but I'd long since stopped seeing the funny side of the whole awful process. At the same time I just wanted it over and done with, so as soon as the house was empty I starting doing that filthy stuff right there on the kitchen floor.

Over the course of the next 72 hours, I discovered that my children have reached the age where a furiously foul-mouthed father is not to be feared but pitied, then sniggered behind. All that angry, contorted squatting also endowed me with the life-blighting industrial disease, Wheelwright's Arse – my first experience of an occupational condition since student-era flirtations with Asteroid's Finger and Miser's Bowel.

My brother, a more considered cyclo-technician with much related experience to call upon, came round on day two to advise me. The pursuit of roundness was, he said, a matter of delicate adjustment, a clockwise quarter twist of a spoke here, an anti-clockwise semi-tweak there. He explained the physics – tightening a spoke pulled the rim towards the edge that spoke was laced through, or something – then offered a demonstration. Complete with tilted head and gentle half-smile, this brought to mind a kindly piano tuner at his wise old work; ten minutes after he left me to it I was once again wrestling the wheel like a roaring-drunk pirate captain in high seas. I dragged the colossal bike stand indoors and bitterly rammed a rim into the LFD frame's rear-axle dropouts, the better to monitor my doomed quest for circularity. Great armfuls of angry lock with the spoke key stripped the threads off many an ancient nipple and began to ease my shoulder joints asunder. My thumbs burned and my haunches screamed for their lives. When my wife returned to find the kitchen commandeered by an apprentice wheelwright and the many tools of his unmastered trade, her cry of protest was muted by one glance at that terrible red face, aglow with rage, sweat and WD40. The family retreated to the front room with a takeaway, then filed silently upstairs to bed.

Five hours later I followed them on all fours. I had built a wheel that span without lateral deviation, but at a price: pulling the stubbornly warped rim straight had required a novel blend of spokes, thirty-two of them one size, and the other four half an inch longer. I can't imagine Sheldon would have approved, and there was a definite egg thing happening when I span the wheel and appraised its side-on profile, but it didn't look that bad. Certainly better than the second rim, which I had done my best to buckle into a scale model of that Anish Kapoor sculpture outside the Olympic stadium.

'Do you know what a Mobius strip is?' asked my son three days later, when it was safe to mention the wheels. I Googled it and saw what he meant. Then I put the rims, and everything to do with their stupid fucking adjustment, into a big plastic crate and hid it at the back of the shed.

CHAPTER 3

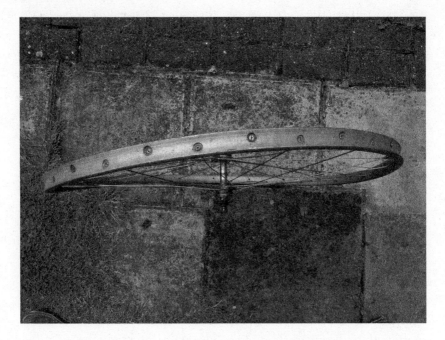

'Please, Mr Coppi, sir,' asked the wide-eyed young reporter, 'could you tell us what it takes to become such a great champion?'

'You must do three things,' replied the campionissimo, *leaning forward and speaking in a significant, confidential murmur. 'Ride your bike' – and now those around pressed in to hear – 'ride your bike, ride your bike.'*

Ahead lay many ordeals at There Cycling's wheel-trueing jig, but to cleanse my soul in preparation for these I now belatedly decamped to my training retreat. This state-of-the-art facility featured an exercise bike and a big telly, and was handily located in our loft. With a forty-eight-tooth chainring to power, I apparently had an awful lot of physical conditioning to do, and it is no exaggeration to say that in the following weeks I did some of it.

The cornerstone of my regime – in fact, all its other stones, plus its roof, front door and windows – was pedalling along to live coverage of real bicycle races. The 2012 Giro d'Italia kicked off on 5 May – in Denmark, obviously – and I was in the saddle from the prologue onwards, reacquainting my legs with prolonged rotary exertion and my loins with the unsettling sanitary-pad sensation of a chamois-cushioned gusset. I threw open the Velux, stripped down to shorts, socks and shoes, and lined up water-filled bidons on a bike-side table. What a stirring training-montage video sequence it would have made. I was there, spinning away furiously, when Mark Cavendish came horribly to grief at 70kmh near the end of stage three, eventually wobbling over the line with his left leg looking ready for a butcher's window. I was there when he somehow recovered to win the following bunch sprint. Up in the saddle and forcing round the pedals with the magnetic-resistance knob set to max, I was there for the 'queen stage' – a fearsome multi-Alp parcours that climaxed atop the 2,800m Stelvio Pass, a climb that pretty much did for me when I'd tackled it nine years previously, at the wheel of a Peugeot 206.

However, I wasn't always there. In fact, never once did I manage to complete more than three hours of any single stage – it was simply too dull. Beyond my manifold physical shortcomings, I was if anything more troubled by a total inability to match the peloton's relentless focus: my self-discipline was feeble and my powers of internal motivation seemingly nonexistent. I'd get distracted by the gorgeous scenery, or the race doctor's absurdly voluminous hair, then at misty-eyed length gaze down and note that my legs had stopped turning. And if the choice was an hour on the exercise bike up in the attic or an entire afternoon staring gormlessly at bits of La Française-Diamant on the patio, gormless staring won out every time.

I tried at first to keep a pedalling tempo sympathetic to Eurosport's enthusiastic main commentator – *Will anyone catch the big Dane? I don't think they will, I don't think they can!* – but inexorably fell into step with the unexcitable, often unintelligible monotone of his ex-pro sidekick Sean Kelly. How fun it was trying to square Kelly's feats of tarmac-ripping indomitability as the hardest of the 1980s hardmen with the faltering Gaelic-zombie mumble that earns him his living today. When Sean said a rider was 'uh, majorly suffering there' – as he did at least a dozen times every stage – he summoned all the vocal drama of Melvyn Bragg humming 'Blue Monday'. I tried to majorly suffer, really I did, but the image of Sean's great Easter Island head lolling towards the microphone put lead in my pedals. It didn't help that the space between me and my televised fellow riders was entirely filled by an open sofa bed strewn with squashy pillows.

As my virtual Giro petered out, I attempted to put a positive spin on its multiple disappointments. Twelve years before, I had set off to ride the Tour de France route with about 19 training miles in my legs. Wouldn't it be fascinating, I told myself, to find out if a man of my advanced years could still get away with doing almost no preparation for a mammoth physical undertaking? Fascinating and perhaps of ground-breaking medical significance. One man's monumental laziness is another's bold and selfless scientific experiment.

My training schedule was flatlining, and the restoration programme now suffered two reversals. I was in Jim's workshop one afternoon, on my knees with the figure-of-eight wheel wedged in his trueing jig, when Lance popped in.

'Of course authenticity is important,' he said, frowning at the wheel, and the stack of mismatched spokes I was preparing to cajole into it. 'But so is comfort and safety.' He stooped to inspect the rim. 'Is that woodworm?' I told him I thought it might be. Lance drew himself upright and tugged the cuffs of his immaculate overcoat straight. 'I love a risk, but I wouldn't ride on those rims down to the shops, let alone all round fucking Italy.'

A second opinion was waiting in my inbox when I came home. One of Jim's regular customers, concerned by what he kept seeing me try to achieve on the trueing jig, had put me in touch with Harry Rowland, doyen of British wheelbuilders. I'd emailed Harry some photos of my wayward wooden rims, along with the old spokes and nipples. His response was succinct: 'Last wood rims I built was twenty-five to thirty years ago but even then I had problems. Looking at what you have there I would go for new spokes and nipples and definitely new rims.'

I accepted these expert verdicts with a heavy heart. My quest for slavish replication was over: my hundred-year-old bike would not be 100 per cent authentic. Two days later this percentage took a rather more serious hit. I'd emailed Roger Rivière some update photos, proudly showing off the repainted frame and close-ups of rejuvenated components, and received a brief reply requesting a photo of the La Française-Diamant badge affixed to the bike. This was a pièce-de-résistance ceremony I'd wanted to save for last, but offering up that golden starburst to its home on the head tube for Roger's benefit I grasped the full and horrid significance of his enquiry. The rivet gaps on the rear of the badge completely failed to align with the requisite little mounting holes in the frame. I clattered out a panicky email, to which Roger responded with a gentle enquiry: had I noticed the word stamped into the cranks and saddle? I had indeed, but my assumption that 'BRILLANT' denoted a top-of-the-range La Française-Diamant model was now Rogered to death: Brillant, he explained, was an entirely unrelated manufacturer of complete bicycles.

I Googled it and found myself presented with promotional posters of Brillants in period environments. The era was right but the scenarios were not. LFD adverts had depicted Garin and other moustachioed 'giants of the road' barrelling around banked velodromes or smoothly outsprinting rivals at a crowd-thronged stage finish. A Brillant, on the other hand, seemed pitched at the easy-going customs official with a lot of windmills to gaze at. The only poster to depict a Brillant in action showed one being piloted by a terrified caricature strongly suggestive of Kenny from *South Park*. There was no online evidence of a Brillant cycling team, or that any Brillant had ever been competitively raced.

I shuffled wanly out to the patio, and looked at my bike through new eyes, the eyes of a less gullible imbecile. Of course that saddle – broad enough for a shot-putter's arse and stretched over a monumental double-sprung chassis – wasn't a racing saddle. The same went for those weighty, indestructible cranks, and the handlebars, distinctly more sit-up-and-beg than head-down-and-hurtle. Roger and I had both been confused by Max's bewildering assortment of stuff, and deceived by his warm credibility. The old dog had sold me a pup.

'Fuck-trumpets' seemed as good a word as any to describe this development, though I also tried out a number of loud alternatives. All that time invested, all that acid infused, spilt and inhaled, all that hard sodding cash spent – on a pig-iron clunker built to lug some fat-faced district nurse about her rounds. But I was in too deep now, and no amount of garden swearing could get me out of it. I'd have to make the best of this very bad job, and get the bike formerly known as LFD back on the road and primed for the creaky, cumbersome sloth it was designed for. Bloody Brillant.

*

The history of transport is bound up with the twin human urges to invent, then recklessly compete. The horse and cart swiftly begat the chariots of Ben Hur. When dragon boats first raced on the Yangtze, over 2,500 years ago, fatalities were obligatory: if nobody fell overboard and drowned, crews put down their paddles and pelted each other with rocks until someone stopped breathing. In 1784, just months after the Montgolfier brothers launched a sheep, a duck and a cockerel into the Versailles sky, an inaugural balloon race for over-venturesome humans was held at Heveningham Hall in Suffolk. As the prevailing wind would have swiftly ferried competitors beyond the coast of the North Sea, it's perhaps no surprise to find history drawing an embarrassed veil over the outcome.

So it was with the velocipede – the 'speedy foot' whose very name implied something racier than just a practical means of getting about. The first bicycle was patented in 1818 by Baron

Karl von Drais, in response to a famine that had decimated Germany's horse population. His pedalless 'Draisine hobby horse' was propelled by pushing those aristocratic tippy-toes against the ground, a prancingly foolish spectacle that would have raised louder chuckles in the upper Rhine valleys if von Drais hadn't been collecting taxes on behalf of the local Grand Duke. And with unparalleled haste: the Draisine was clocked at an ear-bleeding 12mph, enough to have it banned from the streets of Karlsruhe by a terrified citizenry.

The baron's invention sparked off a velocipede craze that swept through Europe and the US in 1819. The 'dandy horse' was so nicknamed in honour of its popularity with the fast young ponce about town, venting his Mr Toad tendency and wearing out his boot soles in lunatic pedestrian-slalom speed trials along city pavements. One London manufacturer sold 320 in the first few months of the year, and ran two riding schools in Soho and the Strand. But hefty £2 fines for dangerous riding, ratcheting public abuse and unsustainable cobblers' bills killed the dandy horse off in a year.

For half a century the velocipede receded from memory, a pioneering false dawn in personal transport later emulated by heroic, ridicule-resistant early adopters of the Sinclair C5 and the Segway. It wasn't until 1867 that a Parisian blacksmith, tinkering with an antique hobby horse in his workshop off the Champs-Elysées, made the advance that overnight transformed this defunct prannet's plaything into a rapid utilitarian conveyance. By the standards of steam-age engineering, Pierre Michaux's innovation wasn't exactly *Rocket* science: taking inspiration from the handles that rotated his grindstone, he stuck a couple of iron cranks on the hobby horse's front axle, and bolted pedals to them. The bone-shaker was born, and almost immediately put to breakneck competitive use.

The first races were held before the year was out, and in November 1868 several thousand spectators packed into a Bordeaux park to watch the inaugural women's championship (after a 'superhuman effort' on the home straight, Mademoiselle Julie overhauled Mademoiselle Louise and won by a nose). Even before Michaux's new firm organised the first international velocipede race in 1869, the need for two-wheeled speed had already claimed its first fatality: a fifteen-year-old boy lost control of his boneshaker on a steep valley, plunging straight into the Rhone and drowning.

This tragedy and the others that swiftly followed exerted precisely no moderating influence: however fast you rode a bone-shaker, it was never fast enough. Proposed braking systems were laughed off drawing boards around Europe in the quest to squeeze more speed from Michaux's design. The principal drawback of his propulsive mechanism was that every full revolution of the pedals corresponded to a full revolution of the front wheel to which they were fixed. Try to get any sort of speed up on a toddler's trike and you will understand this limiting correlation, before being asked to leave the playground. Boneshakers in consequence featured steadily larger front wheels – not yet penny-farthings, but certainly 10p-5ps. The advent of steel spokes opened the way for massively huger rims, and thus massively faster machines. And so the development of the bicycle was once again hijacked by cocksure speed-merchants. Penny-farthings were self-evidently difficult and dangerous to get on, let alone ride – but they were fast, and that was all that mattered.

Speeds soon topped 50kmh, with a world hour record of 38.17km set at Herne Hill velodrome: no mean feat when you consider that well over a century later, despite giant technical strides and regular ultra-punishing attempts by almost every champion of note, the hour record still stands in the 40s. Wheels grew ever larger – some penny-farthing riders sat 9 feet above the ground – and frames ever lighter. One high-end manufacturer sold a track machine that weighed in at under 6kg – an achievement you'd struggle to better in today's era of titanium, carbon fibre and non-idiotic rim diameters.

Wobbly, featherlight enormity, increasing speeds and the persistent absence of brakes incited a steady growth in ghastly accidents: routine and regularly fatal over-the-handlebar meetings of road and skull earned the casual nickname 'headers'. One published history of the bicycle includes the curiously precise but manifestly appalling claim that any penny-farthing collision with a pedestrian at over 12mph carried a 100 per cent mortality rate, and that during the machine's peak, over three thousand people died in this fashion every year.

That obsession with haste and the high-tech means of increasing it also made penny-farthings ruinously dear: a market-leading Starley cost more than an average worker's annual salary. Michaux's boneshaker – simple, practical, cheap – had promised a bikes-for-all revolution. The exorbitant and suicidally imbecilic penny-farthing pitched this dream straight over its handlebars.

Launched in 1885, the Rover Safety Cycle was a game-changer for a game that badly needed changing. Safety bicycles were so called by virtue of their equal, modestly sized wheels, which lowered the centre of gravity and allowed riders to place their feet on the ground at rest, thereby greatly reducing the probability and severity of a 'header'. The Rover broke little ground itself: the first safety cycle had gone on sale ten years before. And it wasn't even cheap: manufactured in Coventry by J. K. Starley, nephew of the penny-farthing king, the first Rover retailed for £20 15 shillings, which for the purposes of pointless comparison could have bought you five hand-tailored suits and 310 gallons of pale ale.

JK's creation was, in essence, no more than a considered aggregation of all the best bits from its many unsuccessful 'safety' predecessors. A diamond-shaped frame, handlebars connected to a front wheel supported by forks, pedals below the saddle powering the rear wheel via a chain and gears: it was to prove a stunningly durable design. You could put a silhouetted Rover on a no-cycling sign anywhere in the world today, and no one would give it a second look. Some achievement, especially when you consider that 1885 also saw the launch of the first successful petrol-powered motor car: the three-wheeled, handle-steered Benz Patent-Motorwagen, which bears as much resemblance to the vehicles of today as a tramp does to a banjo.

Starley's guiding principle was a machine in which 'the rider could exert the greatest force upon the pedals with the least amount of fatigue'. In comparison to walking, a Rover required 80 per cent less human energy while increasing speed four-fold. Courtesy of this astonishing and unimprovable efficiency, Starley's Rover Safety Cycle has survived almost intact through the bewildering developments of the last century and a quarter, surely the most profound overhaul the human race will ever experience in such a timeframe.

Paired with John Dunlop's new inflatable pneumatic tyre, Starley's bike was a smooth and easy ride. You didn't need to be daring, youthful or male to get your leg over a Rover: women could now pedal around in comfort without the twin risks of imminent fatal head injury and showing everyone their pants. And for the first time they could set off into town, or even miles and miles out of it, minus a chaperone: Susan B. Anthony, America's Emmeline Pankhurst, wrote that 'the bicycle has done more for the emancipation of women than anything else in the world'.

Booming sales brought down prices, and by the turn of the

century, Starley and his many imitators were shifting a million Safety bicycles a year in Europe alone. When Edouard Michelin introduced a detachable tyre that could be easily repaired or replaced at the roadside, a social revolution was born. The boundaries of commuting were hugely extended, and leisure was transformed. Countryside picnics, day trips to the city or seaside, touring holidays: all were now in universal reach. And though the Safety wasn't as fast as a penny-farthing – not yet – it was certainly better adapted to the emergent craze for tremendously long transnational bicycle races. I would therefore like to conclude this brief history with an expression of deep personal gratitude to J. K. Starley, for the invention that did away with the penny-farthing, and thus prevented me having to ride one for over 3,000km in the company of Europe's worst drivers, and dying in the process.

*

As depicted in Paolo Facchinetti's 1914 photos, Alfonso Calzolari looks even less like a champion athlete than the stork-like Fausto Coppi. A clean-shaven, diminutive fellow with thick, slicked-back hair and a squarish, slightly too large face, in the saddle he seems frail and shell shocked, old before his time: caked in road-filth, malnourished and weathered by the vicious elements. But bathed, fed and besuited for the post-victory celebrations, Calzolari looks cocksure, squat and tough, like one of those 'you got it, Boss' Mafia sidekicks. A five-foot man with watermelon bollocks.

The son of a carpenter, Alfonso Calzolari was born in 1887 in Vergato, 40km south of Bologna. The family moved to the city soon after, where the teenage Alfonso found work in a bed factory. He bought a rickety second-hand bike with his first savings and, encouraged by his father, rode every day after work to do a few laps of the Montagnola cycling track near Bologna station. Alfonso was keen and showed impressive resilience in his first amateur events,

though no one but his parents would describe his competitive progress as more than steady. He didn't win a race until he was twenty-two – a local club event – and only attracted the first stirrings of attention after finishing eighth in the national amateur championships the following year.

Drawing upon the indefatigability that would stand him in such good stead in 1914, Alfonso persevered despite his ongoing lack of success in the saddle. He was still working full time at the bed factory, and being unable to afford trains, spent the weekends riding his old clunker to races all over northern Italy, coming tenth and riding home. After bagging a few podium places in early 1912, he was finally awarded a 'junior professional' contract. Though not a very good one: after his L'Italiana team entered him in that year's Giro d'Italia, he had to beg the bed factory for time off. He was back at work within a week, having only lasted four stages.

Calzolari didn't chuck in his job until 1913, when at the advanced age of twenty-six he was finally awarded a proper contract with a proper team. Stucchi, one of the pre-eminent bike manufacturers of the time, expected results from their pro riders, but Alfonso was only able to give them one that year: a win in the regional Tour of Emilia. A broken collarbone made a mess of the season, and he started the Giro before it had properly healed, failing to complete the first stage.

The next year began with a run of solidly unremarkable results: a tenth, a seventh, a fourth. For a rider of twenty-seven, this was the kind of form that looked like the beginning of the end of a pro career. As the 1914 Giro approached, Alfonso Calzolari was hardly prominent in any discussion of pre-race favourites: in the unkind assessment of one Italian cycling historian, 'nobody needed an abacus to count the victories of that little man from Vergato'. The 1914 Giro, he said, 'elected its king from among the lowly actors of cycling'.

Paolo Facchinetti based his book on a meeting with Alfonso Calzolari back in April 1972. It was the old champion's eighty-fifth birthday, and Paolo had requested a commemorative interview. The man he met at the reception area of an old-people's home near Genoa was even tinier than he'd expected, with a full head of silver hair and a restless manner. Alfonso's greeting incorporated casual mention of his recent visit to Bologna, where he'd spent a day riding between various press engagements. 'On my road bike, of course.' In the evening, he'd signed on to enter an amateur race organised by one of his old home-town cycling clubs, before being talked out of it by the officials. 'I just wanted to see if I could hold their wheels: if I still had it.' As Paolo would conclude, this was 'Fonso' Calzolari all over: 'a fellow with unstoppable get-up-and-go, who spent his life exploring his own limits'. A small man with a big heart, and other such patronising clichés.

The two talked all afternoon. Paolo was intrigued to hear Fonso's memories of 1914 littered with French road-slang, the lingua franca in pro cycling's early days even for a rider who never left Italy. Riders were *'routiers'*; *'suiveurs'* the following caravan of officials and journalists. Calzolari also referred to his bicycle solely as *'la macchina'* (literally the machine, but these days the default colloquialism for a car) and called tyres *'palmers'* – the name of the American company that had just patented and introduced the first rubberised cord fabric. To Paolo's immense excitement, the old man then brought out his scrapbook, filled with yellowing photos and cuttings and his own handwritten reminiscences of that terrible, glorious 1914 Giro.

The journalist was astonished by what he read and heard. 'A fable, an adventure of true pioneers, when a stage was not a race but a journey of hundreds of kilometres, a journey that began at midnight and ended at dusk.' For three hours Calzolari held forth on the filthy weather and dirty tricks, the relentless mechanical and human carnage, the miraculous escapes with the hand of God upon him, the pain piled upon pain. 'It was a massacre that only eight of us survived,' he said when he was done, 'and somehow, in spite of everything, I beat them all.' Then he shook Paolo's hand, gave him the scrapbook for safekeeping, and walked away from what seems to have been his final interview.

Listen to the sporting reminiscences of a pole-vaulter or a National Hunt jockey and though you will certainly be impressed by their exploits, you probably won't wish to emulate them. But riding a bike down the road without falling over is a humdrum core skill that everyone possesses, unless there's something badly wrong with them. 'The bicycle is democratic,' wrote one of pre-war Italy's many self-styled cyclo-philosophers. 'You just get on, start pedalling and enter an ecstatic dimension.' Easy, tiger! That's him off my tandem list. But hearing about Paolo's encounter with Alfonso Calzolari, I knew exactly what he meant. The 1914 Giro had been dreadful beyond imagination, almost humanly impossible, yet its eventual victor was no more than a plucky journeyman, bagging his place in history by doing something we all do, but doing it harder.

The final photo in Paolo's book showed Alfonso at ninety, waving from a stage in his Sunday best. I looked at it and felt a lump in my throat the size of an avocado. His was a generation that knew what to do when the going got tough. As a member of mine, I went shopping.

CHAPTER 4

Wooden bar grips, 22mm interior
Double bidon handlebar holder, 2x metal bidons
B/B: bearing cups? Locking ring??
Stem bearings/cups (?)
Toe-clips
Butterfly axle nuts
Chain tugs
Cotter pins – knackered one too fat, other one too long, need
  9mm/9.5/10??
Crochet-backed gloves
Twat hat
Twat goggles

A singular blend of wisdom and cluelessness, this was the shopping list I took to the Anjou Vélo Vintage festival. Even before my champion's-choice road racer was outed as a rustic potterer, I'd been looking forward to this event; now the enhanced urgency for properly authentic components and remedial period accessories had elevated the AVV cyclo-jumble 'brocante' into a last-chance mission-saver. I'd even experienced a related dream, one of those typically male Aladdin's Cave jobs, in which naïve, profit-averse stallholders slouched behind trestle tables strewn with boxed new-old-stock kit and antique memorabilia. The absurd highlight was a framed display case containing an ancient but pristine Stucchi jersey, as worn by Alfonso Calzolari in the 1914 Giro. This item's €13 price sticker made it very hard not to shriek myself awake.

Roger Rivière had sold the AVV to me, and in the interests of company and informed input, I'd sold it to Jim and Matthew. At the end of June, the latter drove us down to the Loire in a car that seemed more than big enough for the task in hand, but in the event wasn't.

Based in the winsome old riverside town of Saumur, the festival announced itself as a magnet for those with an interest in old bicycles and pillbox-hatted *'Allo 'Allo!* extras in seamed stockings. Except for a temporary softening of the frontal lobes brought on by over-exposure to trad jazz, the three of us enjoyed our weekend there tremendously.

To calm myself before the orgy of grubby burrowing in the open-air brocante zone, I spent the morning of that fateful Saturday browsing the festival's display of fabled vintage machinery. This was introduced, almost insultingly I felt, by the very La Française-Diamant on which Maurice Garin had won the 1903 Tour de France. Running my eyes over its hateful blackness, I throttled back a Max-eating growl, which at length evolved into a puff of relief. A single fixed gear, and no brakes whatsoever! All hail eleven years of technical development: the 1914 Peugeot nearby sported familiar caliper brakes, and a switcheroo flip-flop hub that gave the rider access to at least two gears, even if changing between them meant stopping to take the back wheel off and turning it around. Perhaps more crucially, one was a freewheel, which would have allowed him to descend mountains without taking both feet off the crazily spinning pedals (the unnerving Garin method) or having his legs puréed by the rotational frenzy.

I left Matthew and Jim talking to some penny-farthing owners in deerstalker hats and tweed knickerbockers – Jim had acquired fluency while riding as a semi-professional in France for a few years – and set off to do a first pass of the brocante tables. Two hours later I came out the other end €74 lighter and with a third of my shopping list crossed off. By far the dearest purchase was a wire-frame twin bidon holder to be mounted on the front handle-bars in the daft but period-correct manner: a brittle and shriek-ingly cack-handed assemblage of welded coat hangers that I sadly accepted was the only one I'd ever find. Some other vendor had a set of original tin bidons, but they didn't fit in the rack, would probably have given me botulism and were priced at €250 the pair.

I was halfway through another pass, haggling over some tan-suede string-backed gloves, when Jim tapped me on the shoulder. 'A few lovely old bikes being flogged here,' he said, reminding me of a plan to extend his shop's retro range to include actual vintage machines. I'd noticed a few stalls selling complete old bicycles, but transfixed with the micro-management of my kit and components I hadn't paid them much attention. But how very flattered I was when Jim – bike-shop-owning, semi-professional Jim – now asked if I'd run the rule over a few that he had his eye on. I thought back to an autoroute discussion the three of us had shared about old bottom-bracket designs – really, you should have been there – during which it became apparent that I was no longer a completely stupid idiot.

'The one you really want to avoid is a Thompson,' I heard myself say, informed by the many comparative discussions I'd waded through online over previous weeks.

'A what?' Neither of them had ever heard of it.

Jim was especially interested in *porteurs* – old grocer-boy bikes with baskets over the front wheel – and together we assessed a few, rubbing chins and sucking our teeth doubtfully in the traditional manner. One was on a stall nominally overseen by a pair of stubbled, bleary and very French men, both preoccupied with running their oily fingers through their unabundant slicked-back hair and refreshing themselves from the crate of beer under their table. We'd just dismissed this duo's overly knackered *porteur* when Jim nodded at a bike hidden away at the back of their pitch. 'Go and check that out,' he advised.

I did so. It was self-evidently ancient: filthy, liberally pocked with rust and unburdened with brakes. The tyreless wooden wheels were horribly warped and delaminated, and half their spokes had rusted clean through. But it was a racer, and of appropriate vintage. The head-tube was pitched less rakishly than a Garin-era machine, but more so than the 1920s bikes in the AVV display zone. The chrome drop bars were finished off with copper-trimmed wooden grips. Most conspicuously, the distressed Brooks racing saddle was supported by one of those funny V-shaped seat posts that the less ignorant, more dull new me was aware had fallen from favour after the First World War.

Jim called out to the stallholders, cocking a thumb at the bike. '*Quelle année?*' The nearest one yawned massively, massaged his scalp, drained his Kronenbourg and at length rose. En route to us he disappeared into a fearsomely dishevelled van and emerged with a crumpled bit of paper. In place of an answer, he vaguely uncrumpled this and handed it to Jim. I looked over his shoulder: it was a photocopy of a monochrome page from an old bike catalogue. Page

207, to be precise, headed 'HIRONDELLE 1914' and largely filled with a meticulous line drawing of a bicycle, labelled 'No 7 COURSE SUR ROUTE'. The sweep of the handlebars, the profile of the forks . . . the briefest geometrical comparison suggested the bike in the catalogue was the bike before us. Some judicious rubbing with my newly acquired glove lifted enough dirt to confirm it: there were the backgammon-board darts – green on black in full-colour reality – that embellished the drawing's down and top tubes; there, most definitively, was the head-tube brass nameplate. *'Manufacture Française d'armes et cycles,'* read Jim, *'Saint-Etienne.'* I rubbed a bit harder to reveal the swooping bird that filled the space between these words. 'That's a swallow,' said Jim. *'Une hirondelle.'*

I swallowed in sympathy, excited but a little frightened, and above all terribly confused. I'd come here to get the final bits for my – hawk, spit – Brillant, and had already got most of them. I'd rebuilt that bike from rusty scratch, stripped it down, painted it up, marinated the sodding thing in my own sweat and man-tears . . . but, but, but, but it almost certainly wasn't built in 1914, and it definitely wasn't a proper road bike, and this here Hirondelle was demonstrably both. I restrained a screech of flustered frustration, or tried to: the vendor recoiled slightly at the high-pitched gargle that forced its way through my pursed lips.

'C'est combien?' asked Jim, carelessly. Quite a large part of me wanted a lofty four-figured answer, one that would neatly seal off this unsettling new avenue.

The vendor once again savoured the feel of grubby fingers on threadbare skull. *'Quatre cents.'*

Four hundred euros – bum-nuts on a rope, right in the sweet spot.

'Trois cents,' I blurted. At this he cranked up the Frenchometer with a terrific huff of offended exasperation, followed by many fast words.

'He says the handlebars alone are worth that,' Jim translated. 'How about we tell him to take them off and offer a hundred for the rest of it?' It was a brilliantly tempting suggestion, but ten seconds later, in the time-honoured fashion, we'd split the difference and shaken on it. In a daze I shuffled off to find a cashpoint.

Ten minutes later I was counting seven fifty-euro notes into a blackened palm and feeling markedly more at ease. Yes, I was back to square one, and yes I had paid through the arse for the privilege, coughing up €350 for a knackered and incomplete bicycle to replace a €400 predecessor to whose restoration I had devoted (read: wasted) most of the previous two months. Yes, now that I inspected this new acquisition in detail I could see that the chainring and pedals were all wrong, that the rear sprocket and both hubs were rusted to a buggery beyond citric redemption, that the bottom bracket – yes, really – was a non-original bloody Thompson.

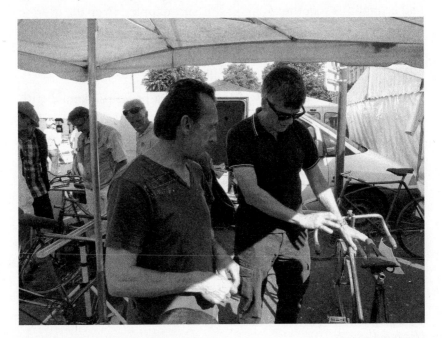

But, as I shouldered the filthy thing and set off with Jim through the funny-hatted throng, all this stuff began to seem less and less important. On a humdrum practical level, Max's tins and boxes contained most of the period bits this Hirondelle lacked or would need to have replaced – brakes, bell, pump, hubs, axles, pedals, sprockets. All those patio hours had not been in vain: many, in fact most, of the components I had so painstakingly revived would find a home on my No 7 Course sur Route.

Above and beyond such mundanities, though, this bike was the tits. It just looked right and felt right. So very right that the events of the past hour were already beginning to resemble some out-take from that pre-festival Aladdin's Cave dream. With my fingers round its crusted crossbar and its Calzolari-era catalogue-double folded tenderly in my back pocket like a billet-doux I already felt a connection I'd never felt with its ill-fated forerunner. Serendipity had brought us together, here in this sun-dappled riverside avenue full of twits in trilbies and shonky old tat. My Hirondelle was The One; this was meant to be. I'd gone on holiday to France and fallen in love with the ropey old village bike.

The balance of the weekend passed in a haze, thickened with new passion and lunchtime drinking. We spent that evening in a neat square full of bars, watching on a tiny outside screen as France went out of Euro 2012; celebration evolved seamlessly to wake, and along we went for the boozy ride. I'd leaned the Hirondelle next to my chair, and as we stumbled to our feet and made to leave, a suave young festival-goer walking by with a shiny 1950s racer stooped down for a look. '*Ah, une Hirondelle!*' Assessing our general unsteadiness he continued in English. 'Zees bicycle were super-populaire wiss ze police in, uh, old times.' I nodded glassily. 'It's, in fact, ze old familiar name for police *en France – les Hirondelles.*'

It wasn't exactly what I wanted to hear – shades of the windmill-watching customs' officer in that Brillant poster – but I smiled broadly all the same. I was still smiling, though more palely, when we coerced the Hirondelle into the back of Matthew's car the next morning, along with a colossal Anjou Vélo Vintage placard I'd seen fit to liberate from a fence on the way back to the hotel. I think I must have been showing off to my new girlfriend.

The festival's finale was a thousand-strong retro-ride around the Pays de Loire, and before setting off home we drove up to watch them head out. It was a blowy morning: all those vintage floral skirts were now pleasing liabilities, and to great cheers one of the cardinals on a three-seat tandem lost his red cap. As the fancy-dress peloton wobbled gingerly by, dinging bells and parping horns, it occurred to me that this 30-mile ride round the country lanes was as tough as it ever got for these well-loved but wonky velocipedes. As tough as it ever got for their twat-hatted riders. I tried very hard to imagine that in two months' time, both me and the crusty antique making a terrible mess of Matthew's upholstery and the back of Jim's neck would be ready for a rather sterner challenge. That we'd be breaking through that 30-mile finish line and pedalling on, away towards the horizon, for another 2,000 miles. Forrest Gump on a daft old bike.

Inspired to the point of terror, I came home and revived my training regime, branching out into attic 'biathlons' in which I performed one sport (exercise-biking) while watching another (football). When the Tour de France began I pedalled along in earnest, head down, watching sweat drip from my chin onto my distorted reflection in the exercise bike's shiny black frame. To bolster motivation I competed against the future Sir Wiggo and friends with what seemed a fair handicap, trying to keep my speed – as indicated on the exercise bike's little digital screen – at half theirs. I don't mean to boast, but under this weighted system I actually finished third in the stage-nine time trial.

Momentum was building, and necessarily: my departure deadline could now be most sensibly measured in weeks rather than months. I contacted Ghisallo, the Italian wheelbuilders who were the solitary manufacturer of wooden rims, and ordered a pair of six-layer, lap-jointed beech-wood wheels with the correct period profile. Cerchi Ghisallo seemed like a splendid concern. It was named after, and located next to, the famous Madonna del Ghisallo 'cyclists' chapel' above Lake Como, and had been run since 1946 by a family of grumpy craftsmen. Their avowed aim: never to produce fewer than five hundred rims a year, or more than one thousand. I found an interview with the elderly boss in which an enthusiastic questioner was repeatedly frustrated in his attempts to portray the fabrication of a Ghisallo rim as a painstaking labour of love.

'Could you describe the technical variations between the nine different rim designs you offer?'

'There aren't any.'

'Really?'

'Yep.'

'But how about your special reinforced model, the Rinforzato?'

'Hah! That's just a name.'

With a heavy sigh I got to work stripping all the many bits off my old-old bike that I'd need for my new-old bike. And with an even heavier one, I bowed my head and grimly embarked upon the most dreadful task of all. To pay meaningful homage to the 1914 Giro competitors meant doing everything as authentically as possible. To suffer as they suffered I must go where they went, ride what they rode and wear what they wore. So it was that I now set about kitting myself out like a giant cock.

The Internet's ability to unearth definitive, hyper-detailed answers to even the obscurest question is a double-edged sword. Its shinier, stabbier edge had proved very useful in pinpointing the precise design of wooden wheels preferred by pre-war professional bicycle riders, and contact details for the only firm who still made them. My quest to find out how these riders dressed caused the other edge, all rusted and jaggedy, to slash me right across the buttocks.

A *tonton* named Emile nurtured a particular fixation with the minutiae of vintage peloton fashion, and hosted a website that displayed his enormous collection of replica kit. Emile's 1910–20 outfits made for especially difficult viewing. Jerseys of this period were long-sleeved, roll-over cowl-necks fashioned from heavy wool, like something you might have worn to catch deep-sea fish in the *Whisky Galore!* era. What fun that promised to be when I was toiling round Italy in the dog days of late August.

A price tag of €175 for my pair of wheels didn't seem outrageous for something hand-crafted by Italians, certainly in comparison to the slightly larger sum I now paid a Parma resident called Fausto to knit me a woolly jumper. Like Ghisallo, Fausto was the only show in town: Emile had assured me that nobody else offered bespoke replica jerseys from this epoch. Along with my PayPal dosh, I'd sent Fausto a convoluted series of requested measurements, and an instruction that the jersey should be of plain white merino wool. He offered to embroider an age-appropriate team logo across the front at no extra cost – Calzolari's cursive, copperplate 'Stucchi' would have made a majestic chest-spanner – but I was hamstrung by my slavish-ish pursuit of authenticity. 'Participants in the 1914 Giro were divided into three categories,' wrote Paolo Fachinetti. '*Accasati*, affiliated to professional teams; the privateer-professional *isolati*; and *aspiranti*: amateur adventurers, little more than cyclo-tourists, almost all of whom failed to finish the first stage.' Reluctant as I might be to align myself with these doomed no-hopers, doing so was the only honest option. I was an *aspiranto*, and as such could only wear the simple white jersey that the Paolo-transcribed rules dictated.

I'd have to wing it with the woollen shorts and socks, which no one bothered replicating but seemed pretty unremarkable. Shoes – mincing little black lace-ups – didn't seem to have evolved much from the dawn of cycling time until the 1970s; leboncoin and French eBay turned up several antique options. The real horrors kicked in from the neck up. Emile's site and the photos in Paolo's book on the 1914 Giro brooked no argument: my Internet history was soon besmirched with searches for 'vintage blue lens goggles' and an 'eight-panel white linen baker-boy hat'. I could have saved time by typing in 'terrifying Seventies pervert'.

The bulk of my waking hours, though, was still spent out on the patio, making what could kindly be described as steady progress on the bike clamped in the stand. For three years I'd been promising to redecorate the house, and when my wife now subcontracted the task to a Polish bloke, I felt in no position to argue (though obviously did anyway). This fellow seemed tremendously interested in what I was up to out there. At the end of his first day he came into the garden to clean his brushes, walking curiously around me as I prodded ineffectually at the bottom bracket.

'Is old,' he declared at length.

I agreed that it was.

'Why you not put in rubbish?'

Lying in bed the morning after my return from Anjou, I'd experienced a sort of epiphany. '*Dans son jus*' was a phrase familiar to me from the *tonton* site, and one I'd heard severally around the AVV stalls. 'In its juice' meant unrestored, original, as-is. A relation of the eBay catchphrase 'shabby chic', it was generally wheeled out to cast an alluringly romantic gloss on some woeful rustbucket that had spent thirty years rotting under a cat-piss tarp. The *dans-son-jus* ethos was the antithesis of Lance's showroom-fresh ideal, but I suddenly realised that what I'd wanted all along was a warts-and-all bike, one that had been around the block a few times, a bike that was old and looked it.

My Hirondelle was by no means a race-bred professional machine: having tracked down the firm's complete 1914 catalogue, I'd established that the 'No 7' was their entry-level road racer, pitched at 'young people and any cyclist who loves speed'. At the list price of 160 francs, even brakes were an optional extra. But Number 7 made an endearing underdog, and it seemed instinctively right to leave its edges roughened. No more shotblasting, no more resprays, and certainly no re-nickeling (how close I'd come to spunking £70 on having the handlebars re-plated). I opened my eyes and told my wife: 'I'm going to have her as she is. I want her in her juice.'

This new intention was fast-tracked by another ill-fated dalliance with *la méthode Piotr*. After a brisk dabble exposed the original frame number – 87277, gold stamped on the black seat post – I got carried away, erasing a great swathe of the green backgammon-dart decoration from the down tube. That was that. Instead, I simply rubbed the whole thing down with a damp rag and painted it with that stinking rust-proof varnish. Every acid-scoured component – handlebars, cranks, brake levers, pedals, bell – received the same simple, smelly treatment. When it was done I looked happily around the patio, now bestrewn with sticky old metal embalmed in its own decay. The Polish painter had been monitoring me from an upstairs window; I smiled at him, and he burst out laughing.

The Tour ended; the Olympics began. Up in the attic I was cranking out a big gear for the men's road race, and a slightly smaller one for the beach volleyball. Every couple of hours the doorbell heralded a mad dash downstairs to receive a new delivery. Cotter pins, white grease, another tub of that ruinously dear horse-tackle renovator to revive the Hirondelle's original Brooks racing saddle – svelte and extremely comfortable, but as deeply crevassed as the hide of a dying elephant.

In a state of excited dread I tore open a Jiffy bag plastered in transatlantic stamps to reveal the 'vintage chemist goggles with leather side shields' I'd bought off a Canadian eBayer. My word, they were mad: John Lennon specs for a steampunk welder. I put them on and felt all kinds of wrong. The leather – hefty lateral blinkers plus a protective pad across the bridge of the nose – hemmed the world ahead into a claustrophobic corridor that reeked of musty laboratories. The extraordinary weight of the old clear-glass safety lenses, thick as £2 coins, swiftly caused my head to loll downwards – just as well, with a mirror in front of me. The glazed-millstone aspect was very much improved a week later, when a slightly unnerved optician replaced the lenses with much thinner blue-tinted ones. The view in the mirror very much wasn't.

There was no let-up for our postman. A pair of plain merino-wool socks. Two metal bidons – retro-style, but for health considerations not in any way old (after booting them around on the patio for ten minutes to scrub in a bit of age, I looked up to meet the painter's inevitable steady gaze). Four light-grey, wide-profile Vittoria tubular tyres designed for cyclo-cross use: as I'd learned at Anjou, the closest available approximation to Calzolari's bulbous, cloth-backed 'palmers'. That baggy white linen cap, a true abomination, even more Gilbert O'Sullivan than I'd feared. A vintage-pattern leather-and-canvas saddlebag from a specialist South Korean firm, which looked terrific but also tiny, an improbable home for everything I hoped to take. A pair of old woollen cycling shorts from French eBay, embroidered on each leg with the still-mysterious legend 'DALISTEL'. The elastic was going and the fraying chamois gusset had seen better days – days I really didn't want to think about in any detail. They were high-cut mini-shorts, perhaps from the early Merckx era. I put them on; they fell down.

One day brought two sizeable packages from across the Channel. The first was a box containing the shoes of Gerard Lagrost. I'd found them on leboncoin, and ended up enjoying a chirpy email correspondence with the aforementioned owner/vendor. His winning opener: 'Hello, English cycleman friend! I have 67 years.'

Gerard's shoes, supplied with bespoke wooden trees, were hand-hewn from stout leather – black laced uppers, liberally perforated for ventilation, with soles held in place and reinforced with rusted nails and rivets. Prolonged contact with ridged pedals had left two neat rows of indentations across the front part of each sole, a tribute to my fellow size 42-er's long career in the saddle. Deep into his fifties, Gerard decided to tell me, these shoes had been pressing the pedals on an annual 900km trip from Paris to Perpignan. He sent me photos of the bike on which he'd completed these rides – a yellow tourer inherited from his father – and the 1910 swan-neck Peugeot town bike he still pottered around on.

Gerard Lagrost was from that generation of European males who undertook a transnational bike ride not as some wanky challenge of self-examination – that was my job – but just as a cheap and hearty way of getting from A to a very distant B. His touching need to reminisce was, I sensed, a recognition that this generation was coming to a close.

To reciprocate I emailed him a snap of my Hirondelle up on the bike stand. 'Next month I shall ride this bicycle 3,162km around Italy wearing your faithful shoes,' I typed, my keyboard quite literally aglow with dramatic significance.

His reply arrived within the hour. 'I am happy you enjoy my shoes.'

The second package was rather larger, and contained a shiny, bamboo-coloured pair of Ghisallo wooden rims. Again I felt that double thrill, entranced both by the timeless aesthetic of these varnished birch circles and by the very fact that I should feel this way about them. More familiar emotions rose to the surface when I attempted to marry wheels to bike. Removing the spokes and hubs from the discarded Super Champions was the sweary work of a painter-pleasing morning, with the balance of the day devoted to nearly fitting half of them into the Ghisallos. ('Is wheels from *wood*?' 'That's right.' 'But . . . is new!')

In the morning I inflicted myself once more on Jim, and submitted to another compromise. The old spokes were, we conceded, both the wrong length and dangerously shit; I abandoned them in favour of seventy-two new ones from Jim's stock room. Four hours later I came home with an almost functional bicycle in the boot.

Impatience had been knocking on the door for a long time, and now finally burst inside along with its handmaiden, clumsy haste. With the help of a club hammer, a son and a big length of wood I separated the handlebar stem from the head-tube in a manner that left the patio scattered with bearing cups, locknuts and tiny steel balls. Reassembly was inspired by a technique I had beta-tested while putting the axles and hubs together: fill thin gaps with washers, cram thicker ones with ball bearings, then slather the lot in grease and quickly tighten it all up before too much stuff fell out.

I was stuck with the universally reviled Thompson bottom bracket, which someone – runaway favourite: scalp-scratching vendor – had hammered brutally and thus permanently into the threaded hole at the frame's fundament. Thompsons needed constant adjustment and were a cheap and nasty feature of the cottered crank's end game (sorry, but it isn't every day I get to hold forth about engineering from a position of authority, so just suck it up). Acceptance of this hateful reality unleashed a torrent of frustrated mechanical violence. Having spent a fortnight trying to gently prise the right-hand crank off the axle, I strode out into the street, wedged this stubbornly conjoined pairing in the slats of a drain cover and beat the living shit out of it with a scaffold pole. The red mist went brown when the drain cover flew up into the air, plopping the crank/axle combo into the liquid badness. Without a thought I effected a plunging bare-arm rescue, replaced the grating and smote noisily on. Success, when it eventually came, was celebrated with a spittled, rutting grunt and a distant Polish snigger.

The cotter pins got it next. Again tippy-tappy tinkering gave way to lusty metallic punishment. The left-hander was driven into its hole with no more than half a dozen hammer blows; after its distorting ordeal in the drain cover I wasn't surprised to find the right-hand crank more reluctant to admit its new cylindrical companion. I did my best to force through this introduction, then my scarlet-faced, neighbourhood-desecrating worst. As I battered away, the head of the cotter pin began to bulge and split, like a wooden tent peg after years of mallet abuse. It didn't go very deep into its hole, but didn't look like it would be coming out of it any time soon. Too late now to judge the random assemblage of bearing cups and washers I had stuffed into the bottom bracket: this was a point of no return.

I'd been carefully collating all of Max's ancient brake bits into a Museum of Deceleration on top of the barbecue, but now snatched anything that looked like parts of a matching pair and clamped it roughly to the bike. Levers on the handlebars, calipers on the front forks and seat stays, all connected with age-old cables sheathed in heavyweight coiled metal.

My new mood of slapdash recklessness was a poor fit with the task that now presented itself. The *tontons* had told me that wooden wheels could not be slowed down with traditional blocks: the heat thus generated quickly melted rubber, coating the rim in viscous black gel. The only effective brake-block materials, as used by professionals throughout Calzolari's era and right up to the widespread adoption of alloy rims in the 1940s, were cork and leather.

I emailed Ghisallo requesting a stockist for such blocks, and was promptly informed that none existed. Ugo, my contact at the firm, explained politely that customers who put Ghisallo wheels on their vintage bicycles were collectors, largely senior connoisseurs with no intention of ever taking their treasured museum pieces off the display stand and pushing them out onto the road. Further *tonton*-talk established the ludicrous truth: there was only one solution, and I'd find it wedged in a wine bottle. I went to work at once, hunched over a chopping board on the dining table, Stanley knife in one hand, Rioja stopper in the other. As a measure of how many improbable stupidities my family had recently witnessed me engaged in, my explanation of what I was up to procured no more than an indifferent hum.

Fresh from this sojourn into squinting precision, the next morning I got back into the brutal, insouciant swing of things. I hammered the funny-angled seat post into the frame, then hammered the aged Brooks saddle into the funny-angled seat post. An intention to restore the very knackered copper-trimmed handlebar grips was dumped in favour of a new-old pair in plain dark wood, acquired at Anjou and now summarily squirted full of Evostik and banged onto the bar ends.

I snatched a pair of freewheel sprockets from Max's cog pile –
one with slightly more teeth than the other, offering a change of
gear at the mere flick of an entire wheel – then rashly bunged
them in the white-spirit degreasing bath. When I scooped them
out the larger one revealed the hurtful legend 'FEMINA' stamped
into its surface: sire, you have a woman's gear. Worse, it had seized
solid. I shoved it in the bottom of the oven on a low heat to dry out,
then forgot about it for two days, during which it shared many
super-Celsius hours with a roast dinner and impregnated a lasagne
with the tang of hydrocarbons. Movement, albeit noisy and
begrudging, was restored by a forty-eight-hour soak in a tray full of
leftover automatic gearbox oil I found in the shed. Better than
nothing: onto the flip-flop hub it went, followed by the unpromis-
ingly orange chain.

Matthew came round and together we stretched and bullied the
tubeless tyres onto the rims – a slapstick ordeal, like pulling a
fitted rubber sheet over a greased billiard table. The next evening
I toiled late into the early August dusk, sensing I was on the home
straight and resolved to get it over with. Grab, slap, twist: on went
the old bell, the brass pump, four of Max's elegant but rather
malleable axle wing nuts and that shamelessly rubbish handlebar-
mounted twin-bidon rack, a frail and flimsy accident waiting to
happen.

Wild of hair and eye, gasping raggedly, I staggered back and
beheld the Hirondelle, raised aloft in its work-stand gallows. I had
done it, actually done it, I had put together a hundred-year-old
bicycle with handlebars that moved the front wheel, with pedals
that went round, with a back wheel that rotated via a chain when
you did so, and stopped – woo-hoo! – when you squeezed a lever
that pulled a cable that pressed a craggy oblong of hand-crafted
wine-cork against the wooden rim. With trembling hands I released

the Hirondelle from the stand, then carried it through the house and out into the street.

For the first time I cocked a leg over that ancient crossbar, parked my arse on that ancient saddle, eased a foot down on that ancient pedal. The Hirondelle wobbled forward into the long suburban shadows, feeling unexpectedly light and skittish. My pulse raced and my mind with it. I imagined Number 7's first ride, the pride of some knickerbockered young Gaul, saved up for at two francs a week. I imagined its last, pedalled creakily into the barn, a clunking, human-powered embarrassment superseded by a moped or a 2CV. I wondered how this combination of aged bike and ageing man would cope with what lay ahead, and soon: the date on my plane ticket to Milan lay just two weeks down the road. Most of all I wished passionately that the Polish painter, who had finished the job that very lunchtime, was here to see this. But then the front brake cable tore right through its housing in the lever, and I was extremely glad he wasn't.

The word 'inauspicious' might have been invented to describe this inaugural ride and the half-dozen that followed it, along with 'why', 'ow' and 'bastard clown-flaps'. The next day I hammered the brake lever back into vaguely functional shape and set off to visit Matthew's friend Suneil for a masterclass in the care and maintenance of tubular tyres. Two miles covered at walking pace sufficed to dispatch all four of my wine-cork brake blocks into the gutter, along with three of the silly little springs that returned the calipers to their position when the brake lever was released. Suneil helpfully pointed out that I'd installed all the calipers back to front, but even with this significant wrong righted for the return journey I came home minus one block and two springs.

My next ride round the block ended with the handlebars pointed at the floor; the one after shifted the pedal cranks from the traditional six o'clock position to quarter past seven. A lone, reedy shriek from the bottom-bracket area swelled into a full-bike orchestra of rattling groans. The rear wheel went suddenly off-kilter, and after three hours of soul-draining spoke-fiddle I realised the issue was the axle supporting it, which had bowed in the middle. I found a solitary compatible spare in one of Max's boxes, along with a number of old leather toe-straps, which I lashed round parts of the bike in a mad-looking but generally successful bid to shut them up.

With two days to go I rode the Hirondelle to Lance's workshop in Ealing, packing three extra brake blocks and half a dozen springs from a job lot of 150 acquired through eBay. I only needed one of each but still wheeled it in on foot: halfway there one of the pedals literally fell to pieces, cheerfully scattering the bus lane with fractured metal and ball bearings. Questions of the most fundamental nature were being asked of my ancient machinery, and being answered with a long, splattering raspberry.

Lance had very generously offered to give my bike a last-minute once-over, and though it plainly needed at least a thrice-over, just being in his workshop made everything feel better. It was the stuff of wholesome male fantasy in there, a cosy, oil-stained man-nest dominated by the shell of a Sweeney Jag and an Al Capone-era mobster-mobile, whose roof Lance was loudly reshaping with what I now know to be a cross-pein hammer. Stacked claustrophobically amongst the tool racks were dusty display cases of old Dinky cars, vintage sunglasses, enamelled garage signs, and a naked shop mannequin with hubcaps for tits. And hanging from the low-slung ceiling and the breeze-block walls, bike after bike after bike, a dozen or more immaculate vintage track and road racers.

This was the lair of a man who knew all I needed to know, who could do everything that needed doing. Lance put down his hammer, walked over, stooped down by the Hirondelle and said: 'What the fuck have you done to those cotter pins?'

I was there for the rest of the day, soaking up well-earned reproach and helping to inch the Hirondelle closer to road-readiness. Lance had me remove and discard the surviving pedal – 'no great loss, they're total shit' – and retrieved a far sturdier replacement pair from some buried stash of period components. With surgical force he expelled the half-squashed cotter pin, tapering a substitute to fit the hole via the use of what he called his 'Polish lathe' – an electric drill with an abrasive bit. I watched him delicately tap the new pin home. 'Never use a forearm with a hammer. Got to let your wrist and fingers do what you're seeing in your head. It's a feel thing.' I later found out that the young Lance had crowned his metalworking traineeship at Rolls-Royce by fashioning a cube of steel more geometrically precise than that managed by any other apprentice at the firm before or since.

Still, the cock-eyed, cork-wobble embarrassment that was my Hirondelle's braking system didn't seem to concern him, any more than the various mechanical death-rattles or the ovoid profile stubbornly discernible in both wheels. 'Anything that's bolted on doesn't really matter,' he announced airily. 'Just have it replaced or get some local feller to fix it. Italians will do anything if you wheel out a few *ciaos* and *benissimos* and promise not to shag their sisters.'

Lance plugged in a caged inspection lamp and popped on his Harry Palmer bifocals. 'Structural stuff is different,' he murmured, holding the light close to the Hirondelle's vital joints and squinting at them intently. 'My bikes are old, but this thing's a fucking antique. If any of these frame lugs go, that's the end of your trip.' He lingered over the seat post. 'See that mark?' I tried to, couldn't, but hummed assent anyway. 'Hairline crack. If it starts to go you'll hear it. Old steel's useful like that.' He stood up, and by way of demonstration let out a terrible rending shriek. 'I'm jealous, you're a lucky fucker. Take care.'

It was quite a send-off, and my breakthrough incident-free ride home was crowned with another. Waiting for a green light at the fearsome multi-junction by the end of my road, I heard a distant shout defy the North Circular Road traffic. 'Hey, mate! Mate!' I looked around and spotted its owner, a lightly bearded young man on a plain-black fixie five lanes away. 'Top bike, mate! You doing the Eroica or what?' The only attention the Hirondelle had previously aroused on the street was in agonised response to the blackboard-raking dissonance of its progress.

'Actually!' I shouted back, before the other lights changed and a column of buses passed between us. When they'd gone, so had he.

A strange new mood sidled into my head that evening, hitching a ride with the third glass of red. I went to the back window and gazed out at the Hirondelle, propped against the bike stand and glinting in my neighbour's Stalag Luft patio searchlight. Hope, excitement, anticipation: for the first time, I could imagine myself successfully achieving what I had set out to achieve, piloting that ancient velocipede all the way round Italy in Alfonso Calzolari's ghostly wheel-tracks. Halfway through the fourth glass I under-stood that we had a thing going on, me and that old dear out on the patio. Peas from the same wrinkled pod, a couple of road-rusty veterans shackled together for one last comeback. I may not have mentioned that my family had at this point been away with the Icelandic in-laws for three days, and that by the time they returned I would be gone, off on a mammoth journey of unknown duration. Glass five reminded me.

The next forty-eight hours hurtled by in a nauseous blur of panic. So much still had to be done, most of it incredibly funda-mental for this stage of the game. I affixed the seat-post bracket that would support my saddlebag. I fashioned a canvas insert for the bidon carrier, to dampen the brain-melting milk-crate rattle of metal bottles in metal frame. I rooted out Max's rustiest pair of toe-clips and bolted them on to Lance's pedals, then threaded them with his crustiest pair of toe-straps.

The clips were branded 'Christophe', in appropriate honour of Eugène Christophe, the man who embodied the heroic awfulness of those early grand tours. Leading the 1912 Tour de France up the Pyrenees, Christophe broke his front forks, shouldered the stricken bike many mountainous miles to the next village and forged himself a new set at the blacksmith's, where the several hours he had already lost were supplemented with a further time penalty for receiving illegal outside assistance: a watching official had spotted a local boy pumping the forge bellows. Those were the days. And, give or take a couple of years, those were now my days.

Also, I packed. This wasn't supposed to take long, on the grounds that I wasn't taking much. Twelve years before, the fitter, sillier me had set off to ride the Tour de France route with a bulging pair of panniers crammed full of such featherweight professional essentials as six copies of *procycling* magazine and the 1,123-page *Rough Guide to France*. I had also taken along a wardrobe of après-cycling wear to suit a variety of moods and occasions, an electric razor the weight of a Neolithic hand-axe, and a lucky house brick. (I wish I was joking – and my wish is granted!)

With a combined age of 146, the Hirondelle and I weren't up to that sort of burden, any more than my tiny South Korean canvas bag could accommodate it. At the same time, authentic necessity dictated I carry whatever the bike and I would need to survive. Food, drink, spares, tools, knee-length sou'westers: the 1914 rules decreed you lugged it all. So: no spare kit, whatsoever. I'd wash my entire cycling outfit – socks, shorts, jersey, every fetid, woolly inch of it – every night. Common decency and the probability of being refused service demanded a change of clothes for the evening; I assembled a solitary lightweight outfit. All my shoes seemed too hefty, though, so I went to the TK Maxx up the road with our digital kitchen scales and weighed all their size 42s (you can get away with anything in that place – I once saw an eight-man piggy-back race around homeware).

The 516g pair of hideous canvas slip-ons I came home with filled half the saddlebag. I stuffed one shoe with micro-toiletries: a mini tube of toothpaste, a sawn-off toothbrush, concentrated detergent/shampoo, four disposable razors plus a tiny bottle of shaving oil/chain lube. And a wrinkled, half-empty tube of Savlon, left over from my Tour ride's fight against saddle sores. (How I looked forward to that morning ritual: one handful down the front of the shorts, another down the back, and off down the hotel stairs for an oily-loined breakfast.) The other shoe could swallow no more than those non-authentic but sadly unavoidable contemporary companions, phone plus camera plus chargers. I scrunched and punched my pitiful capsule wardrobe into what little space remained, wedged in two 1:200,000 maps of northern Italy and Paolo's book down the sides, then with empurpling effort yanked the bag straps into their final notch.

Max had furnished me with an old leather tool bag, angled to fit snugly in the meeting point of top tube and down tube. The bare essentials of daily maintenance – even my lightest pliers weighed almost as much as a hideous canvas shoe – had its ancient seams straining. I glanced helplessly around at the sizeable heap of stuff I had yet to accommodate, then for the penultimate time pushed the Hirondelle out of the front door.

Sixteen hours to go, and this was my first ever experience of toe-clips: impressive unreadiness even by my standards. Easy enough to ram the first foot into its little cage while stationary, but cajoling home the second in motion seemed like a knack it might take 3,162km to master. Extracting at least one foot before coming to a halt was the more urgent skill, though, especially as I'd soon be dressed up like the kind of daft twit who absolutely deserved to topple stupidly onto the tarmac at every set of traffic lights. Perhaps I'd find the clips easier when I was wearing the shoes of Gerard Lagrost. Perhaps by now I should have tried wearing those shoes for more than eleven seconds.

I wobbled round west London for a farewell plunder. I came away from Matthew's with a pair of old cone spanners and an illegally modern multi-tool, from Suneil's with a roll of tubular-tyre tape and a bottle of puncture sealant, and from Jim's with a spoke key of the requisite diameter. Nobody welled up and clamped a quivering hand on my shoulder, the heartless bastards, but I still pedalled home feeling that I wouldn't just be letting myself down if I messed this whole thing up. Maybe this is why, cresting the bridge outside Boston Manor tube station, I suddenly decided to give the Hirondelle its first dose of full beans, standing up in the saddle and forcing those old cranks round, sweeping past two homecoming commuters in high-vis tabards. The whole bike creaked and shrieked and grated and shook, and I pedalled on, harder, ever more astounded that nothing was giving way, and glad that at least when it did I was about seven feet from the Brentford branch of Evans Cycles.

My neighbour Bernie was in her front garden when I trundled up the road. 'So here's the famous bike,' she said. 'Is it really one hundred years old?'

'Not entirely.' I held up a plastic bag containing the recently severed chain, in a hand that might have pulled seagulls out of an oil slick.

'Oh,' she said, frowning doubtfully at the Evans-sourced

replacement chain, then the Hirondelle in general, then me. 'Don't take this the wrong way, but are you absolutely sure this is sensible?'

The postman had been. On the mat lay a vintage postcard depicting an Edwardian lady being upended bloomers-first from her runaway bicycle. It was from my parents, the message on the rear less of a *bon voyage* than a last-minute appeal to reason. 'Go slowly and be careful!' That was in my father's hand, the last two words underlined twice. 'It's never too late to change your mind,' my mother had written beneath it. 'We will love you whatever you choose to do.'

Beside the card sat a slim, transatlantic-stamped package. I tore it open and those siren calls of paternal and neighbourly concern began to recede. Inside: a bespoke black-leather frame bag, just large enough to accommodate a wallet and phone, with stout brass press studs on straps to be slung round the top tube. I'd ordered it two months before; it had arrived with just a day to spare. I held the bag up to the fading light and saw that my special request had been thrillingly fulfilled: just above the bottom seam, stamped deep into the leather in an aptly archaic typeface, were the words 'ALFONSO CALZOLARI'.

Some gland within me squirted a cocktail of raw emotions directly into my spine. Who thought this was a good idea? Not Bernie, not my parents, not me. But I knew a man who did and his name was here in my hands. Then I flung the old chain into the new bag, clipped it to the Hirondelle's crossbar and pedalled straight back to Evans, where I bought a little chain-repair link and failed to obtain a refund for the now-filthied item I'd bought there an hour before.

CHAPTER 5

It had been damp and more than a little nippy when I'd pedalled off into the west London dawn, bound for Heathrow Terminal 4. Here in Milan it was vehemently neither. Down by the lonely 'weird shit' carousel at the far end of Linate Airport's baggage hall, every time a lawn mower or a surfboard parted the rubber-strip curtains, it brought in a sauna waft of outside air. I'd been waiting almost an hour, yawning hugely and contemplating the miracle of impracticality that was my all-white civvy outfit: canvas shoes and trouser hems already streaked with ancient chain oil from the eight-mile ride to Heathrow, shirt cuffs blackened by a protracted ordeal in the Terminal 4 'repack area'.

The Alitalia website offered a helpful welcome to passengers transporting bicycles, but the reaction at their Italian-staffed Heathrow check-in suggested I had turned up with a horse. 'Please, *signore*, how can you *believe* this is possible?' It took twenty minutes to persuade them to consult their own regulations on bikes as baggage, then another forty to package the Hirondelle to their ever-changing satisfaction: tyres deflated, pedals off, handlebars turned in – no, the other way – front wheel off, front wheel back on, bubble wrap, more bubble wrap, even more bubble wrap.

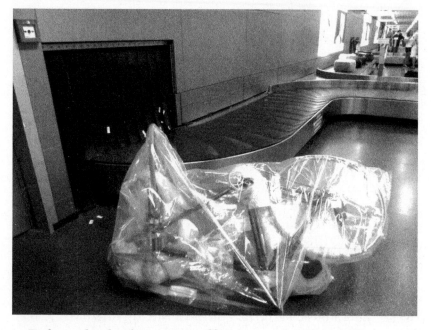

Right at the death, a senior official arrived to demand a 'special luggage charge': the commendably random sum of €118, 'euro cash only, no card please'. None of this seemed at all in keeping with the bike-loving amenability Lance had painted into the national character.

'Would it help if I promised not to shag your sister?'

Nothing in his expression implied that he'd understood any part of this proposal, but the fact remains that the bike and I got on board without an extra penny changing hands.

The carousel conveyor lurched into life and a huge iceberg of plastic sheeting forced itself through the rubber strips. I heaved it off, made a terrible shredded mess, and then, before a gathering throng of baggage handlers and customs officials, laboriously returned the Hirondelle to its pre-Alitalian condition. When it was done I filled the bidons from a drinking fountain and propped the bike and my back against the wall, waiting for the audience to disperse. Bad news for the elderly male cleaner who chose to linger: my final public performance was a costume change, which began with taking absolutely all of my clothes off.

Against the odds, I was at once very glad of those leather-shielded blue goggles, my Robin Gibbs. Pushing the Hirondelle through the arrivals hall with half my face hidden, I felt gratefully removed from the attention, as if somebody else was being stared and tittered at. The heat outside was smothering, and the airport's hinterland typically grotty, but the Gibb goggles bathed the world in a cool and flattering azure wash. Then I pedalled off towards the city centre on a six-lane expressway, taking it easy, and even easier once I'd confirmed a suspicion formed on my 8-mile ride to Heathrow: the application of cork pad to wood rim exerted little influence on the speed of a fully laden Hirondelle No 7 Course sur Route. How very fortunate that on a Thursday afternoon in high summer, the traffic was extremely sparse.

Downtown Milan proved quieter still, a broiled ghost town. Italians, I surmised, adhere to French-pattern holiday traditions: the entire nation spends August on the beach. The shops were shuttered and the pavements empty. A digital display outside a pharmacy told me it was 16.04, and 41 degrees centigrade.

My quarry, as I flap-slapped over tram-tracks up the deserted, flag-stoned boulevards, was the 1914 Giro's start line on the Corso Sempione, and I think you can guess what lead me to it. That's right: smell, the distinctive scent of history itself overlaid with fragrant top notes of heroic accomplishment. Verified, when necessary, by a sat-nav mounted on my crossbar. (I know what you're thinking, but don't worry. This was an absolutely original period device, made out of two pocket watches brazed to a portable theodolite.)

Plotting my route with the help of Alfonso's race diary, as abridged by Paolo Facchinetti, I'd established that the 1914 Giro followed many roads that had subsequently fallen into deep obscurity. Getting lost would certainly be authentic: in that race as in every other grand tour of the era, wrong turnings were an almost daily tribulation. But cycling even 2 feet further than necessary seemed like a young man's game. Plus, in addition to the catalogue of progress-monitoring data that is the very life-stuff of male middle age, this particular sat-nav – I appear to have told a fatuous lie about that theodolite – had a feature that allowed you to race against a virtual competitor who advanced at the rate of your choosing. On the plane I'd calculated and programmed in Alfonso Calzolari's average overall speed – 23.374kmh seemed far from shabby given the 400km stages, the available technology and a booze-centric approach to chemical performance enhancement. A little digital Alfonso now sat astride his pixelated bike, raring to go, on a subsidiary menu of my Garmin 800 Edge – a device that was so much more than the Huret speedometer I never had. This omniscient infoholic on my handlebars would tell me how hot it was and how high we were, and where we were, and where we were going, and when it was getting dark, and how many calories I was burning and my current state of mind via a library of over two hundred on-screen emoticons, from 'pompous sneer' to 'sickening wink'. (Feature not available on real Garmin 800 Edge.)

Have a look online and you'll find some wonderful images of the Grand Ristorante Sempioncino in its gas-lit heyday, mostly depicting Edwardian couples in evening wear waltzing graciously around an enormous palm-lined dance floor. The venue that hosted the 1914 Giro's opening ceremony had, of course, long since been demolished, and squeaking to a drawn-out, corky halt outside the appointed address I understood that 61 Corso Sempione was not going to see me off in style. In place of the Grand Ristorante stood a diligently unmomentous seven-storey apartment block, gazing blandly out across a boulevard lined with thirsty plane trees.

I rooted out Paolo's book and looked again at the photo of the riders gathered outside the Sempioncino with their bikes for final registration. No fisherman's jumpers and sou'westers just yet: they were still in their Sunday best, three-piece suits and straw boaters. One was looking right down the lens with an air of impressive insouciance, hands in pockets, backside propped on crossbar, face half-filled by a mighty handlebar 'tache. The caption identified him as Carlo Durando of the Maino team; I riffled through Paolo's index and was almost tearfully pleased to find him listed as one of the eight finishers.

'A test for none but the strong – and the desperate.' Provided by one of the journalists who would follow the 1914 Giro in a fleet of Fiat Tipo Zeros (my word, Paolo did his homework), this neatly summarised the groundbreaking awfulness of that year's itinerary, and the dreadful poverty that drove eighty-one men to the start line. Pre-war Italy was a place of shocking deprivation: tens of thousands died every year from hunger and deficiency diseases, and half of all Italians were illiterate. No surprise to learn that three million of them – a tenth of the entire population – emigrated to the US in the first fifteen years of the century.

A career in professional cycling was one of the very few routes out of grinding hardship. 'To ride is to work,' said Armando Cougnet, who organised the first Giro in 1909 and ruled the event as race director for half a century. 'Each turn of the pedal is like a blow of the worker's hammer.' Every great Italian rider before the 1960s was raised in extremely humble circumstances, their talent unearthed through epic feats of work-related cyclo-commuting. Take Costante Girardengo, the original *campionissimo*, champion of champions, reared in rural poverty with eight siblings and sent out to earn his keep at a distant factory, a job that involved a daily 40km round-trip ride. Girardengo proved himself a glutton for pedalling punishment, who went on to win the notoriously demanding Milan–San Remo race more times than anyone but Eddy Merckx, and was still riding the Giro – an event he won twice – at the age of forty-three. Four days after the 1914 Giro rolled away from Milan, the twenty-one-year-old Girardengo would come home first in what was and remains the event's longest ever stage, 430.3 non-stop kilometres from Lucca to Rome. Two days later, this self-evidently super-hardcore endurance athlete abandoned by the roadside in tears, undone not by injury or break-down but by the event's soul-destroying relentlessness.

Drawn up by Cougnet in full Bastard-General mode, the 1914 route deliberately set out to explore the very limits of human desperation. The number of stages was cut and the overall length increased, meaning riders faced the unparalleled attritional brutality of covering 3,162km in just eight non-stop stages, averaging very nearly 400km each. Cougnet was encouraged in his devilish work by the Giro's new chief sponsor, a newspaper group keen to promote itself throughout Italy: the 1914 route dutifully encompassed the nation from the northwestern Alps (thanks, Armando) to Bari right down in the southeast. The bike manufacturers who sponsored the pro teams were just as hot on a properly awful ordeal, to showcase the durability of machines that were now being pitched to the mass-market as indispensable work-horses. They were also hoping to impress the military: after winning the 1911 Giro, Bianchi was awarded a Ministry of War contract to supply 63,000 bicycles for Italy's imminent invasion of what is now Libya. In May 1914 it would have seemed a fair bet that other conflicts with even more lucrative potential lay in wait.

As the sour cherry on top of the pain-cake, Cougnet announced that the 1914 Giro would be decided by time alone, casting aside the simpler and more humane points system (riders were previously awarded points for their finishing position in each stage, totted up to decide the overall winner). In this he was inspired by Tour de France director Henri Desgrange, his partner in violent crime, who had recently dropped the points system from the Tour after blaming it for 'a worrying decline in competitive aggression'. Once their finishing position in a stage seemed secure, riders would unsurprisingly take it easy, and there was nothing that infuriated Cougnet and Desgrange more than one of their professionals not flogging himself into the ground. Racing against the clock, every second had to be fought for; in the 1914 Giro there would be no let-up.

What of the carrot that Cougnet dangled before his riders, as he prepared to stripe their buttocks raw with the stick of physical suffering? Well, the winner of the 1914 Giro was promised 3,000 lire, a sum that after adjustment for inflation translates to around €9,000 in today's money. When you consider that Giro victory is now rewarded with precisely fifty times that amount, it's not too hard to understand why Cougnet found himself a few starters short of a peloton. With twelve days to go, he boldly addressed this situation by throwing entry open to all comers. So it was that amongst the hard-bitten, long-suffering pros lined up outside the Grand Ristorante Sempioncino were fifteen of the rankest of rank amateurs. 'Extraordinary young adventurers,' is Paolo Facchinetti's apt description of these *aspiranti*, who turned up in Milan on borrowed bikes with no inkling of what they were letting themselves in for. 'Most were unemployed,' says Facchinetti, 'and all were desperate. Many may have felt they would at least eat better in the race than they could at home.' The youngest, Umberto Ripamonti, was a local boy of nineteen.

A crowd of over ten thousand stood along the moonlit Corso Sempione as Milan's many clocks struck midnight. Every stage of the 1914 Giro would commence at this extraordinary hour, designed to ensure a well-attended evening turnout when the riders toiled up to the finish line eighteen or nineteen hours later. Surveying the massive, peloton-ready boulevard yawning out before me, I could quite easily picture the scene, even though it was August, not May, four in the afternoon rather than midnight and I had several hundred feet of hot, broad pavement all to myself.

This was it, then. In place of a starter's pistol I propped the camera on the seat of a parked scooter and took a self-timer shot. Looking at it now, what strikes me is how very clean everything is. My crisp white cap and jersey, the Hirondelle's shiny grey tyres and varnished rims, the starched black canvas of the saddlebag and the gleaming brass press-studs of my Alfonso-branded frame pouch. And my fresh, pale face with its bloodless half-smile, a gawp of abject disbelief clearly visible through those polished blue lenses.

I double-checked the safety pin holding my shorts up and took a girding swig of sun-warmed airport water. Then I slammed an old man's shoe into a toe-clip and eased my behind onto a dead man's saddle. Off the pavement – *ker-thunk* – and steadily away up the desolate heat-hazed boulevard, northwest into a mighty low sun. 'To ride is to work,' I said to my knees. 'Each turn of the pedals is like a click of the freelance writer's mouse.'

Back in 1914, things started to go wrong almost at once. The clear night sky abruptly vanished behind scurrying storm clouds, and at the satellite town of Rho, after a mere fifteen minutes in the saddle, the heavens tore open. What unfolded in the seventeen

hours ahead has no parallel in sporting history, unless you count Captain Scott's 2,600km Antarctic steeplechase. In faithful tribute, my own Giro took its own rather dramatic turn after fifteen minutes, though of course I wasn't even halfway to Rho by then.

Beyond the virgin fragility of its subject, the other conspicuous feature of my start-line photo is the lopsided heap of stuff piled on top of the saddlebag. My predicted failure to shoehorn everything into that canvas anti-Tardis had left it stacked with overspill, held in place with a strap borrowed from what I've just been loudly informed is – was – my wife's second-smartest evening handbag. An inauthentic micro-fleece top (sorry) and Gore-Tex rain jacket (look, give me a break), a number of the heavier tools, and crowning all this a bulky pair of tubular tyres. It had been my intention to wrap these spares round my torso in homage to the 1914 riders, in fact to every rider in every professional race up to the 1950s. But my reflection, clad thus in the glass doors at Linate Airport, was less noble-giant-of-the-road than the Michelin man's weedy, bullied nephew; I pulled the tyres off, folded them up and strapped them round the fleece.

This bundle had been bobbing gaily about behind me all the way from the airport, but as I swung out to overtake a parked bus it did something else: it fell off, striking some rearward part of the Hirondelle in a manner that caused the back wheel to buck across the shiny flagstones. A corrective yank of the handlebars neatly introduced the front wheel into the slot of an adjacent tram rail, and over we went. My unaccustomed feet did all the wrong things and I slid gently along the road with both of them jiggling help-lessly in their toe-clip cages.

To state the obvious, I wasn't going fast. Together with the persistent absence of traffic and onlooking pedestrians, this meant not even my pride was hurt. Nonetheless, as I strapped everything back together and shakily remounted, I had cause to question my stance on the trade-off between authenticity and responsible common sense, which had meant staying faithful to period peloton fashions at the cost of protecting my brain with a linen cap. Thankfully, in the event everything turned out absolutely fin31^GIUGHHHKJNnnnnnnnn.

It was an otherwise benign reacquaintance with the business of sustained cycling. The old highway out of Milan was straight, flat and empty, giving little cause to regret the absence of gears or any effective means of slowing down. An interest in seeing where I'm going means I generally ride with my hands on top of the bars, but with this zone annexed by bell and bidons I had no choice but to grab the drops. My neck wasn't mad on this arrangement, but rolling through the city's outskirts I began to feel at home down there.

The Hirondelle seemed far happier than a massively overloaded hundred-year-old bike had any right to. Stripped of all luggage at the Heathrow repacking area it had weighed in at 14kg, half as much again as my Tour bike, yet even burdened with an extra 85kg of tools, possessions and middle-age spread the bike seemed anything but cumbersome. Road bikes back then were much longer, their wheelbase typically 1.2m rather than today's 1m. I dare say this stretched profile made them in some biomechanical manner less efficient, but it soaked up the bumps and was certainly kinder on an old man's back. Good work, long-dead frame designers!

Trees began to outnumber buildings and I cranked up the revs. My knees pistoned crazily, the steel rings on the bidon lids launched into a spastic, bin-lid rattle and the blue world before me steamed up at its leather edges. I figured I'd soon be grateful for my easy-spinning, twenty-two-toothed main sprocket, but it did mean I'd never be eating up the kilometres. With my legs a rotary blur I checked the juddering sat-nav and saw I'd just topped 26kmh, barely faster than Calzolari's average speed over the entire race. On the relevant screen, his digital blue-jerseyed homunculus was already pulling inexorably away from mine, twenty-seven minutes up the virtual road. As a race it was over before it had begun; I sat up and coasted down to a sustainable cadence.

This brief effort and the lingering heat brought on a premature pit stop. Part of me could see that Legnano was no more than a run-of-the-mill, mid-sized Italian town, but another part was in charge as I sat outside a café on its main piazza. Slumped in the warm shade with a salami *panino* and a litre of *acqua gassata* inside me, what a profoundly splendid place it seemed, with its octagonal church and its terracotta roofs and its stooped old widows left behind when their families sneaked off to the seaside.

They say the Tour encapsulates the spirit of France, but as an embodiment of its host nation the Giro is clearly the more convincing. In 2011, the organisers marked the centenary of Giuseppe Verdi's death by dedicating each stage to a different opera. Stage winners are routinely required to participate in podium pasta-cooking contests. The Pope blesses the leader's jersey, for heaven's sake. Contemplating all this I expansively unfolded my Touring Editore map of Lombardy, a triumph of handsome, ageless Continental cartography, like something Napoleon would have jabbed at with an imperious finger. Sesto Calende, Lago Maggiore, Biella . . . every stop on my route ahead suddenly beckoned me with the promise of sun-dappled refreshments enjoyed amongst engaging natives in picturesque splendour. This journey, an undertaking that had previously seemed absurd and appalling, now made perfect, beautiful sense.

It was getting dark when I called it a day at Gallarate. Rolling up to the first hotel in town I felt no more than pleasantly well exercised, but climbing off the Hirondelle my legs almost buckled. To my bewildered consternation I found I was utterly spent, so spent that I offered mumbling assent to the receptionist's demand for €72 up front, some way above my daily accommodation budget. 'I know you people like keep bike in room,' she said as I fumbled out the cash. 'You can take in elevator, is no problem.' How things had changed. Twelve years before I'd faced nightly abuse for even suggesting such an arrangement to the hoteliers of France. But twelve years before I was better equipped for the challenge of forcing a laden bike vertically into a tiny lift. I shook my head and wheeled the Hirondelle down into the subterranean garage.

It was a night of many long-forgotten rituals, relived with a twist. There I was again, stooped nude over a hotel bidet, sluicing the residue of human toil from my kit. Only this time it was all hundredweight wool, which clung on to its filth and wouldn't be even half-dry by morning. There I was again, prodding uneaten pizza shards around a plate ringed with beer empties and unsettling fellow diners with my dead-eyed stare. Only this time the pizza was better, and a lot more crows had their feet round the stare. And there I was again, lapsing into a coma while brainless Continental shite pumped out of a hotel-bedroom telly. Only this time in gaudy, tits-out BerlusconiVision.

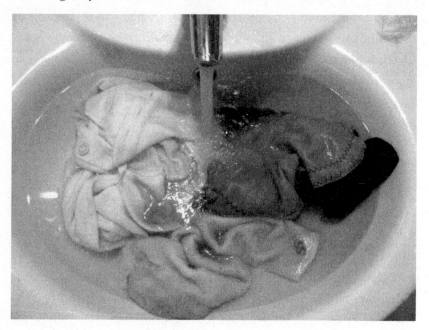

CHAPTER 6

'Hello, Savlon, my old friend,' I sang, wanly enriching my jacksie, 'you've come to torture me again.' The upside of this morning ordeal was that every squirt – of toothpaste and concentrated travel wash as well as genital bactericide – meant there was ever so slightly less to compress into my undersized saddlebag. The downside was thereafter sheathing my smeared nethers in sodden wool; the first coil of musky disinfectant steamed up from my groin as the hotel waitress came over with a cappuccino.

Though few and flat, the previous day's kilometres had wreaked an ominous toll. I drained the cup in a trembling, numb hand – the tips of my four smallest fingers were dead to the world – then advanced to the buffet like a pensioner in a post office. The full and horrid truth emerged as I dutifully ingested icky jam-filled brioche croissants: I had pushed myself as far as I could, but not nearly as far as I would shortly have to. The map revealed that my draining efforts had achieved no more than deliver me from one Milan airport to a place very close to the other. The waitress, via a puckered intake of breath and a steeply inclined forearm, made it clear that the route ahead led me smartly away from the gentle plains of Lombardy. Paolo Facchinetti was grimly setting the scene for the 1914 Giro's looming apocalypse, and when I clicked up to Alfonso's screen on the sat-nav he span round and flicked me the Vs.

That first morning introduced one of the unexpected challenges of long-distance touring on a really old bike: getting out on the sodding road before lunch. As I pushed the Hirondelle up the garage ramp, it fell apart like a clown's car. The saddlebag bracket collapsed, and while attempting to keep the destabilised bike upright, the front wheel somehow worked free of its dropouts. In fact, almost every bolt, screw and spoke that could have loosened itself had done so.

Do you own a bicycle manufactured in the twenty-first century? If so, I would ask that you go and kiss it full on the saddle, right now. My everyday ride is a decade-old ladies' hybrid bought second-hand off eBay for forty quid, chosen largely for its lack of theft appeal. Yet this machine is capable of taking me up and down hills in all weather, in ease, safety and comfort – and doing all this while requiring no maintenance beyond a monthly squirt of air in its tyres. You know what a Victorian cyclist would say to that? He'd say, HOLY FUCKING SHIT.

The point I'm trying to make is that owners of even nominally crappy modern bikes really don't know how lucky they are. I didn't until I'd spent the balance of my morning in that hotel garage, tightening stuff up and trying to get the Hirondelle to roll straight. By the time the bike and I creaked out into the daylight it was gone twelve, and my jersey cuffs were despoiled with black streaks

that accurately looked permanent. On the plus side my shorts
were almost dry.

'*Eh – tutto completo d'epoca!*'

I was wheeling the Hirondelle through a shopping centre in
Gallarate – thanks, sat-nav – and looked up to see a plump chap
of middle years giving me a big grin and the circled forefinger and
thumb of Latin approval. It was a doubly cheering encounter: not
only was someone appreciating my full-monty vintage get-up, but
I understood that he was. *Forza* 1984 Business Italian! The man
came over and positively assessed my bike's incantible wheels of
wood and handsome original sella, then shouted '*Bravo!*' and
clapped me extremely hard on the damp woollen back. Some
upgrade from previous native interactions: everyone from the
airport staff to the hotel receptionist had visibly pitied me, an
ageing loser who couldn't afford proper cycling clothes or a new
bike.

The sun was high, and not far out of Gallarate the road set off
to join it. Enthused by my bravo encounter, I stood up in the
saddle. When I sat down again it gave way slightly, then – OW! –
completely. With something beyond disappointment I turned back
and saw the front two inches of the saddle, its whole nose section,
face-up in the cobbled gutter. The hundred-year-old leather had
torn through all the way round, taking with it the steel end bracket.
I retrieved the severed nose but the damage was ostentatiously
irreparable; I looked down and saw that my nuts were now to be
cushioned by a big rusty bolt.

Grateful again for the absence of witnesses, I flung the
Hirondelle against a tree, sat heavily down on the wizened grass
beside it and tried to feel sorry for myself. It wasn't easy. The very
first time I'd got on this ancient bike a bit of it broke, and with
fewer than 100km covered since, equipment failure was already

into double figures. Getting my leg over this geriatric suddenly seemed an act of perverted abuse: it was old enough to be my grandmother. What in the name of Satan's cock and balls had I been thinking of?

The tanks of gloom were on my lawn, with the stormtroopers of sober realism already kicking the shit out of the rockery. I picked up the severed saddle nose with quivering fingers that could not feel it. After less than one full day on flat roads, both man and machine were falling apart; imminent gradient in both its flavours seemed unlikely to retard these processes. Things were going to go wrong that I wouldn't know how to put right. All sorts of things, involving public disgrace at best, and disfiguring injury at worst. The only sensible, adult course of action was quitting right here, and right now.

I pressed my crochet-gloved hands over my face and screamed into them loud and long. Then I climbed back on the Hirondelle and pedalled tentatively away in a semi-erect half-crouch, failing to admire the glittery splendour of Lake Maggiore laid out beneath me.

By unhappy coincidence, my Giro had started to unravel in almost precise geographical sympathy with the 1914 original. As the storm-sodden peloton rode out of Sesto Calende and away along the shore of Maggiore, a cry rang out from the darkness: 'Watch out – nails in the road!' Too late: the entire field, plus its following motorcade of journalists and race marshals, came to a ragged, hissing halt. Sabotage-related punctures were a feature of almost every major race back then, and more than a few since: the practice enjoyed a memorable revival in the Tour de France I'd just watched, when a scatter of carpet tacks wreaked carnage on a Pyrenean summit. But this was something else. Nails had been strewn in countless thousands along a great length of road, and in the rain-lashed blackness the riders' acetylene lamps couldn't pick them out. The lucky got through with just a couple of flats; others found that the three spares they carried about their person weren't enough. For some of the pros and almost all of the *aspiranti*, the Giro was over before it had begun.

The race organisers had expected serious pointy-metal bother, even offering a hefty 1,000-lire reward for anyone who dobbed in a nail-chucker (dob in four and you'd have out-earned the Tour winner). Sabotage in those days was seldom an act of mindless mischief: people disrupted bicycle races because they really hated bicycles.

In the history of transport, unfamiliarity has always bred Luddite contempt. Let us refer once again to the development of the balloon, and the pioneering experiments of Jacques Charles. On 27 August 1783, Charles untethered the first hydrogen-filled balloon, an unmanned 35-cubic-metre sphere of rubberised silk he dubbed *Le Globe*, from its moorings in the Champ de Mars in Paris. His gasps of delight as he watched it rise up, up and away would evolve to cries of anguish: having come to a rest near the village of Gonesse, 21km north of Paris, *Le Globe* was summarily shredded by a baying pitchfork mob. (In fairness, their fears were well founded: less than two years later, 130 houses in the Irish town of Tullamore were razed to the ground after a balloon crashed and burned.)

Bike-bashing had been part of cycling history from the very beginning, when Karlsruhe's fearful citizens banished Baron von Drais and his pioneering velocipede from their streets. By the end of the nineteenth century, as bikes became integrated into daily life, all manner of spuriously affected parties queued up to despise them. Farmers grumbled that bicycles panicked horses and lowered dairy yields. Embittered watch- and piano-makers claimed they were being driven out of business by the trend for marking special birthdays with the gift of two-wheeled personal transport. Milliners complained that cyclists had stopped wearing hats: a US consortium petitioned Congress to pass a law obliging bike-owners to buy a minimum of two felt hats per year. Shoes didn't wear out when you switched from walking to pedalling; cobblers weren't happy. Theatre owners, innkeepers and preachers blamed time-hungry bicycle touring for a downturn in trade, and – pass the chutzpah – tobacco firms raged that a million fewer cigars and cigarettes were being smoked every day.

Direct action was often alarmingly extreme. Carriage drivers, fighting a rearguard battle against the horseless future, drove cyclists into ditches and against walls. Street-sweepers pelted them with the equine ordure whose impending scarcity threatened their jobs. Things got especially out of hand in Holland, would you believe, where gangs of *'velo kannibalen'* routinely battered bike riders unconscious. Dutch cyclists felt compelled to ride in groups, and cycling magazines carried adverts for a 'handlebar-grip high-calibre revolver', with a handy quick-release holster.

By 1914, all this business had died down in most European countries. Backward and impoverished Italy, however, was not most European countries. Anti-Giro hostility remained intense and widespread, in most cases the product of simple rural resentment. Who did these bloody people think they were, poncing about on velocipedes while hard-working country folk tried to scratch out a living? Let's see how they like *this*.

That night, looking at the photo I'd taken of the sawn-off scrotum-stabber between my legs, I was impressed that I'd carried on at all. Astonishment set in when I saw how much of the map I'd crossed, and how brown and pointy most of it had been. At the lakeside town of Arona I wasted a lot of time trying to cushion what was left of the saddle with my emergency fleece, then set off up a modest thoroughfare that identified itself, in Italian, as 'road of the little Alps'. I didn't think there could be such a thing as a little Alp, and I was right. The trees turned to pine and the road twisted upwards through them. My hands flapped reflexively at gear levers that weren't there; my thighs quivered under full load. When they could support me no longer I cravenly lowered my buttocks down onto the saddle. At once the metal frame and its fixings seemed to gather into a bunched metal fist; rumbling down the brief descents was like being energetically violated by a robot.

The sat-nav let me know that it was stupidly hot, that my speed was into single digits, and that we'd just passed 600m altitude: nearly 2,000ft, higher than almost anything in England, miles higher than I'd been on a bike for twelve years. I kept trying to forget that I probably shouldn't even be up here, that the threadbare itinerary as related by Paolo had left some very widely spaced dots to join, and that I'd eschewed a far more sympathetic valley route out of – yes, really – scenic preference. Sweat blotted right through my cap, and pooled repellently around my woollen waistband. My entire head seemed to expand and contract in time with my lungs. How had anyone ever managed to do this sort of thing on this sort of bike, in this sort of long-sleeve roll-neck jumper? When the sat-nav beeped me off the tarmac and up a meandering red-gravel footpath I was in no fit state to argue. It seemed like a good time to trial that ladies' gear on the other side of the hub, but my shrivelled brain feebly spat out a more appealing plan: I got off and pushed.

'No pizza? No *panino*? No croissant repulsivo con jam?'

I had to find out the hard way that small-town Italy doesn't do lunch, at least not in a form of any use to the dying cyclist. Touring France, I could count on stuffing my big, fat midday face in even the most dismal hamlet. In Italy it seems everyone goes home for lunch, to get their cheeks pinched over a massive bowl of Mamma's pasta. The few village restaurants are rarely open for lunch, and though – as in this case – there's always a bar, you'll be lucky to find one offering more than a sandwich. That day I wasn't even that lucky. I bought the last two packets of crisps in Valduggia and ate them under a roadside parasol, next to a table of old men playing an ill-tempered game of cards.

In between crumbly fistfuls I slaked an obsessive thirst for Coca-Cola, the glucose drip in a can. It seemed almost poignant to find I could muster no enthusiasm for the more potent refreshments that had featured so prominently in my French *déjeuners*. I hardly needed an excuse: almost every rider in the 1914 Giro started each stage with one of his bidons filled with *vino rosso*, and thereafter topped it up whenever possible. Later in the race, an over-zealous customs officer tried to confiscate a bottle of Barbera from Giovanni Gerbi's saddlebag as the race crossed a departmental border. Gerbi was a fêted rider who had finished third in the 1911 Giro, but he was having a bad day and evidently couldn't face the rest of it without his reserve supply: when the officials and journalists drove up they found Gerbi kicking the officer senseless.

The scenery settled, and I rolled along a hot valley dotted with forgotten towns, decrepit Renaissance palazzos cheek by dusty jowl with cement works and abandoned sawmills. All was quiet, or almost all: the Hirondelle pulled a swelling symphony of harsh decibels over the fan-pattern cobbles. The jangling scrape of ancient chain round ancient sprocket, the desiccated rattle of an oven-baked freewheel, the increasingly bothersome *pa-donk* that crowned every turn of the pedals. Every tiny imperfection in the road surface had the bidon lids a-pinging and the brass bell a-dinging. Larger bumps sounded like a slammed cutlery drawer, and presented more serious issues: I bucked over a level-crossing and shed two springs from the brake calipers. Six spares used in a day and a half: would my 150 be enough? All the while draughts of hot, wet sheep rose up from my merino jersey, and the saddle's exposed metalwork enmeshed itself ever deeper into my horse's skull of an arse.

After a stop to sustain myself with a messy fistful of roadside blackberries, I remounted and found pain replaced by a harrowing absence of sensation. It was as if my intimate parts now belonged to someone else: someone who was dead, and had died a virgin. I had somehow coped with a busted sit-upon for 60km, but only now wondered: Why? I hadn't even tried to find a bike shop, and at 5 p.m. with a weekend looming I might have seventy hours to rue that oversight.

In the event I barely had time to burst into tears before looking up to see a sign that read: *Pepebike – tutto per la bici!* The road was passing a rundown little industrial estate marooned between distant towns, and the sign led me to the only unit open for business. If I have another child, I hereby vow to christen it Pepebike. Though after what my reproductive organs endured that day I doubt I'll get the chance.

'Eh – old style!'

Italy's bicycle-repair artists, I went on to discover, come in two flavours – sweet and sour. Giacomo, as this cheery, flip-flopped gentleman instantly introduced himself, oozed glucose – mmm! – from every pore. Before I'd had the chance to fail to explain my predicament, he'd wheeled the Hirondelle into his cavernous back-room workshop and hoicked it up on a work stand, cooing and beaming all the while. *'Super old style – magnifico!'* Three bike-fixing assistants abandoned their stations and came up to say other nice-sounding things, though one of them perhaps enjoyed my outfit a little too much, and later made a 'gurning deviant' face when he tried the goggles on.

With a regretful sigh Giacomo pronounced old Brooks dead; I kept its severed nose and left him the rest. He rooted around under the counter, extracting a proposed replacement. 'Old style?' Well used it certainly was, though the balding fake suede and aluminium rails were hardly period correct. Still, it was the right kind of brown and there didn't seem any gain in quibbling. Not even when Giacomo scratched his stubble, shrugged and asked for fifty euros. Mind you, this did include fitting, and a ninety-eight-year service.

Forty minutes later, with the brakes and bottom bracket extensively overhauled and my reanimated loins the talk of the workshop, I completed a test circuit of Giacomo's car park. My bike would never be quite the same without the Brooks – nor, oddly, ever quite as comfortable – but it now felt markedly more dependable. I shook Giacomo's hand, absorbed a torrent of good wishes, then blurted out a farewell message that combined inexpertly rehearsed phrases with the withered fruit of that Business Italian course.

'I now go a Tour of Italy to the year 940 by a French bicycle from this epoch. Respectfully yours!'

The storm that laid waste to the 1914 field hit its dreadful peak as the bedraggled survivors approached Biella. From this point on, Paolo's account began to sound less like the report of a sporting event than some dread prophecy of the imminent horrors of trench warfare. Uprooted trees blocked the way; bikes and cars skidded into ditches or sank to their axles in the mire; rivers burst their banks. With the road swallowed by flood waters and most of the route signs blown down, many riders found themselves utterly lost in surging tides of mud. Calzolari recalled desperately shouting out for directions from farmers braving the storm to rescue livestock.

As sunrise approached, a group of soldiers spotted 'two mud-soaked ghosts' stumbling hypothermically past their barracks: Calzolari and Luigi Ganna, winner of the inaugural 1909 Giro. The soldiers dragged the unprotesting pair inside and dunked them in hot baths; a while later, the semi-comatose Calzolari was roused by a passing commotion and belatedly learned that he and Ganna had been in the lead, but now weren't. He pulled his soaking kit back on, staggered deliriously out to his bike and set off in wayward pursuit.

Biella, a grubby textile town in obvious decline, presented a suitably drab backdrop to my own more humdrum travails. Once again I ran out of juice right at the death, making such a weary mess of dismounting in the hotel car park that the Hirondelle and I both ended up flat on our backs. A moment later, when the kindly and bilingual receptionist recommended a restaurant outside town and suggested I travelled to it by bicycle, a furious riposte burst reflexively from my lips, along with the boiled sweet I had just taken from the basket on her desk.

'Sorry,' I gurgled, wiping purple saliva off the Formica and avoiding her wide-eyed alarm. 'I've just ridden a hundred and ten kilometres with half a saddle.'

Instead, I shuffled up the street to a garish parade of demonstrably unpopular dining establishments. I went into the only one that didn't have enlargements of glistening fast food displayed outside, and was led into an uncustomered back room dominated by a wall-mounted mega-telly that kept me very loudly up to speed with some spirit-withering junior talent show. As fat-faced young punchables warbled above me, I manfully dispatched a pizza topped with raw oven chips: a necessary carb-fest that may rank as the most challenging meal I have ever completed in southern Europe.[1] My appetite was not improved by Paolo's introduction to the 1914 Giro's post-Biella progression: 'The attack on the Passo della Serra began at dawn.'

I was up before then, driven from my bed by a plague of mosquitoes. Like the 1914 riders I had packed no more than the bare essentials of life on the road, but it's fair to say our concepts of necessity may not have overlapped. An awful lot of my bag-space seemed devoted to tackling or preventing maladies they would have just put up with, like saddle sores, sunburn and tooth decay.

---

1 *Incessant pizza bingeing: an apology. In these pages, the reader will encounter nightly scenes of explicit stonebaked-dough consumption. A devastating spoiler, I know, but it seems necessary to explain my gut-numbing one-track diet in advance. It's all about reliable calories. Replacing the energy expended in cycling all day is not something you want to leave to chance. Order pasta and you might end up with eight twists of fusilli splashed in red water. Meat and two veg could easily mean pushing a couple of florets and a new potato around a lonely chop. But a pizza is, and always is, a hefty open toasted sandwich that packs a generous and predictable calorific punch. Plus, when the manipulation of cutlery proves too much for your trembling, glassy fists at the end of a long, hard day, you can cram it home without tools, which I find isn't such a great scheme with spag bol.*

And insect bites: I now blearily embalmed myself with military-grade concentrated repellent, too tired to recall the warning supplied by the Dutchman who had given it to me in the middle of a Swedish midge cloud many years before. His words burst into my groggy brain when I ran my tongue across sun-dried lips and felt it shrivel and froth, like a slug in salt. 'This is serious shit, my friend: get some in your mouth and it's bye-bye salivary glands.' Thodding bollocth.

A night apparently spent licking oven cleaner off cane toads doesn't seem like ideal preparation for a marathon bike ride, but for whatever reason I was bang on it that morning. I rolled on empty weekend roads towards the foot of the Passo della Serra, then put my head down and ground steadily up its verdant contours. It was no more than a big hill, in fact, though the commanding view from the top made its nonchalant conquest seem more impressive. A giant sparkling lake, a fecund plain ripening in the sun, and in the hazy distance a dim rank of Alps. When the day was done I'd be right at their feet, having pedalled off the edge of my Lombardy map and all the way across its Piedmontese successor.

The fickleness of good form is one of the durable frustrations of long-distance cycling. In the week ahead, Calzolari would win a stage by twenty-three minutes, and lose another by over an hour. It was the same for him and for me: you simply never know if you're about to wolf down the miles or choke on them. All I can say is that through some alchemic combo of a tailwind, two mid-morning espressos, benign terrain and a jersey pouch full of hotel-breakfast buns I covered 142.4km that day – an achievement, I've just established, bettered only twice during my Tour ride.

I can't even hand much credit to the Pepebike pit stop. Giacomo's remedial work was audibly undone before I crested the Passo della Serra, and on the descent the bottom bracket acquired a new double-lurch in each turn of the pedals: *ker-dunk-pa-donk*. Number 7 quite plainly required extensive daily fettling of the sort I was not technically or temperamentally cut out for. The best I could reasonably expect of myself was a cursory morning once-over, an assessment of basic roadworthiness governed by one maxim: fuck it, that'll do. Anyway, that day it did.

Freed from the smothering preoccupations of fatigue, I could for the first time take proper stock of the blue-hued world beyond my bidons. It was properly rural around here, the air heavy with the muscular smell of rosemary and sileage, topped with wafts of gently frying garlic and two-stroke Vespa fumes in the villages. String-vested husbands tended their sunflowers, wives sang in their kitchens, kids filled their paddling pools. Maize seemed to be the crop of choice, crisped-up and harvest ready; it only now occurred to me that all the women I'd seen sitting in field-side camping chairs weren't sweetcorn vendors waiting for a new delivery of produce, but – and a good afternoon to *you*, madam! – prostitutes. Approaching Turin I detected a sad pattern that would be copied at every other city I passed in and out of: Africans furthest out, then old Eastern Europeans, then young Eastern Europeans. Belatedly I recognised the odious brazenness of punters in Berlusconi's bunga-bunga Italy, the well-dressed husbands who'd popped out in the family Fiat for a quickie in between lunchtime courses at Grandma's house, happy to flaunt their sordid roadside negotiations in front of passing cyclists.

Cyclists plural, because now – on a weekend and near a major settlement – I was no longer the only two-wheeled show on the road. When a mini peloton of club riders wobbled towards me out of the heat-haze, my frenzied ding-ding-wave-hail-ding-ding greeting was met with a guarded half-nod. I understood why when group after group of cyclists – some old, some young, but all in matching jerseys and riding machines of recent high-end manufacture – began pedalling by in both directions. By the time I broached the suburbs of Turin I had encountered more proper road cyclists in an hour than I did during my entire circuit of France. I'm guessing this explains why Italian riders have won seventeen Grand Tours since 1990, and the French only one. (Well, this and the ropey doctors who made Italy the cradle of EPO.)

The day before the sun had been a bully; now it was a warm companion. I spent the entire day failing to feel guilty about the persistently glorious atmospheric conditions, by rights a disrespectful affront to the storm-lashed 1914 survivors now inching into an Alpine blizzard. My bidons were drained with refreshing sips, not the desperate gulps of yore. The minute one was empty, a street fountain seemed to magically appear. Turin's were wonderful, cast-iron antiques decorously topped with the city-emblem bull's head. I checked my shadow as I leaned over to fill from one. Big peaked cap, shielded goggles, one foot in the clips and the other on the cobbles: I'd never felt more Alfonso.

'Eh, mister-sir, how you are, bye-bye!'

Clearly I didn't look very Alfonso, though. Funny that 1914 Giro fashion should so accurately identify a twenty-first-century Englishman engaged in some daft challenge.

Turin was even more subdued on a high-summer Saturday than Milan had been on a Thursday. The only shop that had its shutters up was an African grocery, with a sign outside that said: 'Yes – we are open in August!' So it was that I traversed the *Italian Job* city's many-laned avenues without alarm, or indeed excitement of any sort: the cold logic of satellite navigation steered me right through Turin without offering even a glimpse of any centrepiece attraction, picking a route through careworn, undistinguished districts that might only lure a tourist if he had a sewing machine to repair or a sudden fancy for halal kebabs.

Out of town I headed westwards, into the setting sun, towards Alps that reared abruptly from the foreground plain, as if someone had jolted the horizon with a defibrillator. I dispatched the last breakfast bun, soggy with chest sweat, then stopped at a village Spar for what would become my standard late-afternoon restorative: a litre of milk and a bar of Milka Extra Cacao. One hundred kilometres, 120, 140. I settled down in the drops and let the road come to me. Hubris welled unstoppably: this was a piece of piss. It didn't even seem an issue when the rear wheel developed an elliptical imperfection, which, at speed, bounced my buttocks clear of the saddle, as if I was riding a horse. What of it? I raised the revs and bucked into Susa, gateway to the bastard Alps.

Susa was one of those curiously grubby Alpine valley towns, its chalet-roofed apartment blocks streaked grey with glacial grit. It bustled, though, and largely with beach-phobic French holiday-makers: the border lay just behind one of those monstrous flanks of Alpine rock that hemmed the town in on three sides. It wasn't just the number-plates that gave them away. Italians manifestly enjoy life, but a Frenchman on holiday is Eeyore with cancer.

I found a small hotel just behind the main drag, run by a kindly old couple. The wife seemed genuinely thrilled when I suggested that I keep my bike in my ground-floor room, and as I wheeled it past reception her husband fairly jumped to his feet. '*Bella, bella,*' he cooed, the entrée to a jolly chat about vintage cycling, near the start of which he gently corrected the more ridiculous errors in my prepared speech about going the Giro of 940.

I could at least accurately inform him, by parroting the title of Paolo Facchinetti's book, that the Giro I had chosen to retrace was *il più duro di tutti*, the toughest of all. At this his wrinkled face wrinkled further. '*No, no,*' he protested, '*Charly Gaul, Monte Bondone.*'

Having encountered both names while researching famously awful Grand Tours, I knew he was referring to the 1956 Giro. The snowbound Dolomite stage in question was a horror indeed: sixty riders, including the race leader, abandoned in sheer frozen agony, dumping their bikes outside bars and farmhouses and blundering rigidly indoors for warmth. Gaul, a tiny Luxembourger who later earned the nickname 'Monsieur Pipi' for his pioneering achievements in the field of on-the-move urination, had started the stage sixteen minutes off the pace, and would end it with a Giro-securing lead. Amphetamine use was then almost universal, and Gaul later admitted he necked more pills than anyone: prodigious consumption of a drug that raises metabolism and thus body heat probably explains why he rode through the blizzard in a short-sleeved jersey (by the finish it had frozen to his torso, and had to be cut off him).

Throw in the heroic travails of Fiorenzo Magni, as the hotelier now did, and you have the ingredients for suffering-based infamy. Despite riding halfway round Italy with a broken collarbone and humerus, Magni somehow finished second, keeping the pain at bay by gritting his teeth round a strip of inner tube tied to his handlebars. Only forty-five riders finished the race, but that was a lot more than eight: terrible though the 1956 Giro certainly was, 1914 was, like, way terribler. I didn't have the words to explain why, but it seemed a small tragedy that I needed to at all. The 1914 Giro and Alfonso Calzolari meant nothing to even an old man, one who lived on the fateful route itself, right beneath the mountain that only half the starting field would reach the top of. The last surviving Great War veteran died just before I set off, and with an inward sigh I realised the 1914 Giro had now also passed from living memory. In the weeks ahead I encountered precisely no people who knew anything at all about the race. Woollen roll-necks and wooden wheels, twenty-hour stages on strychnine and Chianti: these were now the forgotten tales of dead men.

'*Solo?*'

Slightly less hurtful than 'Just one?', perhaps, but walking into a restaurant alone isn't fun in any language. Once again I was led to a dingy, rearward corner, then covered in an old horse blanket and pelted with slops. It wasn't much better when I went over the road for an after-dinner *digestivo*: the barman placed my thimble of bitters on a distant table underneath a blaring radio speaker, then gestured at me to go over and join it.

I'd brought along Paolo's book to set the scene for my morning challenge: the ascent to Sestriere. Translation was always tricky – my 162-gram pocket dictionary didn't make the packing cut. Trickier still given the barman's fondness for weapons-grade Euroshite pop, tumultuously dispensed by some station with an idiotic English name, like 104.5 Jolly Wellness or Sexy Jeans Box FM.

Sestriere was already notorious to me as the ascent where Horrid Lance won his first Tour in 1999, speeding ludicrously away from the world's greatest climbers to build an unassailable overall lead. What I hadn't properly grasped, until very slowly running my finger along Paolo's words with a head full of New Look Gossip Sound, was the climb's dreadful enormity. 'From Susa to Sestriere it is needed an ascent of 40km.' Forty? *Forty?* That didn't seem possible: go uphill for 40km and you'd surely be, I dunno, in orbit. The sat-nav said we were at 521m, and the map told me Sestriere topped out at 2,035m. The road between the two did an awful lot of twisting about: one ominous compaction of hairpins brought to mind my O-level diagram of the human digestive system.

Sestriere – the cursed mountain. Paolo's heading for his account of the climb didn't help the bitters go down. My stomach lurched as I read that the fun had begun right here, almost bang outside the bar.

Lucien Petit-Breton, a double Tour de France winner and the brightest international star in the field, had already endured more than his share of punctures that night; with the rain now torrential, he flatted again in downtown Susa. At the messiest end of his tether, he tore off first the tyre, then his sodden jersey, yelling at the attendant team car for a dry one. On being told they'd run out, Petit-Breton suffered 'a genuine hysterical crisis', mounting his bike and roaring away up the flooded street, one-tyred and bare-chested. When the team car caught him up, he vaulted out of the saddle, raised his bike aloft and battered it repeatedly against the support vehicle before collapsing into the gutter. 'An inglorious end for a great champion,' said Paolo of Petit-Breton's impressively French abandonment. The Giro has no respect for reputation: this was Petit-Breton's third and final attempt at a race he never finished.

Faithful to the tradition of mountain climbs, it got worse higher up. The rain turned to sleet, then a full-on blizzard. Defeated by the frosted mud, all the surviving riders got off to push their bikes up the path laid by Napoleon's troops a hundred years previously. They were joined on foot by journalists and race officials, fleeing their glaciated Fiat Tipo Zeros to desperately stamp in some body warmth. Racers cried like children and begged the Lord for dry clothes. 'This was a Calvary,' concluded Paolo, and for once the default metaphor for extreme sporting duress seemed apt: if Jesus had been made to ride up Sestriere on frozen gravel with no gears, Christians would now be wearing little bikes round their necks.

On my way back to the hotel it suddenly began to bucket down. I broke into a jog and at once my right knee seized solid, almost pitching me into Petit-Breton's gutter of wet surrender. When I started to walk again the joint wouldn't bend; I made my way back to the hotel like a man with a full-leg plaster cast.

The juddery interface between old steel frame and Italian road had been steadily eroding my sense of touch, and my toes bore blistered tribute to the shoes of Gerard Lagrost, tenaciously preserving the strange contours of their former master's feet. But this was a whole new level of disability. Why now? I levered myself awkwardly down onto the bed, smeared a palmful of ibuprofen gel into the affected patella and tried not to think about what lay ahead. It wasn't easy in a room festooned with wet cycling clothes, and a bike jutting out of the en suite.

CHAPTER 7

A gale banged shutters all over Susa that night, and by the time it blew itself out near daybreak I'd given up trying to sleep. A 40km climb on a disintegrating antique, with one knee and no gears . . . As the church bells struck up, my mind spooled back through all those previous daft journeys of mine, searching for a more doom-laden night-before. Only once could I recall staring up at a dawn-softened ceiling with such saucer-eyed dread: in a caravan being playfully butted by the donkey I was about to lead 500 miles across northern Spain. It now occurred to me that Number 7 was more animal than machine, wilful and needy, primed to exact revenge if I pushed it too hard.

The breakfast room was a study in wordless marital loathing, full of French couples gazing coldly through each other. I swung my unbendable right leg under a table and captured the miserable spirit, bitterly loading up on carbs while staring out the Alpine view. The old *patrono* brought me my coffee with a look of concern, and he was ready with another when I Douglas Badered the Hirondelle past reception.

'Sestriere?'

'The cursed mountain,' I rasped.

He filled his red-veined cheeks and let out a long, slow huff of sympathy. 'Courage, my friend.'

Good things needed to happen, and did. First, I found that bending my knee for the purpose of pedalling was not only possible, but almost painless. Second, I managed to change gear – a process, remember, that involved removing and rotating the back wheel – in as few as eighteen minutes. Third, I cycled several kilometres up, and then back down, the wrong mountain: an invaluable learning experience that helpfully alerted me to the minuscule benefit of my Femina 'mountain' sprocket, and the petrifying uselessness of my brakes. I arrived at the foot of this retraced detour with exhaustion and terror battling it out on my features. When I looked down I saw the brake blocks had been eroded to brittle crescents, smoking gently in the Alpine sun. JOKE: wine corks don't make great stoppers.

The right mountain was bigger than the wrong one. Outside Susa the road dusted its hands and ploughed resolutely skywards, tacking up Sestriere's lower slopes with switchbacks and long, steep ramps. Residual gusts of gale had twice blown my cap off ascending the wrong mountain, but they were long gone now; the sun bore down from a windless hard-blue heaven and swiftly brought my brain to a rolling boil. In between desperate rasping breaths, claggy hunks of the previous night's Euroshite seeped helplessly from my blistered lips: *Ho voglia di dance all night, di dance all night*. Creaking through Gravere (820m, 1,000ft, above Susa) I plunged my whole mad head – goggles, cap and all –

straight into a mossy old fountain trough outside the village grocery. Then I saw that despite being Sunday it was open, and squelched blankly inside for provisions: a Bible-sized slab of stale, Friday focaccia, and a reckless surfeit of Coca-Cola.

On the approaches to Susa I'd noticed a growing number of roadside tributes to accident victims; now there were even more, and I was proceeding sluggishly enough to read them. Every single one mourned a young man, and I had a good idea how most had met their end: at irregular intervals, a Day-Glo pack of huge motor-cycles would tear deafeningly past, two or three abreast, or four if there was a blind corner ahead. How I came to hate those death-centric, me-scaring weekend nob-rockets, and the demonstrably brainless girlfriends who clung to their sweaty leather backs. It's now clear to me that the only reason anyone ever buys a massively engined Ducati is to ride it like a stupid shit then die.

The trees thinned, taking those welcome pools of shade with

them. Each grimacing crank of the pedals felt like a rev too far. Left leg down . . . and . . . round, right leg, left, right, head and shoulders rolling sluggishly all the while. Anything to stay above wobble speed, when you're going so slowly that remaining upright involves a desperate and arthritic seesawing of the handlebars. *Not the wobble – NEVER the wobble.* What a sorry let-down my ladies' gear was proving to be, the difference between towing a drugged sow up this mountain instead of a drugged sow in a hat. How infuriating to have learned, just before leaving, that multi-sprocket derailleur gears had been patented well before 1914, and weren't even banned by the Giro authorities: riders only eschewed them for being possibly unreliable and definitely unmanly.

It was in 1906 that Paul de Vivie, the spiritual father of cyclo-touring, launched a derailleur system that I don't really under-stand, but which did offer dependable access to up to four gear speeds. De Vivie trialled his mechanism in the hills behind St Etienne – home of my Hirondelle – and saw it accorded interna-tional acclaim after a 200km mountain race between a male pro and a female amateur, won by the latter on a bike with a three-speed derailleur. 'She never once set foot on the ground over the entire course,' wrote an astonished journalist, an insight into the age of pushy-up-hillo that I would imminently be reliving. Henri Desgrange, who didn't allow derailleurs in the Tour until 1937, damned this result with the very faintest of praise: 'I applaud this test, but isn't it better to triumph by the strength of your muscles than the artifice of a derailleur? We are getting soft. Come on, fellows: let's say that the test was a fine demonstration – for our grandparents! I still feel that variable gears are only for people over forty-five.' Quick question, Henri: why don't you piss off?

De Vivie, so keen to make cycle touring more accessible that he nobly refused to patent his system, deserves at the very least to have his face tattooed on every adult cyclist's forehead. How grateful I was to have come of age in the post-Paul era of humane uphill assistance, even as I grovelled miserably through a rerun of the era before. De Vivie later drew up a list of cycling command-ments; I'd written these up on the inside cover of my notebook, and consulted them while I cracked off focaccia fragments in the shade of a wooden bus shelter.

Eat before you are hungry. (My score on this: 2/10. But I bet
   Paul never tackled a 2,000m mountain on fossilised
   focaccia.)
Drink before you are thirsty. (1/10 – been thirsty for ninety-
   six straight hours.)
Rest before you are tired. (1/10 – been tired since 1994.)
Cover up before you are cold. (10/10 – hollow laugh.)
Peel off before you are hot. (0/10 – 'Woollen Cyclist's Nude
   Shame.')
Don't drink or smoke on tour. (10/10 – evenings don't count,
   right, Paul? Paul?)
Wear yellow and masturbate every four hours. (Sorry, made
   that up.)
Never ride just to prove yourself. (-400/10 and a thunderous
   honk of the Family Fortunes klaxon.)

Off again, inching upwards. The bipolar sonic landscape was a curious torture: four seconds of heart-punching Ducati scream, then long minutes of huge, hot silence. Lizards scuttling through the sun-crisped roadside brush, the rubbing swish of warped rim on burned cork and a haunting creak from my leather toe-straps, a sound my brain chose to interpret as the groaning timbers of a becalmed slave ship. I'm surprised I didn't go completely mad, though I clearly did a bit. Every time a Ducati howled past I wanted to blurt out a confession for something terrible that I hadn't done. '*HO VOGLIA DI DANCE ALL NIGHT!*' All Coke and no carbs make Tim a strange boy.

Oulx was the last town before the rocky, treeless final haul to Sestriere. I stopped at a petrol station for milk and Milka, then checked the sat-nav: 23km to climb 1,000m. The road swung southeast – a direction I'd be getting used to for the next thousand kilometres – and suddenly wind was howling right in my face. There's an insufferable impertinence about a headwind, shoving you rudely in the chest like some bouncer's massive hand: and where d'you think *you're* going, sunshine? It seemed only right to take this wind to task, and I did so loudly and at length.

This proved a poor use of my depleted reserves; my speed wound down to a shamefully geriatric 7kmh, and I was overtaken by a butterfly. The wobble was with me, and the only thing that kept my feet on the pedals were the chants of encouragement now echoing down from Franco–Italian holidaymakers barbecueing outside their villas: '*Allez! Allez!*' '*Vai, vai, vai!*' From somewhere I found the strength to raise an acknowledging hand, haul myself out of the saddle and force the speed into double figures. Then the final shouts died away, and round the first available corner I dismounted like a Dalek at a rodeo.

'I have no gears and they pushed it up here in 1914.' This, I decided, would be the optimum wording on a placard to be waved at vocally disdainful vehicle passengers, below the headline: 'BUTTON IT, WANKERS.' In the saddle I'd been at worst a silly-goggled figure of fun; out of it I was a hateful, pathetic failure. Cars and motorbikes shot past at aggressively close quarters, strafing me with jeers and whistles. The act of walking reactivated my knee condition, forcing me into a theatrical rolling limp that did nothing to appease my tormentors.

I toiled up unwelcoming, lumpy highlands set in a blue-skied bowl of craggy peaks, the stiff wind and steadily accumulating altitude at least taking the edge off the heat. The gradient was a git but never a total bastard; I could see why Hannibal had chosen this route to lead his elephants over the Alps. My mind wandered, and my gaze settled wearily on the tarmac at my feet. There's nothing an Italian likes more than despoiling a scenic roadside, and extended exposure to discarded packaging presented the opportunity to enhance my stunted vocabulary. After scanning a few kilometres of litter I could picture myself holding court at a bar, intriguing drinkers with gnomic mash-ups of phrases old and new.

'My bicycle is one hundred years old and made with twenty per cent real fruit pulp.' 'Wheels of wood? Enjoy responsibly.' 'The most difficult race of all time causes fatal lung cancer and may diminish fertility.' 'Ribbed for maximum pleasure – I want to dance all night in your cursed mountain!'

When my knee hurt too much to walk I climbed back on the bike, grinding out a couple of hundred metres until progress congealed and the handlebars began to shimmy and twitch. And so the ascent of Sestriere took its place amongst the most dreadfully protracted ordeals of my life: double maths, the *Archers Omnibus*, my late forties. It's no exaggeration to say that it was literally the worst thing anyone has ever had to do.

When the 1914 frontrunners reached Sestriere at midday, they expected to find nothing but a signalman's cabin and an obelisk erected to mark the recent centenary of Napoleon's crossing. The team cars were floundering distantly up the slopes, but astoundingly, a group of diehard fans had braved the conditions and stood in wait for their heroes with hot water and dry clothes.

Back then, as Paolo says, 'nobody ever went up to Sestriere'. They didn't until the 1930s, when the Fiat-owning Agnelli family built a winter resort at the top. The cylindrical hotel towers they put up still dominate the town, and indeed the lengthy video footage I took during my final approach, hoping to persuade all the Sunday strollers that I had a valid reason to be walking. The show-piece hotels and cafés at the head of the pass were aswarm with the wrong kind of bikes; I remounted and trundled through the hinterland of 1970s ski-lodge apartment blocks. Most betrayed the dark and shuttered look of seasonal mothballing, but I found one that didn't. Its front desk was manned by an Eastern European lady who spoke just enough English to bring a bad day to a dis-piriting close.

'So you are lonely man, without friends?'

I agreed that I was.

'I have only big apartment, but is no problem. You complete register here. Not this section, is for family, and you are lonely man.'

She led me and the Hirondelle to a three-roomed self-catering suite fit for seven skiers, at the building's furthest, gloomiest extremity. I had to make my own bed with a pile of provided sheets, and the absence of toiletries meant a shower with concentrated detergent, washing my kit underfoot like an aged peasant stamping on wine grapes. My first pee since breakfast bore grim tribute to a hot, hard day: a painfully extruded dribble of Tizer.

I hobbled out to see what kind of people take their summer holiday in a ski resort. Answer: people who go to bed at 7 p.m. Plazas that were teeming when I'd rolled through an hour before now lay bleakly deserted, and as soon as the sun went down the temperature followed it like a stone. I dully mused that this tends to be the case at 2,035m. The only other diners in the only open restaurant were a French mother and her son, a boy of about ten. She droned away into her phone for the entire duration of my meal, and way beyond the duration of her son's, who finished his *gelato* just as my pizza arrived. At length he tired of staring listlessly out at the chilly, unpeopled street, and directed his attention to her untouched glass of lager. The first sip was nervously surreptitious, but success and its alcoholic bounty soon led to disinhibited, chugging draughts. He drained his mother's beer before I was halfway through mine; I raised it in appreciation, which he acknowledged with a glassy wink. Walking past the window after I left I saw *Maman* still yammering on, and her son's chin sinking to his chest.

Back in the lonely man's apartment I thought of my own family, and the substance abuse that its neglected juveniles might be seeking solace in during my absence. They would all have returned from Iceland that day, I realised, and when a text bleeped in I grabbed my phone and stared at it with desperate, reddened eyes. 'Hello,' I read, 'we think you may be entitled to compensation for an accident that was not your fault.'

The radiators were now roasting hot – for the first and only time I would hit the road with a bone-dry gusset – but I shivered all the same. The entire day had been an accident that was all my fault, from the sat-nav defying navigational stupidity that began it to the woeful lack of physical conditioning exposed thereafter. Those hours up in the loft might have readied my legs for the flat miles, but as soon as the steep stuff pitched up I'd died on my wet woollen arse. I'd managed just 54km that day, and my average speed had sunk to an ignominious 15.4kmh. Alfonso was now 6 hours 17 minutes up the road, and whereas I was about to collapse into my fourth bed since Milan, he had yet to stop. For the 1914 boys, a bad day was four punctures in a blizzard. For me it was walking up a hill and having to make my own bed. I clicked off the light and once again shook my head in Butch Cassidy-pattern disbelief: Who *were* those guys?

'Look, bicycle has bedroom also!' joked the receptionist the night before, but tough love meant the Hirondelle had slept in the kitchen. I looked him up and down while breakfasting on a packet of Tuc biscuits some skier had left in a cupboard above the fridge. Many a clumsy leg has been hoisted over that rust-blistered top tube, I thought, but I bet in all his ninety-eight years he's never been as high as this. High enough for frosted windows in August, and for the altitude-based throb belabouring my skull. 'Chin up, Gramps,' I said, to myself as much as the bike. 'All downhill from here.' At this a mouthful of Tuc lodged in my throat: Sestriere was the roof of my route, and I was about to ride off that roof with only four slivers of singed wine cork to slow me down.

Operation Corky McBrake-o-Carve was always going to be a rum affair, and the decision to leave my kit warming on the radiators rummed it up to the max: I executed the procedure entirely naked. The six corks I'd collected en route should have been enough for twelve replacement brake blocks, but a heavy touch with the apartment's bread knife procured just five. Out with the old, in with the new: the poking, jabby work of an hour made a terrible mess of my hands, chest, thighs and the kitchen floor. When it was done I pushed the bike out of the door, then pushed it back in again and got dressed.

'Goodbye to the lonely man,' said the receptionist as she handed back my passport. 'Only the nature is his friend.'

I silently begged to differ: glorious as the crisp and cloudless mountainscape outside undeniably was, it would soon be doing its un-level best to kill me.

Seeing the road fall precipitiously away just beyond the apartment complex, I took the opportunity to pre-test my overhauled brakes in an adjoining car park. No point in dainty half-measures: I got up a decent head of steam and slammed the anchors on. The

emergency stop that ensued jerked the back wheel off the ground and smacked my sternum into the bar bidons. That should have been perfect, but the cacophony of scrapes, shrieks and rending twangs that accompanied it suggested otherwise. I looked down, then at the gravelled skidmark behind me, and established that I had just broken every single component of my braking system.

The cable-restraint mechanism that had pulled through its slot in the lever on my first ever ride had done so again, but more dramatically, flanging the metal inside out. Three of my new cork blocks had been wrenched from their carriers; one lay in two halves. All the springs had sprung. Most dramatically, the front right-hand caliper was bent almost double. Its cork-less block carrier now sat jammed between fork and rim, garnished with a neat coil of shaved beech wood that explained the suddenness of my halt.

I retrieved the blocks and propped the stricken Hirondelle against a wooden Christmas tree, one of several stacked up at the side of the car park for off-season storage. The caption to this pathetic scene: 'Festive Greetings from the Lonely Man and his Dead Friend'.

I sank to my haunches and absently noted that my knee had stopped hurting. An old body can heal itself with use, but an old bike cannot. Running my fingers along Number 7's scabbed and ancient crossbar, I thought: You didn't ask for this, you poor old sod. What way was this to treat a ninety-eight-year-old? My wife's great aunt Lilja is only ninety-two, but I wouldn't make her give me a piggyback up a mountain. Even if I did, I'd surely have the good grace not to make a fuss when her ankles popped.

Doubt and defeatism had been whispering in my ear all the way up this enormous mountain; I'd made it to the top and now they were shouting right in my face. That grinding 40km ascent was about to be reversed at unthinkable speed, and entrusting my downhill well-being to this disintegrating antique was a suicidal folly. Would it really be so shameful for us old-timers to take early retirement, here and now? Bail out atop Sestriere and we'd still have made it further than most of the 1914 crew.

With some heat in the air I might have sat there feeling sorry for us all day, but shuddering Alpine cold soon enforced activity. Fumbling frozen pliers in numb fingers, I bullied the caliper back until the manufacturer's name faced forwards. Stamped into the blackened metal in cursive, Edwardian script: *Le Bambin*.

For some reason I began to sing these two words, loud and often, in the fruity fashion of Maurice Chevalier. For some reason this performance caused misgivings to recede. As I worked on I warmed up, in heart and soul: doubt gave way to faith, and fear to bravado. Satisfied with a set-up that at least applied some cork to some wood, though much more of it to rubber tyre and thin air, after an hour I bundled all the tools away and pointed Number 7 downhill.

Prudence beseeched me to walk the bike down to the valley floor – I'd have done it by lunchtime – but I didn't listen to her. Life-shortening though it might be, no way in clicking heck was I missing out on the zoomy reward for all my Alp-ascending toil. Going fast downhill is kind of the whole point of cycling; it's what makes it better than walking.

Momentum built exponentially, and unstoppably. As I joined the main road the valley opened sumptuously beneath me, a post-card panorama of retreating snow-veined pinnacles and chuckling Alpine water. The momentary distraction of this beckoning prospect was enough to accumulate more speed than I could ever hope to get rid of. Cattle, chalets and frost-cracked mountain tarmac flashed past; the rear-wheel bobble hit a million RPM, delivering perineal punishment of a very specialist order. My goggles claimed their first victim, a large UFO that splattered the right lens with bits of abdomen. A quick-fire, half-glance down: 51kmh on the speedo, and painted names strobing crazily by on the blurred roadway below, a legacy of the previous year's Giro. I began to feel strangely detached, as if someone else was enduring this crisis, no doubt because I really, really wished they were.

Snatching at the brake levers, as I'd just discovered up in the car park, was not a recommended course of action. *Nibali's such a classy descender, Phil, you can see him just feathering the brakes through these corners . . .* Drawing deep from all those years of exposure to Tour commentary, I curled two fingers round each lever and squeezed tentatively, hoping at least to slow down to a pace that might allow me an open-cask funeral. Fifty-two, 55, 57 . . . feathering be damned. Not very gradually I squeezed the levers hard, harder, hardest, like a man trying to juice potatoes in his fists. *Sproink!* The right-hand lever suddenly slackened: I was in no position to confirm it, but I knew I'd just shed one of my rear blocks.

If you're going to die in a bicycle race, chances are you'll do it by losing control down a mountain. Chances are that mountain will be in Italy. More riders have died in the Giro than in any other race; the most recent victim was Belgium's Wouter Weylandt, who in 2011 paid the ultimate price for looking over his shoulder while descending a Ligurian peak at 80kmh. In the pre-helmet, crap-brakes age, the toll was truly grim: every mother with a son in the 1914 Giro would have known that six professional cyclists had died on Europe's tracks and roads the year before, a casualty rate never exceeded before or since. Frozen mud made their descent from Sestriere especially exciting. Of the forty riders still in the race, most fell at least once; one shattered his bike beyond repair and abandoned.

Maurice Garin had won the first Tour de France without any brakes at all, slowing himself via the application of shoe to road. This technique was still widely used as an auxiliary brake in 1914, and after a soul-freezing brush with oncoming traffic at the first tight bend I knew there was nothing else for it: with wind and G-force pleating my cheeks and the road beginning to oscillate I drew my feet out of the toe-clips and eased my buttocks forward off the saddle. Sixty-one kilometres per hour . . . The thought of voluntarily planting parts of my body onto this savagely abrasive surface at juddering high speed seemed an outrage against reason. But then a sign flashed past warning of an imminent *tornante*, which I'd found out the day before meant hairpin, and Gerard Lagrost's thin leather soles hit the deck hard.

A very short while later I scraped to an inelegant halt in the village of Pragelato-ruà. Friction warmed my feet uncomfortably, and a number of the little tacks that affixed shoe upper to sole were now denting my flesh. I hadn't turned a pedal for 10km, but nervous exhaustion meant my breaths came hard and fast. There was a bar opposite: I shakily dismounted and tottered inside for restorative sustenance and predicament analysis.

What to do? There was still an awful lot of Alp to hurtle down: the sat-nav said we were at 1,411m, higher than Ben Nevis. I looked out past the window-box geraniums and spotted a ski jump, and at once imagined myself skittering helplessly down it on the bike, both feet on the floor and scrabbling for purchase. Foreboding and double-espresso jitters got to work, and with a stifled dry retch I remembered that the brake block I'd just lost was my last.

'*Sughero?*'

My conversation with Giacomo and his fellow mechanics had unearthed a few key words, and this one was supposed to be 'cork'. The barman had other ideas, first pointing at the toilet door, then proffering a bowl of sugar sachets. In the end I had to mime pulling one out of a bottle in the traditional stance, which let me tell you now is a procedure open to serious misinterpretation.

When the nervous laughter died down I pointed at the Hirondelle leaning against his threshold. '*Sughero per la bici?*' I said in a very small voice. At once the barman splayed out his hands and made a eureka face, then ushered me out into the sunlight and gestured at the shop next door. I had somehow previously failed to notice the two bicycles chained up outside this establishment, or the others filling its window, and most unforgiveably the large banner above it which read, in English, 'FREE-BIKE'. I went inside, and didn't come out for six hours.

Free-Bike was a one-man seasonal operation run by a shy, unabundantly haired young man called Fabio, a mountain cyclist who led off-road tours, hired bikes and – oh, sweet mother of YES – fixed them. He was fascinated by the Hirondelle, and at a wonderfully loose end, a magic combo that catalysed a full-scale mechanical overhaul. Number 7 went up on his work stand, and for the balance of that morning and most of the afternoon, I watched the earnest and kindly Fabio make it all better.

He popped out the cotters, wrapped each in heavy tin foil and tapped them back in: 'No more clack-clack now,' he said in his commendable English. He nipped to the bar and came back with lunch and several prosecco corks: 'Is more 'ard, better for make stop. *Sughero* for brake – *bizzarro!*' While he sculpted these into shape, and rebuilt the problematic brake lever, and properly straightened the bent caliper, I settled into my own task: trying very hard not to kiss him full on the lips, over and over again.

I very nearly cracked when Fabio noted and remedied several accidents I hadn't even noticed waiting to happen. The bucking-bronco rear-wheel action had, he spotted, caused a three-inch lesion to spread along the tyre-wall. Tufts of bare fabric poked out through the rubber; I'd been no more than one pothole away from a catastrophic downhill blow-out.

'*Ciclo-cross* tyre,' he murmured, easing it off the rim. 'OK for grass, no for road.'

'Yeah, but they look really good,' I said, unlashing a spare from the saddlebag. As I did so, Fabio noticed that my modern replacement saddle was already failing to cope: he cable-tied a fat rubber brake pad under the chassis to prevent it collapsing further.

His headline achievement, however, and one that detained this loveliest of men for most of those many hours, was making my wheels the right shape. Neither had been especially round even before absorbing 409km of fully laden punishment. I watched Fabio squat down at his wheel-trueing jig in a mood of bitter-sweet déjà vu. Been there, done that, torn the oil-stained T-shirt to angry shreds.

We talked as he twiddled. Fabio admitted he didn't care much for road-race cycling, but seemed keen to hear about my journey and the 1914 Giro. 'In *eroica* time, true spirit, no doping,' he said, waving away my talk of strychnine and red wine. 'Today in Italy . . .' He shook his head sadly and told me that despair at endemic drug use had compelled him to give up what sounded like a promising career in competitive mountain cycling. 'Even one small local race, prize was a salami, and I see doping!'

The sun was low when Fabio put down his spoke key. We agreed that it was probably unwise to head on down the mountain; he recommended a hotel just up the road. As I feared he refused payment for all those hours of expert labour, though after much insistence suggested €50. I gave him €60 and shook his oily hand. 'Wait, two thing. First is, ah, some *poesia*.' He wiped his fingers on his overalls and fired up the laptop on the shop's counter. 'Here – read. It is about you.'

I bent down to the screen and saw it filled by a poem, translated from some unknown language into approximate English. *Dies slowly he who transforms himself into the slave of habit*, it began, *repeating every day the same itineraries*. Fabio's head nodded significantly beside mine. *Dies slowly he who does not risk the certain for the uncertain, to go toward a dream that has been keeping him awake*. How very moved I was: to think that a free-spirited young off-roader like Fabio should look up to me, suburban, middle-aged me, as the standard bearer of flinty-eyed solo adventure. Moved, then ashamed. *Dies slowly he who passes his days complaining of his bad luck and the incessant rain*, ended the poem, words which might have been lifted straight from the introduction of *How to Be Me* by Tim Moore.

Fabio's second thing was no less touching: he wanted a go on my bike. We took the Hirondelle out into the long, rapidly cooling shadows and I watched him pedal gingerly up the road and back.

It was the first time I'd ever seen someone else ride Number 7, and would be the last.

'Is . . . fun, maybe a little strange,' he said after dismounting, jiggling his wrists on an imaginary set of unsteady handlebars.

'It is,' I agreed, inwardly delighted that it wasn't just me.

We shook hands again, then I rode slowly away towards the hotel. The Hirondelle felt like a different bike, tauter, smoother, younger. With the Alps behind me – or at least beneath me – I felt much the same. Slightly disheartening though it was to have completed only 10 kilometres that day, we had just hugely improved our chances of completing the 2,700 that remained.

CHAPTER 8

Dies quickly he who rides his bike really fast into a tractor.

Fuelled by gravity and impatience, the next morning I covered just over 40km in the first hour. An imprudent rate of progress: even my Fabio-tuned cork brakes could do no more than delay the onset of terminal velocity. I leaned rakishly through tunnels and swished in and out of villages, sometimes risking a half-wave at one of the club pelotons crawling miserably up to Sestriere. Who in their right mind wouldn't cheat in order to mitigate such drawn-out torture? I could hardly think ill of the two rank-amateur *aspiranti* who were nabbed being towed up Sestriere by a car in 1914; far easier to hate the spiteful officials who waited for the pair to finish the stage, more than seven hours behind the winner, before announcing their disqualification.

The road settled into a gentle valley, then bee-lined across a vast alluvial plain carpeted with trim plum and apple orchards. Behind me the Alps were slowly smothered by warm haze. Before me and beside me, a new challenge took loud and wayward shape: it was Tuesday, and with August all but over, the roads were for the first time teeming with Europe's unmellowest traffic.

Those with experience of both will understand the divergent mindsets of driving a car and riding a bicycle. On a bike, momentum is precious, something effortfully acquired, often painfully so. It's therefore more than bad manners when some cock in a van cuts you up, and your hard-won product of mass and velocity is lost in a squeak of brakes. But the desire to chase this cock down and teach him a lesson is tempered by the second principal difference: if a collision ensues, he loses his no-claims bonus, and you lose your legs.

These simple rules of engagement, I now discovered, are less simple in Italy. By the time I stopped for lunch, inexplicably at a garden centre, I'd enjoyed a detailed overview of the more nuanced relationship that exists between the Italian motorist and his pedal-powered road chum. Its basis is respect, and the rather touching assumption that every cyclist is as good at riding a bike as he is at driving a car. There's just one snag: he isn't good at driving a car. Or a lorry, or a bus, or a combine harvester.

British drivers don't like cyclists, but being British they tend to grudgingly recognise their personal space. 'I'd really rather you didn't drive too close to me' – this is the understated message I try to transmit as I ride through London traffic, and with general success. Italians, however, simply don't understand why anyone, in any circumstance of human life, would want or expect a wide berth.

The first time a speeding vehicle shaved my elbow with its wing mirror that morning, a shriek of terrified abuse burst from my lips. It was the same after my initiation in the native arts of being eased into kerbs, street furniture and parked vehicles, and when I paid the price for respecting one traffic signal too many. That shriek would be lying in wait at the back of my throat for the balance of my journey. Indeed longer than that: the night I came home, my wife was woken up at 3 a.m. when in the depths of sleep I very coherently shouted: 'Why don't you ever fucking indicate?'

It isn't malicious. I soon learned that in contrast to their British counterparts, Italian drivers hold cyclists in great affection, employing their horns to communicate greeting and encouragement, not Anglo-pattern reproach or irritation (though I could really have done without the encouragement of HGV drivers: the sudden and terrible blast of their thunderous foghorns generally caused two or three of my vital organs to swap places). It's actually a tremendous compliment when they career past down a medieval alley, allowing you up to 1.8cm leeway between speeding metal and ancient wall. Anything less would be an insult to the deft proficiency of your bike-handling skills. An Englishman who lived in Italy once told me it was considered very poor form for a passenger to put on a seatbelt: the driver would take the implication of perceived danger as a slight on his abilities.

Let's try to be fair: Italian drivers have been raised in a claustrophobic motoring environment. Most towns are a compression of tight old streets, and even major arterial roads are often proportioned in sympathy with the era of fun-sized Fiat 500s. Motorists frequently have no option but to cut things fine, and even if they wanted to give you enough room, it probably isn't there.

Now let's try to be honest: Italians are an appalling liability at the controls of any conveyance, from Vespa to cruise liner, because their main preoccupation – way above arriving with all passengers alive and body panels intact – is showing off.

This infuriating attribute is underpinned with a thick seam of impulsive recklessness. Italians are fundamentally shambolic. Their what-the-heck, go-for-it spontaneity is fantastically well suited to catering and public celebration; less so to negotiating a roundabout. I dare say that the rash expression of daring artistry is consistent with the heady lust for life articulated in Fabio's poem, even though I've just found out it was written by a Brazilian. To me, though, it seems like juvenile hedonism, the helpless indulgence in life's simplest pleasures: yummy ice cream, playing ball games on the beach, watching ladies with big boobies on telly, and getting in a shiny red car and going *brumm-brumm-BRUMMMM*. Plus every Italian has a frankly childish aversion to doing what they're told, whether it's declaring taxable income or looking even one way when pulling out from a side road.

The only exceptions to all these rules are female drivers over the age of sixty, who sit at the wheels of their ancient Fiat Pandas with but one simple thought in mind: crushing me to death.

All of this business would quite regularly force me off-piste. South of Saluzzo, on a busy road that I alone felt wasn't wide enough for two lorries and a bike, I soothed my nerves but not the sat-nav by plunging off down a rural side-turning. It was delightful at once, a sleepy lane that meandered through the shade of towering maize plants, and in sort of the right direction. I paused to take a drink on a little bridge that vaulted a bend in a broad and shallow river. The sun glinted off my bidons and the stilled waters, silvery olive trees shone beneath a cloudless canopy of deep metallic blue, crickets buzzed above the rushing hush of a distant weir. I thought: Thank you, bicycle, for bringing me to this wonderful place. And then I thought: Sod you, Henri Desgrange and Armando Cougnet, for snatching the priceless gift of free-range bike touring, and perverting it into a fiendish torture.

I reached Cuneo just as the markets were winding down, and 97.244 years after Angelo Gremo led the thirty-seven surviving riders to the end of that first and most attritional stage. Paolo didn't specify a precise finishing point, but I figured it would probably be the Corso Nizza, downtown Cuneo's workmanlike main thorough-fare. I trundled up its bike lane, clicking through the sat-nav screens to find that Alfonso Calzolari was now 162km ahead in our silly virtual contest, having required less than eighteen hours to do what had taken me almost exactly five days. Calzolari came in third, but was hailed as the 'true revelation of the race': an unknown amongst the big names who finished in front and just behind. The Red Devil (the wine-loving, customs-officer-kicking Giovanni Gerbi), Lucien 'The Invulnerable' Petit-Breton, Carlo 'The 'Tache' Durando (who rolled in second and flaunted his bushy lip furniture in that start-line photo): this was an age of compul-sory sporting nicknames, and the next morning's papers intro-duced Calzolari as 'Fonso la Mort'. I can't imagine his parents were too happy to see their son christened 'Fonso the dead', any more than I was when I read Paolo's account of its derivation: Calzolari's unearthly capacity for suffering seemed beyond that of any living soul. I'd planned to spend the night at Cuneo, but it felt like the right thing to channel some of that impervious spirit. I rammed my feet into the toe-clips and banged out another 30km to Mondovì. It was what us blank-eyed pedal-zombies did.

In common with a distressing majority of the towns I'd be sleeping in henceforth, Mondovì was positioned atop a towering rock. My distance that day would be a new record, but nothing in the first 146km I covered prepared me for the 147th. The sat-nav's predilection for crow-flying directness led me to an over-grown track that threw itself recklessly at the slope; soon I was staggering through vertical brambles with my bike on my back. At

7 p.m. the heat was still withering. My sweaty hands struggled for grip on the varnished frame, and body brine coursed painfully into my eyes.

Pensioners tended to greet my time-warp appearance with a double take, and the black-headscarved widow who saw me lurch out of the upper Mondovì undergrowth recoiled as if she'd seen a ghost. It must have seemed as if I'd been holed up in there like one of those forgotten Japanese soldiers, an impression I probably didn't dispel by tipping the entire contents of both bidons directly over my head.

By the time the last finisher rode into Cuneo, nearly seven hours behind the winner, everyone had packed up and gone: after enduring twenty-four straight hours of historic awfulness, poor Mario Marangoni had to pedal all round town looking for an official to clock him in. More than half the field had by then abandoned the race, amongst them all but three of the *aspiranti*, who wobbled together into Cuneo not long before Marangoni and then faced the nightly task of sourcing their own food and lodging. Feebly slapping a filthy glove against the locked door of Mondovì's only hotel, I had an idea how they must have felt.

'You hopeless cock-warblers,' I mumbled drunkenly, when it became clear no one was going to answer. I put my face right up to the door and strafed it with a long, messy raspberry, then turned round to find a woman jingling a big bunch of keys at me. In mind of what I'd just said about and done to her establishment, I waited for these to be forcibly inserted into my nostrils. Instead, she took in my oily, brambled derangement with a look of motherly concern and said: 'Oh, *poverino!*' You poor thing. An hour later, laid flat out on the double bed of a huge apartment suite as my kit sloshed round in a washing machine, I thought I probably didn't deserve Italy.

It was a thought that crystallised in the hours ahead. Showered and ravenous, I set up shop at a table outside one of the half-dozen bars and restaurants arranged around the wonderful main piazza, an encirclement of arched colonnades bookended by vast Baroque churches. The sun went down, the streetlights blinked on; a carafe of local *sfuso frizzante* and a rocket-garnished pizza the size of a bin lid were placed before me. Thus began my inspirational and modestly shit-faced vigil.

I'd never heard of Mondovì, and judging from the spirited, snazzy crowd I watched slowly gather on the sheaf-patterned cobbles before me, neither had any other non-Italians. A full moon sidled into position above the pantiled roofscape, and an off-key clonk of ancient bells rang out the quarter hour. It all seemed so perfectly theatrical, right down to the cast: dapper rogues, young guns, giggling girls, grand madams gazing superbly down from their balconies. 'Riding the Giro is like living in Italy,' an unnamed rider told the *Guardian* the week before the 2013 edition rolled out. 'Nothing is straightforward; there are surprises around every corner, good and bad.' Mondovì was a cracker.

I left an extravagant tip, and weaved through the boisterous chatter to a neighbouring bar. Here I pointed vaguely at the strangest-looking bottle behind the counter, from which the barman decanted an unexpectedly colossal glass of herbal booze syrup. Halfway through this alcoholic challenge, I spotted a man I'd earlier seen wearing a white coat behind the till of the piazza's pharmacy. Passers-by nodded at him with evident respect as he made his way across the cobbles to a sleek new BMW, and I suddenly thought: Why can't I do that? Why can't I earn a handsome living and the esteem of a grateful community in exchange for dispensing medicated shampoo while gazing out at this wonderful, wonderful view?

I sighed, belched and drained my overproof cough linctus, then meandered back to bed with a lazy grin smeared over my face, along with a load of tomatoey stuff that I didn't notice until the next morning.

Not nearly enough hours later I was looking back at Mondovì, perched winsomely above the plain on its little hemisphere of rock. I missed the town a little, but the plain a lot more: at 9.45 a.m. I was already off and pushing up the first of many enormous inclines.

It was a naked Michael Gove of a day, one that had begun with the horrible, hungover realisation that I'd left all my kit in the apartment's washing machine overnight. I suppose it could have been worse: I could have been sexually assaulted by a giant scorpion. I wrung everything out until my fists shrieked, then rolled it tightly up in all available dry fabric: towels (sorry), bedclothes (sorrier), curtains (sorriest). Then I put it all on, and stood for a long time with my entire body set in a rictus of damp disgust.

The morning after the 1914 Giro's apocalyptic first stage, race director Armando Cougnet was asked if he regretted the severity of a challenge that had already wiped out half the field. 'Not at all,' began his cheery riposte. 'As long as one rider finishes the race, that's enough for me!' A century on, those dreadful words still echo: as recently as 2011, over a quarter of the Giro's starters failed to finish. It is, and has always been, the most terrible ordeal on the racing calendar.

In the hours ahead – and then the days and weeks – I came to understand how the Giro earned its fearsome reputation. It's horribly simple: Italy is riddled with vast hills. With the northern plains behind me, I now had a good 2,000km of rolling, rearing up-and-downery to deal with. My kit had just about been baked dry by the sun when I swept up to the first hairpin below Montezemolo; by the time I creaked out of the last it was sodden once more.

The woman at the village's grocery clearly didn't like what she saw, pressing a bonus brioche into my hands with a look of grave maternal concern. I accepted it like the brave little soldier I was, recalling that something very similar had happened the day before, when the waitress at the garden-centre café had surreptitiously served me both the options on the lunchtime menu. The last time I looked as if I needed feeding up, I couldn't even ride a bike.

Montezemolo's attempt to drown me in the milk of human kindness intensified as I ate my charity handout on a bench by a roundabout outside the village, trying to ignore an overview of the very lumpy terrain that lay in wait. A silver-haired chap on an expensive-looking road bike clocked me as he passed; after a cartoon-grade double take he did a full circuit of the roundabout and pulled up at my feet. Off came his suave Marcello Mastroianni shades, exposing his suave Marcello Mastroianni face.

'Has one hundred years and without gear-change,' I began,

wheeling out some new catchphrases, then wheeling them back in when it became plain he wasn't paying attention. He leaned his bike against the bench, placed his hairy brown hands on his shaven brown thighs and stooped down to inspect the Hirondelle.

'*Incredibile*,' he said, shaking his silvered head. '*Tutto incredibile*.' Then he rose, turned to me and spread his arms wide. I stood up, and leaned uneasily into the proffered embrace. As he'd just cycled up all those hairpins in the midday sun, and in a sleeveless, unzipped gilet, this was a very warm place to be, and a slightly moist one. '*Coraggio*,' he breathed into my ear, one arm tight round my waist and the other berating my shoulder blades hard and often. '*Bravo, coraggio*.' At length he released me, remounted and bid farewell with a brisk, military nod.

That day I had begun to chronicle my progress via voice recordings, rasped into my phone on the move. This soon became standard practice, but it seems I had yet to master the technique, because after dictating a shockingly dull appraisal of some abandoned glass factory, I failed to press the stop button before dropping the phone into the front pocket of my jersey. The consequence was a covert forty-eight-minute aural slice of my journey, which is sure to prove a game-changing archival asset for anyone who doesn't like me.

The first thing that strikes the listener is the constant and maddening shake, rattle and roll of the Hirondelle in motion, the difficult sound of an elderly machine at war with itself. Focused on the ongoing miracle of my self-healing knee, I clearly hadn't noticed that just two days since St Fabio had done his stuff, Number 7 was once more coming apart at its rusty seams. A mammoth descent suggests a spin drier full of gravel and bottle tops, rounded off with the protracted, creaky halt of an old locomotive ending its final journey. Extraneous mechanical noises regularly pass through the soundscape: the whining drone of a Vespa, articulated roars and rumbles, car after speeding, honking car.

Then there are my own sporadic contributions, an unwholesome medley that I now present in full:

'Fuck socks.'

Flob.

Yawn.

'Ya-hey!'

Flob.

'Oh JESUS.'

'What's that supposed to mean? I want to go to the *centro*.'

'Row, row, ROW YOUR BOAT, gently down the . . . WHAT THE NAKED FUCK ARE YOU DOING, YOU DAFT OLD SOW? THAT WAS TERRIBLE FUCKING DRIVING.'

'Dear oh dear.'

Long yawn.

'I really am massively, massively hungry.'

'Ow, that was bad, OW.'

Truly enormous yawn.

'Coming through, thank you, ladies, *ciao bella*.'

'Oh, wow, there it is.'

And, wow, there it was – the twinkly, sun-spangled Mediterranean. I coasted to a halt by the railings on Savona's elevated promenade, and looked down at the late-afternoon beach scene: a fat dad wrestling the air out of his lilo, a vanilla-faced tantrum, many irksomely brilliant displays of gel-haired keepy-uppy. For the first time it seemed like I'd come a properly long way, from ski slopes to seaside, from pines to palms, right across two large maps. I turned to the brooding peaks behind and suddenly felt a surge of proprietorial conquest – that was my horizon, those were my hills, this was my beach. I've defeated them all with my own fair legs, I thought, then realised I really needed to eat something.

Two snack-shack paninis later I was off eastwards down the Riviera seafront, now gawping up at a ten-deck cruise ship, now weaving through a mob of flip-flopped Scandinavians, now catching my reflection in the window of an amusement arcade and understanding why mothers kept pulling their kids away as I approached.

The coast road wasn't nearly as flat as I'd have liked, hewn sometimes high into the cliffs and regularly meandering to face a stiffening breeze that propelled eye-stinging particles of sea through my goggle shields. I swooped into and laboured through a very Italian assortment of Riviera towns, some full of bougainvillea cascades and heart-stoppingly desirable cliff-side villas, others all derelict warehousing and football-shirted goatherds driving scabby flocks along dried-up river beds. In between were stretches of beach, a gruelling psychological challenge. Why couldn't I be lain out under a parasol with a word search over my face? Almost everyone out there looked too fat to deserve it. For once I had it worse than the 1914 boys, kind of: having started out from Cuneo at 3.45 a.m., they would have pedalled past these beaches during the less inviting breakfast period. And in a refreshing downpour, the jammy bastards.

Having savoured it at trundling close-quarters, I can recall almost every inch of my passage through the Italian countryside in photographic detail. Cities, though, passed in a panicked blur, knuckles whitened around bars, eyes taking in nothing beyond the murderously wayward traffic. I can tell you almost nothing of Genoa, not even my route through it: engulfed by flyovers and speeding metal boxes the sat-nav lost signal, so I just went with the flow, swept helplessly along like a pooh-stick in a tsunami.

After an hour I washed up at a suburb named Nervi, coaxed out a hollow laugh and called it a day.

The hotel I found was fantastically schizo, a Renaissance villa with a palm-lined gravelled drive and marble balustrades, which appeared not to have been updated, redecorated or possibly even cleaned since the Hirondelle rolled off the St Etienne production line. A ceiling fan like a Lancaster propeller almost brushed both walls of my room, which was otherwise dominated by an aged basin the size of a cattle trough. The bathroom, just a humiliating towel-wrapped trudge away down a wonky corridor, was a wonky corridor. I sluiced my kit in the trough, strung it up on the ancient shutters and went out to bring the day to a Nervi ending.

The town's otherwise rather lovely piazza had a thunderous,

decaying flyover slung across it – a popular downtown look in these parts – but I wandered down to the seafront and found a delightfully inviting seafood restaurant, looking out at the moonlit Med and patrolled by waiters in white dinner jackets. I surely deserved a reward for not being smeared along the wall of a Genoese underpass, so ordered double chips with my burger at the bar next door. Palming this lot into my face while reading a book about an old bike race didn't seem like the look of love, but that didn't stop me being pestered by one of those rose-in-a-plastic-tube salesmen. I told him I had brakes of cork and he went away.

Paolo's roll-call of the stage-one fallen read like some sporting premonition of the ghastly war that lay just months ahead. The cannon-fodder *aspiranti* had been decimated, along with two-thirds of the independent *isolati*. Fonso was left with just two Stucchi teammates, and the pre-eminent Bianchi team lost almost half its riders. Most shocking of all was the total annihilation of the strongly favoured Atala squad, led by Lucien Petit-Breton. None of its six riders finished the stage, amongst them the first British rider to ever start a Giro, Frederick Henry Grubb.

An eccentric and rather difficult Londoner, Grubb had made his name by setting a number of long-distance solo records: his time of 5 hours 9' 41" for the 105-mile ride to Brighton and back stood for fourteen years. This was an age when being a non-smoking teetotaller marked Grubb out as a sporting maverick, and he went the extra mile by riding in the colours of the Vegetarian Cycling Club. As 'the most talked-of cyclist in Britain', Grubb was the first name on the team list for the only cycling event at the 1912 Olympics, a murderous but entirely era-appropriate 315km time trial round the lakes of Stockholm. Grubb's silver medal – he won another for the British team's overall contribution – attracted the attention of pro teams, and in 1914 he was finally persuaded to take the money and ride. 'F. H. Grubb has returned his amateur licence to the National Cyclists' Union,' reported *Cycling* magazine. 'He will take part in all the big Continental road races, and should prove a very worthy British representative abroad. He is twenty-five years of age, and scales 12st stripped, and when he gets accustomed to the Continental methods there is no reason he should not shine as a star of the very first order in the professional ranks.'

The Giro represented Grubb's first experience not just of professional racing, but of cycling in a pack of other riders, rather than alone against the clock. His bid to get accustomed to the Continental methods would end in retirement at Susa after just eleven hours on the road – undone not by the insufferable conditions, but his own arrogant aloofness. 'Conceited and temperamental, Grubb quickly created many enemies on the road,' reads one Italian assessment of his experience.

For a sport that's about destroying opponents by any means necessary, road-race cycling has always been curiously companionable. There's a brothers-in-arms unity in all that communal suffering, and an honour-amongst-thieves complicity in all the devious means of reducing it. It never pays to properly fall out with your rivals: you never know when you might need a bit of help in a breakaway, or a drink when your bidons are empty. As a foreigner, Grubb was already a target – indeed, none of the five non-Italians in the field would survive that first stage. As a wine-averse, hoity-toity Olympian lettuce-muncher who failed to work with other riders or in any way fraternise with them, his fate was sealed.

Everyone suffered some form of equipment failure that day, but only Grubb's 'mechanicals' were the result of enemy action. He returned home chuntering bitterly about 'the Continentals' and their beastly ways: 'They would stick an inflator in your spokes as soon as look at you.' Disillusionment was instant and impressively profound: after an eleven-hour career as a professional cyclist, Grubb retired – aware that having returned his amateur licence, this meant he would never be able to compete in any sort of race ever again. Instead, he set himself up as a lightweight frame designer and builder. 'At first he struggled in business due to his unlikeable character,' records one online authority, but Freddie Grubb bikes were still being sold in the late Seventies.

I toasted Friendless Freddie with a Sambuca – along with that burger, it's what he wouldn't have wanted – then walked back through a delicate sprinkling of raindrops. In the alley behind the hotel I passed an alfresco mass, or possibly some foully Satanic call to arms, being delivered by a droning little baldy to a semicircle of shiny-eyed acolytes. I pressed awkwardly through the chanting throng, wondering how Alfonso Calzolari would have interpreted this manifestly significant episode. Unusually devout and superstitious even by native standards, two days before the race began Fonso had visited a Bologna prophetess, miracle healer and all-round holy superwoman named Sampira. Placing her hands on his head, Sampira announced that great glory lay ahead for their hometown: its archbishop would be the next Pope and its recently founded football team would win the national championship.

'Um . . . ?' said Fonso.

'Sorry, yeah, and after enduring untold suffering and facing death and that, our proud city's sole representative in the race will claim victory in the 1914 Giro d'Italia. That's you, by the way.'

Almost sixty years later, Calzolari trembled as he related this prophecy to Paolo Facchinetti. You won't be surprised to learn that Sampira went on to score a predicto-hat-trick, though Bologna FBC did keep her waiting for eleven years.

My own future looked rather less glorious when I woke up four hours later with a wet face: horizontal rain was gusting in through the shutters, and the small gaps between my formerly drying clothes. Things were about to get 1914 on my ass.

GENERAL CLASSIFICATION - STAGE 1[2]
(Milan-Cuneo, 420km)

1. Angelo GREMO 17:13:55
2. Carlo DURANDO +13:55
3. Alfonso CALZOLARI +13:55
   Timothy MOORE +9:45:10
   Stage starters: 81
   Stage finishers: 37

---

2 Please see the appendix for a full breakdown of results and a list of riders.

CHAPTER 9

The true pleasure of the bicycle is freedom. You may go where you wish and when, stop wherever takes your fancy, as carefree as a horse rider, not confined and constrained by railway carriages and timetables. The bicycle now allows us to conquer space and time . . .

Marinated in grim irony, this was the quote with which Paolo Facchinetti chose to introduce his account of the utterly appalling 1914 Giro. When the critic and social commentator Alfredo Oriani penned his poetic eulogy in 1897, he was articulating a widely held faith in the horizon-busting, spirit-unshackling potential of a machine that another Italian writer dubbed 'the poor man's space-ship'. Compare and contrast Oriani's rosy insight with Albert Jarry's dystopian novel *The Supermale*, published just four years later, which describes a 10,000-mile race between teams of riders literally bolted to five-man bicycles – their 'external skeletons' – and fuelled with a generally fatal cocktail of alcohol and strychnine known as 'Perpetual Motion Food'.

Jarry appears to have been a gigantically slappable Pete Doherty-pattern pain in the arse, who referred to himself in the royal plural, insisted on calling his own bicycle 'that which rolls', and once expressed his love of absinthe by riding through Paris painted green, firing two revolvers in the air. However, unlike Pete Doherty, Jarry was a true visionary: beyond the artistic overstatement, his dreadful forecast of cycling's competitive future proved compellingly prescient.

It was partly the manufacturers' fault, and partly our great-great-grandparents'. Hell-for-leather track racing still had its appeal – six riders died in velodrome crashes in 1907 alone – but bicycles were increasingly considered long-distance tourers, not speed machines. Gruelling endurance events promoted the hardy reliability of this new breed of bicycles, and fed into a burgeoning public fascination with the spectacle of drawn-out suffering.

Mankind's most conspicuous physical asset is neither speed nor strength, but stamina. We're built for marathons, not sprints. Anthropologists agree that our fledgling species prospered through 'persistence hunting' – the capture of four-legged prey by pushing them to exhaustion over long distances. Most mammals need to offload the dangerous heat of intense exercise by stopping to pant; only we and horses can sweat it out on the move. Our sub-Saharan forebears were no match for an antelope in a savannah dash, but could gradually haul one in over many hours in the midday sun, hare-and-tortoise style.

The impulse to express this unique talent for endurance built throughout the Victorian age. In 1871, brothers John and Robert Naylor became the first to walk from John O' Groats to Land's

End. Four years later, Captain Matthew Webb dived off the pier at Dover and splashed away towards France. (After this famous success, Webb went on to fashion a career from unlikely feats of aquatic endurance. He floated in a tank of water for 128 hours, and ten years after his Channel triumph, attempted to swim across the rapids at the foot of Niagara Falls, an endeavour perceptively described as suicidal.)

The craze for exploring the limits of human stamina came of age at the 1908 London Olympics, when the first marathon was held. 'As I led the field into the stadium the pain became impossible to bear, and I fell to my knees,' said Dorando Pietri, reluctantly reliving this event's terrible finale. 'I got up automatically and launched myself a few more paces forwards. I no longer knew if I was heading towards my goal or away from it. They tell me that I fell another five or six times.' Yet for the spectators, Pietri's delirious, stumbling indignity was as good as it got. The marathon's arcane official distance – 26 miles 385 yards – was cemented that year, the consequence of a route specifically laid out to allow royal enthusiasts the fullest view of the ongoing agony: the race started at Windsor Castle and ended in front of the royal box at White City Stadium.

Watching Pietri wobble towards coma, the very excited Queen Alexandra 'beat a tattoo on the floor of the stand unrestrainedly with her umbrella'. All around her, the Italian runner's grotesque ordeal was savoured with a baying relish that would have made the Colosseum blush. Arthur Conan Doyle spoke fondly of 'this fascinating struggle between a set purpose and an utterly exhausted frame'. 'The most thrilling athletic finish since that Marathon in ancient Sparta,' gushed the *New York Times* the following day, 'where Pheidippides fell at the goal and, with a wave of triumph, died.' Pietri was disqualified for being helped over the line, but the next day Queen Alexandra awarded him a special silver cup in recognition of his entertaining near-death experience.

The new sport of professional road-race cycling appealed like no other to these unedifying base instincts. 'In the ideal bicycle race,' wrote Henri Desgrange in 1903, 'there would only be one finisher.' As the creator of that year's inaugural Tour de France, Desgrange had a fair crack at bringing this grim vision to life: the 2,500km itinerary accounted for two-thirds of the field, and in his post-victory interviews, La Française-Diamant's Maurice Garin could speak only of pain and distress. 'A single thing sticks in my memory: I see myself, from the start of the Tour de France, like a bull pierced by the toreador's spears, pulling them along with him, never able to rid himself of them.' Prompted to expand, Garin croaked, 'I cried all the way from Lyon to Marseille.'

Garin's convict-of-the-road ordeal seemed vividly reminiscent of the infernal, endless, hamster-wheel torture foretold by Albert Jarry, though he was at least spared the fate of Jarry's winner, whose reward as the triumphant 'supermale' was to be shackled to an electric love machine, which then literally shagged him to death.

But one cycling race came closer than any other to realising Jarry's awful prognostication, punishing its competitors with a brutality Desgrange may have dreamed of but never quite mustered, and it's perhaps no surprise that it was held in the land that fathered both Maurice Garin and Dorando Pietri. No sporting challenge of the post-Spartan era can hold a candle to the solar fireball of suffering that was the 1914 Giro d'Italia, which covered 3,162km in circumstances that made Garin's boo-hoo ride to Marseille look like a charity fun run. How it tickled me that the victorious supermale of this attritional apocalypse was a pint-sized Bologna bedmaker.

Getting rained on as I slept was at least a small step towards empathetic hardship with the 1914 Giro's storm-tossed, frostbitten survivors. Over breakfast a rather more impressive menace revealed itself: there had been a military coup. Wherever Italians gather to eat you will find a colossal television hoisted above them, and I looked up from my small mountain of Perpetual Motion Krispies to see this one filled by a heavily decorated nine-star general. His face was sombre and so was his tone. 'Fellow Italians,' he was probably saying, 'there is amongst us a British cyclist unaccustomed to Continental methods. You know what to do.' Then he strode across to a big map, and pointed at several stylised lightning zigzags superimposed on Genoa and its environs.

Later I came to love the roster of Pinochet-uniformed air-force officers inexplicably hired to do the breakfast weather on Rai Uno, the main state channel. But that day, Group Captain Grim had nothing but bad tidings: storm clouds were unmetaphorically gathering over northwestern Italy. I stuffed my jersey full of bread and strode briskly to the dry-goods larder, where the Hirondelle had slept chained to a crate of beer. We had a tempest to outrun.

Up from the sea to a town perched high in the coastal cliffs, down to the sea, back up again – unhelpful terrain for a getaway. Thunder rumbled from behind; I dropped my head, tightened my fists round the wooden bar grips and tried to force the pace. Doing so without gears meant a journey into the red zone. Worryingly vivid images marched unbidden into my head: the Polish painter's disembodied smirk; a toasted club sandwich on a bed of prawns; Alfonso, out of the saddle, number 18 flapping on his filthy back, caning past without a glance. No surprise to hear a demented mantra grunt forth from my sagging jaw: 'Cat-piss tarp, cat-piss tarp,' in a monotone loop of the *Postman Pat* theme.

I came back from the dead at Sestri Levante, courtesy of sugary fluid and a thousand stone-baked calories. Slowly the scrag end of the Riviera came into focus, an Italian Skegness with ranks of empty sunloungers marooned between container terminals. It seemed as flat as Lincolnshire, too: how glad I was to have put those dreadful coastal cliffs behind me, and to have stayed ahead of the black clouds that now shrouded them. I pulled out Paolo, ready as ever to take solace in how much worse it was in 1914.

Stage two had begun before dawn in lawless chaos. As the riders saddled up outside the Cuneo tavern where they'd gathered at 3.45 a.m. for breakfast, the landlady was heard loudly complaining that half of them hadn't paid. Her grievances rose to furious yells when she noticed that all the hams and salamis hanging up in the rafters to cure were now conspicuous by their absence. The innkeeperess ran out into the street just as the starter fired his pistol, giving her a rearward view of thirty-seven jerseys with some very funny lumps in them disappearing at speed. The high-minded, herbivorous F. H. Grubb would have despised this episode in its every detail, had he not already given up and gone home.

Conditions remained tirelessly appalling. A cocktail of fog, rain, mud and bone-chilling cold had everyone hitting the deck: Girardengo after running over a dog, Alfonso after slamming knee-first into a guard-rail, an incident that would add a little top-note of pain to every pedal revolution from then to the finish. Up the coast out of Savona a galloping wind hurled facefuls of sea at the riders, and at his team feeding-station just outside Genoa, Girardengo – in the lead but paying heavily for his effort – stopped for seven long minutes to devour everything on the table. Calzolari and two Milanese riders took the opportunity to escape, pulling out a lead through towns that were freshly familiar to me in Paolo's roll call: *Nervi, Rapallo, Chiavari, Sestri Ponente, Poi il Bracco.*

Then the Bracco. The Aubisque, the Izoard, the Galibier . . . I was unhappily aware from my Tour ride that a definite article isn't something you want to see attached to a geographical obstacle. I remounted, let out a rippling Fanta belch, and pedalled off into the tranquil early afternoon, hoping to get all my serious uphill pushing done while everyone was still slumped over their thirds at Mamma's lunch table.

Italy never smells of nothing. In the airless dry heat of days gone by I'd inhaled aromatic nosefuls of herbs and barbecue. Now, after a little splash of rain to freshen up the biological juices, it was shit and death. Outside Sestri, the stench of brewing nappies gave way first to slow-cooked farmyard ordure, and then – as the road wound ominously upwards – extra-mature roadkill. Some kind of weaselly thing, a flat cat, many hedgehogs and a poor little bloated mole, its fat pink feet raised to the grey heavens. At 300m I saw my first ex-snake, its skin deeply worked into an aerosoled exhortation to Damiano Cunego, a celebrated Italian rider. Any doubts that this climb had been recently massed with indigenous cycling fans were banished by the tarmac artwork I rode over round the next corner: a jaunty parade of spunking cocks.

Alfonso Calzolari made his name on the Passo del Bracco. When he told Paolo the story over half a century later, the details were still vivid in his mind. The moment he turned to face his two Milanese rivals on the lower slopes, and saw – even through the masks of mud – their deep grimaces of fatigued distress. How, thus emboldened, he pulled the trigger and rode off. By the head of the pass Fonso the Dead had built a six-minute advantage, and would extend that steadily over the balance of the stage.

Calzolari had set out from Cuneo in third place, fourteen minutes off the lead and still an unknown to most Italians. Astonished by his own performance, he crossed the stage-two finish line laughing in disbelief – an exercise repeated up and down the country once the full results were published. Alfonso Calzolari now headed the Giro's general classification by over an hour, and his hands were already being pressed into a metaphorical square of wet concrete on Italian cycling's walk of fame.

I paid what homage I could with a mojo-battering slog up the Bracco, or anyway large parts of it. Six hundred and fifteen metres sounded miserably unimpressive, even when I reminded myself that the climb had begun at zero metres, down by a sea that was – oh – now lost in a curtain of black rain. The first fat drops hit the tarmac just as I sped past the foot of the Bracco in the Hirondelle's default runaway manner.

'*Al controllo di La Spezia . . .*' Paolo's words, for no sensible reason, had fired within me an irresistible determination to reach La Spezia that night. So the 1914 riders passed through a checkpoint there – so what? If only I'd thought this as I ground soddenly past hotel after dry and welcoming hotel. A bad time for the day's many hills to catch up with me: even after the old milk 'n' choc pick-me-up I was still weaving about the road. A sign fuzzed out of the downpour; I wiped rain off my goggles with a greasy glove and squinted at it. 'LA SPEZIA 7.' Right, I thought, failing to stifle an extravagant yawn, I can do this.

Fatigue is a generous contributor to the cause of road-traffic accidents, and not just on four wheels. The steady upturn in Grand Tour wipeouts over recent years can be most plausibly explained by the clampdown on EPO and its ilk: in the Armstrong years a peloton could ride hard all day with no lapse in concentration, coordination or all the other mental symptoms of exhaustion. Watch a stage race these days and you can expect regular spills or pile-ups, especially in the run-in. When the heavens open at the Giro, carnage generally ensues, with riders sliding painfully about on the tarmac at every downhill corner. In the 2013 edition, Sir Bradley of Wiggo suffered such a crisis of confidence after one wet wipeout that he thereafter, in his own words, 'descended like a girl', losing long minutes and any hope of victory. (Lord Wiggo retired two stages later – for a handy encapsulation of the relative challenges posed by Tour and Giro, consider this: in five attempts at the latter, Wiggo has finished no higher than fortieth.)

Anyway, the point of all this is that the 7km that lay between me and La Spezia were all very, very steeply downhill, two-thirds of them soaking and the rest enclosed in a hectic tunnel that I can still see when I close my eyes. Still hear it too: the echoing judder and scream of my wine corks, the madly clattering bidons, the terrible Doppler blare of passing horns, the gutless, defeated whimper that somehow segues into a drawn-out vocal preparation for sleep. I have been more tired, and more scared, but never at the same time.

You know how sometimes you pitch up in a strange town and just instantly fall for it, knowing that however long you spend there won't be enough? La Spezia was not one of those. I suppose it just looked like what it was: a big port that took a fearful pasting in the war, and was then rebuilt by distracted Italians out of reinforced porridge. It didn't seem worth trying to find anywhere nice to stay, not that I could have summoned the wherewithal for a search. Thus I groggily sloshed my way to the station and stumbled into a hotel that looked as tired as I felt.

'Ah, bici antica! Bici di Binda!'

Not a bad guess: Alfredo Binda won a stack of Giros in the Twenties. Ongoing vocabulary issues prevented me from correcting the proprietor, a tubby old gent in a vest, but I had a few new phrases to try out. 'I am sorry, saddle not original,' I told him as he handed me my key. 'Bicycle in the room of me, is possible?'

The room of me proved unastonishingly disagreeable. Mosquitoes lined up in wait all around its scabrous walls, all but three of them too high up for a man standing on a chair to get at with a shoe. Drifts of hairy lint were piled up along the skirting boards, and the dismal sloosh of rainy traffic seemed louder than it had been four floors down.

Undisputed lowlight was my antique en suite, which incorporated an imaginatively repulsive shower/bidet combo. I climbed lethargically into it, yanked my kit off and hit the taps: a mighty jet from the intimate spray nozzle shot bum-water straight into my face. This really is no place to linger, I thought a short while after, slumping bonelessly onto the grubby bedspread and instantly crashing out.

Twelve hours later La Spezia ensured I came away with the worst possible impression, pitching me unfed into the breakneck obstacle course of the morning rush hour. Darting, ever-erratic scooters buzzed me into collapsed drain covers. Lorries blasted hydrocarbons into my face at point-blank range. I was pursued through two tunnels by the bendy bus of death. Following some evident shift in the street hierarchy since my last visit to Italy, pedestrians now showed up as serious players in the irresponsible urban-transit scene: newly empowered and congenitally Italian, they swaggered out into the mad traffic at will, protected by a forcefield of cocksure bravado. My brakes, such as they were, proved to have no respect for this forcefield. I'd like to pretend this upset me.

I was into the final ranks of shabby tenements when a Fiat Punto shot out of a side road 6 feet from my front wheel, its driver gazing at me with placid curiosity. 'Hmm, it seems I may be about to cause this cyclist serious injury,' his expression said. 'Honestly, what am I like?' I emptied my lungs at him and careered onto the pavement. At this stage I was pretty much resigned to ending up as a dusty plastic bouquet cable-tied to a lamp-post, but please God: not a La Spezia lamp-post.

With the city at last behind me I trundled for hours through sombre, under-peopled beach resorts. This was summer's end game: the sands were annexed by battalions of private-hire sunloungers, but not one sagged under a mahogany fatso. Plenty of cyclists, though, most of them high-end amateurs with flash bikes and peloton-issue wraparound shades. An especially smug pair rolled by me in a manner that somehow seemed appallingly dismissive; I suppose some men would have risen to this bait and taken them on – men like me, twelve years ago on a proper bike. Ferocious battles with rival strangers were now off the agenda, unless I fancied blowing away some granddad on a shopping bike, which I did.

After the regal old villas and hotels of Forte dei Marmi, the road turned inland; shedding *panino* crumbs over the map outside a bar, I realised I wouldn't be seeing the Med again. I spent the rest of the afternoon in marble country, dumbstruck by the extraordinary mountainside quarries twinkling in the sun off to my left. They've been hewing Carrara marble out of the Apuan Alps for over two thousand years, and these days are doing so at the rate of a million tons a year. When it runs out there's going to be approximately 100 per cent unemployment in this area. Every single town seemed entirely beholden to the stuff: cutting it up, polishing it and fashioning it into tombstones, floor tiles and abysmal representations of dolly birds getting their kit off.

Rather unnecessarily, I felt, my route then swung right at the Apuan foothills, vaulting them with a pocket bastard of a climb. I freely confess to having every intention of tackling much of this on foot, but it was not to be. A van driver took a shine to me at the first hairpin, overtaking with a volley of supportive toots, and as I crawled up to the second ready to throw in the towel there he was again, pulled over by the side of the bend with a Borat smile and a raised thumb. *'Forza l'eroica!'* he bellowed, and though my legs were already quivering I did my best to appear nonchalant, a poker face as hopeless as the one my neighbour's cat pulls when he tries to look like he isn't curling one out in our flowerbed. My new friend wasn't there at the summit, which at least saved me a dilemma: give him a tearful hug or punch his friendly lights out?

The stress of this effort punished both man and machine. As the descent flattened out I became aware that the 'missing link' in each pedal revolution – previously no more than a modestly jarring *ba-tunk* – had grown to a yawning dead spot that occupied almost a full quadrant. Having paid close attention while Fabio addressed this problem, I now knew exactly what to do: find someone to fix it.

Almost at once a large bike shop appeared by the roadside. I pulled over, walked the Hirondelle in and found myself presented with a most promising spectacle: a bald man in overalls at a loose end by a wall-mounted display of semi-vintage road bicycles. Lady Luck was at my side, and when this man interrupted my idiot mumblings in competent English, she tore her top off. Then put it back on and punted me deftly in the nuts. 'Old bicycle is for *collezione*, for *museo*, for like this,' he said flatly, nodding at the Hirondelle while jabbing a thumb at the machines on the wall behind him. 'For touring? No.'

'For touring *yes*,' I insisted, explaining that I'd already covered the thick end of a thousand kilometres on this particular museum piece, and appealing to his sense of the eroica by wedging in some inspirationally colourful details from 1914. 'I am following the most difficult race in history,' I said imploringly. 'Eighty-one men started that race and only eight of them finished.'

He considered this for a moment. 'On such bicycle you are not number nine.'

After the storm-lashed, carpet-tacked horrors of the opening leg, the stage from Cuneo to Lucca was a picnic. One of those steal-your-own-salami picnics, held in a rolling downpour over 340 non-stop kilometres. It claimed ten further riders, whittling down the field to twenty-seven. These days, Giro riders don't always need much encouragement to pull out: in the 2013 race, Lord Wiggo and a number of other competitors retired citing 'head colds', 'flu-type symptoms' and similar conditions of the sort that I wrote in my mum's handwriting when I didn't fancy PE. Contrast this with 1914 race leader Angelo Gremo, who fainted at La Spezia due to 'unbearable pain in the legs and kidneys', yet still tried to climb back on his bike when he came round. 'I can make it to Lucca if I pace myself,' he croaked to the gathered reporters. But his two surviving teammates had just abandoned, 'weeping like children', in Paolo's preferred manner, and the driver of the team car told Gremo to forget about pacing himself: he had no intention of accompanying him in darkness through the Apuan foothills, an area then notorious for murderous bandits. Gremo, yet another tough old bugger who rode the 1926 Giro at the age of thirty-nine and finished eighth, dropped his head, then shook it. Now *that's* a retirement.

I last passed through Lucca as a student interrailer, and remember the city as a gem of walled Renaissance gorgeousness, where I bought a two-litre bottle of Lambrusco that shattered inside my rucksack. This time I was viewing the place through a different tourist prism, but what I saw thrilled me no less. I'd always planned to stay in Lucca, which as the stage-two finish marked my quarter-way point, and the shop I chanced upon just outside the city walls sealed the deal.

It's hard to think of any single way that Ciclidea could have excited me more, though I suppose a bag full of complimentary sweets and money slung from the door handle might have done the job. A bustling little concern in a bustling little street, the place was like B & L Accessories of Ealing run by hyperactive Fabios, dashing about fixing bikes behind a window full of dusty spare parts and racing trophies. Two things seeped out of the door: the smell of oil and new rubber, and a queue of old people holding variously stricken bicycles. A drop-in surgery! In a state of quiet wonder I took my place at the back, behind a tiny chap in a trilby with a one-pedalled sit-up-and-begger.

The action inside was breathless: when you got to the front of the queue, one of the Fabios grabbed your bike and lashed a steel rope round the crossbar, before another hoisted it up on a ratchet to eye-level. At once a third got to work with the spanners and screwdrivers, a new chain here, a set of pads there, a tweak, a squirt, back down to the ground and off you go. Most were processed in under three minutes, with a purposeful lack of ceremony that called to mind carcasses in an abattoir. Sod the cosseting, overblown romance of all that *eroica* cobblers – this no-nonsense bike-betterment was just what I wanted.

I was on the shop's threshold, second in line, when the youngest Fabio walked up and raised his eyebrows enquiringly. 'I have a problem with my central movement,' I said, which sounded like a prim euphemism for constipation, and was delivered in an aptly strained tone. No rope-hoist for me: he leaned down and brusquely appraised my undercarriage where I stood. Diagnosis was crushing and instant: '*Non ne abbiamo cosi in Italia.*' We don't have those ones in Italy.

I'd learned from Fabio, my One True Fabio, the original and best, that this was indeed so – he'd never seen a Thompson before –

but I also knew that to any experienced bicycle mechanic, the almost shockingly basic workings of a Thompson bottom bracket should hold no fear.

'*Chiavelle?*' I wheedled, in a semi whimper. The native word for 'cotter pins' was now a conversational cornerstone, the 'two beers please' of my weird holiday vocab.

'*Chiavelle?*'

His rather challenging look added the unspoken words, 'I'll give you *chiavelle.*' Then he went inside and came back with a club hammer and a nasty smile.

Why was this happening? Standing at the window I'd seen a couple of the Fabios sharing a me-directed snicker, but that was no more than par for the course given the goggle-faced retro-twit whose reflection lay between us.

'*Chiavelle,*' he said again, then knelt down by the Hirondelle and as I grabbed the bars belted it smack in the cotters. CHONK! KRINK! A lusty hammer blow on the end of each pin. My hands were still vibrating when he stood up and said, actually almost spat, a single-word command: '*Vai!*' Go. Just go. Go on, *go*.

I'd covered a sorry 82km since breakfast, and in the last hour Number 7 had first been deemed unfit for purpose, then beaten up. With no gain for its pain: I pedalled listlessly away from Ciclidea to find the *pa-donk* merely retuned to a *ker-snick*. How *dare* they treat my proud old steed like that? This was personal: that was my bike that I'd built, that I'd suffered with and slept with. Hit my bike and I bleed. Diss him and you diss me. After so many shared travails I sometimes felt we were evolving into one of Albert Jarry's half-man, half-bike supermales, welded together, mechanically married for better or worse.

A thoroughly dispiriting day segued inevitably into a miserable evening. Or at least should have. Instead, six hours later I was feeling so much better about my lot that I rounded off the night with a beer from the minibar – in my book, an Elton-grade indulgence. Reasons to be cheerful: Lucca had proved even lovelier than I recalled, my guesthouse was liberally adorned with goblins, and over the course of a well-fed night out, defeatism had been steadily overpowered by defiance.

Was I an F. H. Grubb, who let the native nasties get into his head and bully him out of the race? Or was I an Alfonso Calzolari, shrugging off the snow and punctures, the pain that pulsed through his injured knee with every turn of the pedals, the dirty tricks that as race leader would henceforth be his daily due? Yeah, OK, well obviously I wasn't even slightly him. But I still clicked off my goblin-helmet bedside light with flinty resolve, thinking: Know this, oh snide and sceptical bike-fixers of Tuscany – wobbly wheels, dicky cotters and all, I shall get this job done.

GENERAL CLASSIFICATION – STAGE 2
(Cuneo–Lucca, 340km)

1. Alfonso CALZOLARI 31:54:15 (including a 10 minute penalty)
2. Costante GIRARDENGO +1:05:07
3. Enrico SALA +1:30:01
   Timothy MOORE +16:09:30
   Stage starters: 37
   Stage finishers: 27

CHAPTER 10

Bedroom goblins counted (a.m.): 19

Minutes in post office arranging repatriation of redundant maps and cold-weather clothing: 195

Minutes savouring heart-stopping piazzas, vaulted colonnades, august ecclesiastical splendour, Shakespearian ambience, etc.: 560

Carafes: 1.5

Bedroom goblins counted (p.m.): 38

Kilometres cycled: 0

CHAPTER 11

The knives were out for Fonso as soon as the enormity of his lead became clear. Professional road-racing was routinely rigged back then, a carve-up between the larger, wealthier sponsors brokered by organisers who knew which side their bread was buttered. On the rest day in Lucca, Calzolari was slapped with a ten-minute penalty, following a belated complaint from person or persons unknown. His offence? A trumped-up charge of 'unauthorised assistance' during the previous stage: his team car had been sent on ahead to La Spezia to source sugar tablets and a dry pair of shorts.

I read Paolo's jaded account of this episode under the sinister, degenerate caricatures of Snap, Crackle and Pop grinning down horribly from the breakfast-room walls and ceiling. (When I'd broached the goblin issue with the receptionist the night before, I was hoping he'd grab me wildly by the lapels and blurt, 'You see them? You see them too?' But in disappointing truth, the art was no more than a tribute to local folklore.)

'For me, cycling is today not an honest sport.'

It was the proprietor, a twinkly-eyed fellow who spoke excellent English and served even better coffee. Moments earlier he had made the mistake of not lapsing into a coma when I started to explain what I was up to, and had consequently been forced to suffer the unedited highlights of my adventure to date. Now it was my turn: as I tinkered with the Hirondelle's brake springs on the guesthouse patio, he leaned against his French windows and held forth on the commercial cynicism of modern professional cycling, its chicaneries and tedious predictability, and – a particular bugbear – 'these idiot helmets everybody wear in the *chrono*, sitting in that stupid not normal position'.

It was difficult to keep silent about 1914's grubby plotting: bar the idiot helmets, every one of his gripes had blighted pro cycling since its birth. But I'm glad I managed to, because as I saddled up he told me that I should think of myself as the ambassador for an epoch of romance and excitement.

It was a cool, grey day, my goggles-off entrée into the world of peripheral vision. The roads were busy with Sunday club cyclists; the undulating landscape around grew ever more Tuscan, full of spindly, noble cypress avenues and farmers burning stuff in olive groves. Even the uglier towns were blessed with vintage wonders: I passed a hypermarket set in its own Renaissance moat. I also nearly died.

Since leaving Milan I had escaped perhaps half a dozen speculative assassination attempts by the Fiat-driving granny hit-squads, but in the latter part of that morning they upped their game: this was *The Day of the Panda*. The red one that shot straight across my bows at a village mini-roundabout was no more than a nerve-shredding softener, the white one that clipped my saddlebag in a traffic-light queue just a range-finding sighter. On the outskirts of Castelfranco di Sotto, a rearward grinding of gears and a volley of angry horns alerted me to the imminent master assault.

Intuitively I bumped off the road and up onto the pavement, a manoeuvre that would save me having to dig out my E1–11 European Health Insurance Card with one hand and half a face. At once a flash of mint-green metal and curly white hair hurtled waywardly through my hastily vacated portion of tarmac, kissing the kerb hard with its front tyre, then slaloming crazily up the road for a hundred yards before planting itself into a stone gate post. The impact, preceded by none of the usual sounds of emergency deceleration, was a tremendous whoompfing crunch that filled the sullen air with milky steam. I pedalled into this cloud and straight out. Perhaps I should have stopped to check if the driver was all right. Then done something to make sure she wasn't.

Number 7 wheezed and groaned eastwards, its orchestra of woe now supplemented with a frail, high-pitched bleat from the bottom bracket, as if I had a newborn animal welded up in there. All the same, it was music to my ears. Strange but true: I'd been suffering withdrawal symptoms after just one day of not pushing myself and my geriatric bike to the brink. It had become my duty to do so. In a funny way, every new creak and judder spurred my determination to get this ailing crock over the line and stick it to those naysayers. *Old bicycle is for* museo. The words were lodged in my head, like a dismissive headline pinned up by a football manager on the dressing-room wall to spur his players on.

The 1914 survivors rolled out of Lucca at midnight, seen off by a huge crowd of spectators waving multicoloured lanterns under the first clear skies since Milan. A memorable start to what would be the longest day in Giro history: the stage finish lay

430.3 non-stop, gravelly kilometres away in Rome, the equivalent of London to Newcastle. Today's pros, riding multi-geared bikes that weigh less than a kitten, are rarely asked to cover even half that, on smooth tarmac. Mario Marangoni, who had trailed home a distant last in both the previous stages, told reporters he wasn't expecting to finish this monster in under twenty-four hours. (He actually did it in twenty-two, but would be last again, over four hours behind the winner.)

Professional cycling's longest-ever solo breakaway began at a level crossing 15km outside Lucca. While the rest of the field waited at the closed barrier, Bianchi's Lauro Bordin sneaked away from the clanking bells and red lanterns, then ghosted through a gap in the fence under cover of darkness, carrying his bike over the track just in front of a lumbering goods locomotive. It was a standard ruse, rendered a disqualifiable offence some years later when riders began scuttling under slow-moving trains in the deathly pursuit of advantage. (This being pro cycling, laws are there to be broken: three of the top four finishers in the 2006 Paris–Roubaix were disqualified for nipping under a closed level-crossing barrier.)

The train took four long minutes to trundle by, and because no one had noticed Bordin slip away, no one gave chase. By Fucecchio, where I ate a takeaway kebab in a cemetery, he had built up a handy lead. Here the rest of the field learned of Bordin's escape – but still did nothing about it: with 400km to go, it was dismissed as a nutjob's folly. When Bordin sped into Florence, his advantage had stretched to twenty-five minutes.

'The crowded riverbanks were gaily bedecked with acetylene illuminations': even at 2 a.m., the Florentines knew how to welcome a cyclist. Under a slightly leaky sky I discovered they still do. It seemed a nutjob's folly to pass through without having a peek at the city's astounding cathedral – my entire adult life had elapsed since I last stood unworthily before it – but with its mighty terracotta dome just a piazza away, I found myself mobbed by camera-toting well-wishers.

Rain-resistant crowds clustered around a giant inflatable arch, a grandstand full of trophy-toting dignitaries: I had blundered up to the finish line of a bicycle race that to judge from the increasingly excitable Tannoyed commentary was imminently due to cross it. As I nosed the Hirondelle through the spectators, they parted before me; heads swivelled and compact zooms came out. Larger lenses turned to face me when the tabard-clad professionals, gathered inside the crowd-control barriers, noted my approach. A barrier was unhitched and by some unstoppable process I was semi-ushered, semi-shoved through the gap, and onto the finish line itself. The snappers formed themselves into an arc before me, and got to work. Amongst their ranks was a freckled woman who raised her voice and said, 'Now this guy has *got* to be a Brit.' With an uncertain smile I looked out from the celebrity pinnacle of my life to date: a paparazzi photo-call at the 2012 Women's Tour of Tuscany.

When they were done, the English photographer came up and explained that my entrance had serendipitously filled a gap: in a massively native turn of events, the entire field had got lost outside Florence after someone switched a few route signs. The finale of this four-day race had in consequence just been neutralised – the Tannoy commentator wasn't building to a climax, just being Italian – and the riders were now rolling slowly towards the finish. We tutted indulgently, then I asked how she'd guessed at our shared nationality. 'That hat and those hairy legs, mate.'

It would be some time before a pissed-off peloton rolled over the line, and I spent most of it being patted on the back, photographed and giggled at. Armed with the keystone verb obligingly supplied on request by the bilingual Englishwoman, I was at last able to tell people – amongst them many local journalists – what I was up to. '*Faccio il Giro d'Italia di 1914*,' I said proudly, though this seemed to ask more questions than it answered, predominantly: 'Why?'

Italy's bountiful stock of senior cycling enthusiasts was as ever to the fore. A silver-haired mob cooed and clucked over the Hirondelle, taking especial interest in my cork brakes, worn down once more to crusty nubbins. One portly chap in a yellow jersey came up brandishing a little photo album, flicking through it to show me his lifetime measured out in bicycles: from monochrome, Brylcreemed youth to over-coloured, well-fed middle age, posing proudly astride or beside road bikes of increasing sleekness.

I confess this was a rather affecting encounter. '*Bici, no,*' he said, when I used this word to describe the Hirondelle. '*Questa e una* bicicletta.' He patted my saddle, then his heart: this is no bike, it's a *bicycle*. I liked that very much: as a gentleman of a certain age, Number 7 deserved a more respectful term of address.

We chatted on, after a fashion, until the rain built to a cobble-clattering crescendo and he toddled away in search of cover, calling out words like *'avventura'* and *'passione'* over his shoulder. After this I hardly minded getting utterly, utterly drenched, or having my subsequent view of the cathedral restricted to a smeary impressionist watercolour.

The rain abated, but the topography didn't, and the ego-boost that propelled me away from Florence petered out in Chianti's khaki humps. Rolling hills really are the most hateful of all cyclo-terrains, half the agony of riding up a mountain with none of the rewarding sense of summit achievement. Gasping over the bars at the crest of yet another punishing but unimpressive eminence, I was appalled by what the sat-nav kept trying to tell me. How could these gently billowing olive groves and vineyards be over a thousand feet up in the air?

Greve-in-Chianti wasn't as far as I'd hope to get that night, but I felt an urge to stop there after passing a family having a stand-up row in the street, dressed as ostriches. Round the corner I caught up with a carnival float upon which five large men in full drag were scooping facefuls of soft cheese from a giant treasure chest. I followed them down a narrow street which opened into a long, thin square teeming with garish insanity: water polo players in boxing gloves, women dressed as bananas, bellowing Renaissance nobles. Never would I feel less conspicuous.

A single hotel overlooked the scene, and incredibly it had a spare room, though less incredibly I had to loiter at the desk for half an hour while the receptionist found this out. A small boy showed the Hirondelle and me to a rearward bike shed, then led me back through a kitchen in which a floppy-hatted chef was doing his stuff over an enormous open fire. By the time I'd showered, laundered my kit, changed and helped myself from a wicker basket decoratively filled with robust and durable vintage Chianti corks, the party was all over bar the shouting.

What shouting it was, though. Seated outside with a plate of fire-singed pig bits, a stirringly ageless bacchanal unwound noisily before me. The square – more accurately a yawning cobbled trapezium – was bordered with canvas pavilions, each medievally bedecked in colourful standards and massed with chanting revellers. The waiter deferentially explained the spectacle in English, which was very good of him as I later realised I'd asked my question in Spanish: this, he said, was the annual celebration for Greve's eight local districts, each represented by a tent decorated with their respective crest and banners. 'Every year our *festa* has a new subject, a new *tema*,' he confided, which rather surprised me as the only theme I'd detected was the refreshingly mad absence of one. 'This year, is, ah, how it is, "a glass of fantasy".' That sounded pretty appealing, so I ordered one for a digestif, and woke up trouserless outside a bus station in Naples.

Because that simply isn't true, I came round in my hotel bed to the sloosh of very wet traffic. Not a cheery reveille for any touring cyclist, particularly one facing the challenge I had set myself: today I was going to do it 1914 style, riding on gravel tracks now being audibly churned into peat bogs.

Chianti's fabled *strade bianche*, its white roads, are rare survivors of the unmade byways that were Calzolari and Co.'s daily lot. The swishing crunch of tubular tyre on loose chippings is what draws the Eroica to this region every October, an amateur sportive open to road-racing bicycles built before 1987. The first Eroica, not coincidentally, was held in 1998, the year the Festina affair blew the lid off EPO; the event now draws three thousand nostalgic enthusiasts to celebrate the hard-bitten heroes of a nobler age. It's only supposed to be a bit of fun, but given the indomitable spirit they're trying to recapture it's no surprise that every year some push themselves too far. Eroica veteran Lance McCormack had told me of several riders taken away by ambulance, and a tragic pair by hearse. But he'd also told me that even at the ragged edge of hard-core authenticity, common sense prevailed: 'Don't remember seeing a rider on wood rims and cork blocks. No one's that fucking daft.'

Paolo's unusually threadbare itinerary allowed for generous leeway through these parts – he didn't name-check a single town between Florence and Radicofani, 140km to the south – and before leaving I'd laboriously planned a route that would maximise my contact with bleached gravel. Eating breakfast out on the covered balcony, how I wished I hadn't. Through a curtain of drips I watched cagouled binmen sweeping rain-mulched party detritus off the cobbles below. The hungover waiter looked like he'd swum into work. The Giro d'Italia planners still like to stick in an occasional *strada bianca* for old times' sake, and this was a bad moment to remember the last time they'd done so. Watching the sodden 2010 race, I'd seen just how much fun you could have on these roads in a downpour: half the field slid from gravel to ditch, though a uniform slathering of mud meant the commentators couldn't tell which half.

As General Galtieri had predicted in his breakfast TV weather slot, the skies soon cleared. With the sun out, I could sort of see why this area earned the nickname Chiantishire. Aside from its popularity with my loaded countrymen, it looked like the Cotswolds left a bit too long in the oven: everything had browned and risen. And risen, and risen. By mid-morning I had toiled up to 700m, higher than I'd been since the sodding Alps, the leaden weight of sweat-soaked merino wool pulling me back downhill. Then, with a pre-programmed warble, the sat-nav ushered me off the tarmac and up a forlorn track that meandered away through the spindly oaks. An introductory parade of red triangles transmitted one overall message: shit road ahead.

Yet my introduction to the famous brown roads of Chianti, as they were that morning, proved almost disappointingly benign. The emergent sun swiftly hardened the mud into a firm paste that seemed annoying at worst; certainly less of a challenge to the business of staying upright than the chalky granules I'd trained for. Revised for, at least: for months I'd been collating tips from anyone who'd ever ridden on a *strada bianca*. 'Don't let the camber drag you over to the edges, it's like sticking your front wheel in one of those kids' ball pits' (Lance McCormack). 'Use the ears and the eyes, when *bici* start to slide you hear it first' (off-road wizard Fabio). 'Oh, *orribile*, oh, *difficile*, oh!' (that old feller at the Tour of Tuscany finish line).

None of that now seemed relevant, not in these conditions and at the speed I was going. A far greater test was working up any appetite for the big bag of raisins that was all I had to fuel myself. (Raisins offer the endurance athlete an unbeatable balance of yumminess and calories per gram, or so I'd read on some website – I think it was liesaboutraisins.com).

By mid-morning the sun was really getting to work, kiln-baking the road into something slightly less brown and more gravelled. At last I stopped going uphill, tracking the brow of a desolate eminence that offered a view of scrubby, ill-tended farmland. Away from the Cameron/Blair 'wanker belt', here was the old Chianti, the region that in 1914 found itself cursed with some of the most desperate poverty in all of Europe. It was extraordinarily remote, just me and the occasional walnut-faced farmer in a three-wheel pick-up, half a tree and a caged goose bumping dustily about in the back. At times the track all but disappeared, leaching seamlessly into the rocky undergrowth. It hadn't been *bianca*; now it wasn't even a *strada*.

Down we went. Whee – look at me go! Woah – look at me fail to stop going! Flap-bollocking-arse-funnels no no no no OK I've got it I've got it no I haven't *skeeeeeeesshhhh* OW.

I looked up at the oak trees through a cloud of beige dust. This time I'd managed to wrench my shoes out of the toe-clips, and had even improvised a speedway-style foot-slide, which took off a few kmh before I lost it and hit the deck. I hauled myself aloft and took stock. The bidon rack had shed its load and I'd lost three more brake springs. Otherwise the only damage was a small tear in the side of my shorts, and some impressive gouges in the craggy railway ballast that had annexed the road surface on the winding descent, precipitating my fall.

Fifteen minutes of more guarded progress took me down to the floor of a small and peaceful valley. Here the track ran along an innocent little brook that had plainly been up to no good in the night. A bridge over it was festooned with muddy branches, and flash-flood detritus lay in ugly clots all over the meadows around. The track followed this stream into a forest, and soon I was threading the Hirondelle through big brown pools of standing water. After a while it became a challenge to distinguish brook from road, and I was off and pushing, mud up to my ankles. When at last we squelched away from the riverside, what a sight the tyres were: thickly encrusted with gravelled clay, like Ferrero Rocher doughnuts.

Two hours of dust-scrunching, wheel-slipping white-road action confirmed it: I'd pulled a reverse Goldilocks. My first stretch of *strada bianca* had been Just Right; the ones that followed exposed me to uncomfortable extremes. Ew: too muddy. Ow: too dry. Profitable employment of Lance and Fabio's handling tips did at least mean I negotiated the punishing corrugations without falling off again, though what a stupendous relief it was when my front wheel at last nosed back onto bitumen. The deranged percussion of bell and bidons fell silent; the scenery stopped vibrating. Oh, the velvety miracle of tarmac! It felt like stepping onto the dock-side after a storm-lashed voyage, a joyous relief the poor 1914 riders would never experience.

The enemy was now above, not below – a blazing sun that scorched away all trace of the previous night's deluge and brought a billion flies to life. Most seemed very keen to investigate the inner workings of my ear; I defended myself in a manner that would have alarmed passers-by. There weren't any though, nor a single town or hamlet where I might have acquired cold fluids and something to eat that wasn't a warm raisin. Only the descents kept me going, those delicious gusts of cool air blasting sweat off my messy red face, bending back the brim of my cap to ventilate the plastered scalp beneath. Bonus refreshment came courtesy of the carbonated water I'd filled my bidons with that morning: at down-hill speeds above 40kmh, the juddering front-wheel bobble agitated the contents so violently that a fine spray forced itself through the screw-top threads and all over my thighs. Then the road flattened, and rose, and an airless, broiled silence ruled once more.

By now I was deep in the kingdom of the über-villa: palatial wrought-iron gates by the road, glittering infinity pools glimpsed through surgically maintained olive groves and vineyards. The contrast between the unseen occupants' pampered sloth and my slow-roasted suffering seemed unbearable, especially when the bidons were drained and my brain began to boil. In a moment, or perhaps an hour, I saw myself shaking the manicured hand of a linen-shirted German industrialist, who had hailed me from his villa's gates in refined Bond-villain English. 'My good friends,' he was now saying to his poolside house guests, 'may I introduce Mr Moore, who I believe you will find a rather remarkable gentleman.' Later: 'I am glad you rested well, Mr Moore. Might I offer you a chilled Calzolari?' And: 'This is Mr Thompson, who will be redesigning your bottom bracket tonight. Silence, Thompson, you snivelling dog!'

I crawled into Siena in limp-home mode, my face scabbed with sunburn and raisin husks. Coke, salami *panino*, Coke, Extra Cacao, milk, water and more water: it all went down in the shade of a grocer's awning. Feeling much less dead, I weaved off through the rearing streets and alleys. This was the twisty, banked realm of the Palio, the age-old stampede that hoofs through the city twice a year, clattering to a finish in the wondrous square that now opened before me: Renaissance palazzos and grand civic buildings arranged around a vast sloping shell paved in red brick and travertine marble, the scene crowned with the slender, soaring Torre del Mangia, one of the medieval world's loftiest structures. Siena's Piazza del Campo ranks amongst the most noble public spaces on earth, and as such was thickly carpeted with gormless foreign oafs holding Apple teatrays above their heads.

Not for long, though. The absurd heat had been building to some sort of climax all afternoon, and now hit it: the heavens abruptly blackened, and a terrific whip-crack of thunder ricocheted off the ancient walls. Shrieks and giggles begat a multinational stampede in the aquatic bombardment that followed at once. Perched under the archway where I'd been standing to admire the scene, I had a splendid covered overview of the scurrying panic. In moments the machine-gun rain had the piazza all to itself, and I was sharing my very compact recess with two dozen bedraggled refugees.

'Get a load of that feller with the bike,' whispered one of them, in Australian. 'Is he for real?'

'Negative, master,' I blurted in a loud, robotic monotone, without looking round. This riposte satisfied me immensely, for perhaps three seconds. Then, in preference to enduring an unknown period of claustrophobic awkwardness, I pushed the Hirondelle out into the pitiless monsoon and pedalled slowly across the deserted square. A wolf whistle rang out from some distant rain shelter, followed by a radiating smatter of silly whoops, fitful applause and all the other trappings of a traditional idiot's ovation. I hoisted up a sodden glove and kept it waving, thinking: If I fall over now, I'm ditching the bike and going straight to the nearest airport.

I've always been quietly proud of my mastery of the touring cyclist's core skill: being asleep while it's raining. Clearly I was out of practice. Just past Siena's city walls I ducked under a bus shelter and for the first time unlashed and donned my shriekingly twenty-first-century bright orange rain jacket. I waited there for a while but it got worse, the heavy-metal sky overflowing helplessly, as if God had fallen asleep in the bath with the taps running. Oh, nob goblins: I splashed back out through the gutter rapids and pointed the Hirondelle south, into the headlights and double-speed wipers of the evening rush hour.

Each passing car flung a bucket of grey-brown *acqua da strada* hard at me; the honking lorries unloaded a brimming wheelie bin. Number 7's front wheel ferried a constant sprinkle from road to face, like a massively annoying child with a water pistol. My feet quadrupled in weight; every heavy revolution squelched out little dribbles of sock-water through the ventilation holes in Gerard Lagrost's shoe uppers. Through some perverse osmosis, rain endeavoured to saturate my saddle, from where it was eagerly blotted up by my chamois groin pad. My waterlogged rain jacket was soon doing no more than preventing the escape of body heat; I pulled over and angrily tore it off. It wasn't all bad: in minutes, every trace of the morning's *strada bianca* pebble-dash was jet-blasted clean off the Hirondelle.

The sky assumed the exact colour of wet Italian tarmac, hurling forked lightning into the hillsides. Farmhouse drainpipes gushed like fire hoses. Every bridge I crossed was struggling to contain a torrent of churning chocolate, up to the top of its arches in furious brown froth. Having long since concluded that nothing could possibly make my brakes any more shit, I now found sustained heavy rain proving me wrong. Presently I greeted my fate with a Hamlet-ad sense of resigned acceptance, channelling the spirit of every famously unflappable character I could think of. Mr Spock, Angela Merkel, my brother, Alfonso Calzolari: your boy took one hell of a soaking.

I threw in the filthy, wet towel at Buonconvento. It was a solemn, rather neglected little place sulking behind a clumsy slab of medieval wall, with a mood-compliant old hotel. The ancient proprietor put his hairless head through a beaded fly curtain as I stood there in the austere hall, pooling cold tea on his age-worn quarry tiles. It was probably the most 1914 I'd ever look, and certainly the most pathetic. Captured in sepia mode I'd have made a great poster boy for distressed retro berks. 'This is Tim. Just £250 could buy him a proper bike.'

My request for a room was granted with a palpable lack of enthusiasm, and only after I'd agreed to dine in the hotel's restaurant. When I went out and wheeled the Hirondelle inside I could see him – and indeed hear him – bitterly regretting this decision. '*No, signore, no, no!*' With sudden vigour he all but vaulted over the desk and bundled the two of us out into the street. I could hardly blame him: sodden and rust scabbed, Number 7 might have just been roused from a long slumber on the bed of an urban canal. Scrabbling out a key from the huge bunch tied to his belt, he hobbled over the road and battled open a door that sounded as if it had last been closed in 1973. It was like some mausoleum of broken crap in there, a cobwebbed jumble of discarded appliances and one-legged chairs. I should have felt guilty leaving Number 7 alone with those dusty ghosts, but then skanky dishevelment was his thing: propped between a radiogram and a listing hat-stand he looked more at home than he ever had. It seemed far more awful to drag him back out into the rain twelve hours later.

CHAPTER 12

I will never forget the day I climbed the Puy Mary. There were two of us on a fine day in May. We started in the sunshine and stripped to the waist. Halfway, clouds enveloped us and the temperature tumbled. Gradually it got colder and wetter, but we did not notice it. In fact, it heightened our pleasure. We did not bother to put on our jackets or our capes, and we arrived at the little hotel at the top with rain and sweat streaming down our sides. I tingled from top to bottom. What a wonderful tonic!

What a deranged freak! Paul de Vivie might have invented gears, but it was difficult to admire a cyclist who harboured such wrong-headed perversions. Would Paul have tingled from top to bottom to find his kit still heavy with yesterday's filthy moisture when he put it on the morning? To find his sodden shoes warped and thickened, his bike's every moving part shrieking with corrosion? Yes,

Paul, cycling is often great. But there really is no point denying that sometimes it's shit.

I sloshed on down the Via Cassia, a major Roman artery enjoying a new lease of life with lorry drivers who don't like paying autostrada tolls. What a lot of them there were! Soon I was forced hard up against the calf-slashing roadside brush, where the fraying tarmac was cleaved with long crevasses comfortably broad enough to swallow my front wheel. Doing my Tour thing I'd been regularly appalled by French road surfaces; they were hugely worse here yet so far I'd barely noticed. Reason: in the intervening twelve years, Britain's roads have deteriorated to a condition some way below most of our Continental rivals. Cluster-bombed tarmac is now the British cyclist's daily lot. It's a dull but damning indicator of national decline: in the pothole chart, we're now duking it out with the Mediterraneans.

Crevasse-monitoring vigilance restricted my scenic appreciation, and when I did snatch a glance around I usually regretted it. Drizzle fuzzed out the background, and the foreground was filled with fields of withered sunflowers awaiting harvest execution, their crusty, black heads bent down to the mud. Yesterday's chirruping blackbird was today's malevolent cawing crow; the broiling pre-Siena sun was now an 11-degree mist, so frigid I had to pedal hard to get some warmth in. It was an extraordinary about-face, as if somebody had just pulled a big lever and turned summer off.

The going was heavy, uphill into an insolent headwind that flung handfuls of chilled drizzle in my face. I couldn't believe I would ever rue posting my fleece home from Lucca, and already here I was, rueing it bad. The road steepened. The Hirondelle shrieked through its rust like Laurel and Hardy's railroad handcart. I slumped heavily into the handlebar drops and ground on towards one of cycling's definitive tribulations: that cook-chill marriage of rain and sweat.

I turned left off the Via Cassia; the lorries vanished but the gradient pitched up yet again. We were soon pushing 700m across blasted moorlands flanked by shadowy peaks. I passed a confidence-bothering sign for a ski resort, here in the middle of bloody Italy. What was going on? It was treeless, cold and wet: I kept waiting for the Brecon Beacons to call and ask for their weather and scenery back.

'Bordin's solitary journey passed from night into dawn; at San Quirico he was welcomed by the town band and the cheers of a crowd who came to salute his courage.' As I pedalled through the scene of Paolo's spirited description, a road-sign told me that Lauro Bordin would still have been 194km from Rome. To be honest, by this point I was almost immune to the 1914 Giro's monstrous scale: it literally defied belief that the riders were barely halfway through that absurd third stage.

The least I could do was stick faithfully to their route. I knew I'd regret it if I didn't. On the second day of my Tour de France ride, I blithely snipped off a 600km loop in order to spare myself the damp hills of Brittany. As nobody, least of all me, imagined I was up to tackling more than representative chunks of the route it didn't seem a big deal at the time. It very much did once I'd somehow managed to complete almost every remaining kilometre: the joy of pedalling into Paris was tempered with contrition, a niggling shame that I would never be able to boast of having ridden the entire route of the 2000 Tour de France (I still do, though, all the time). Anyway, never again. I set off from Milan vowing to eschew all short cuts and half measures, a vow that was put to its most severe test yet when I saw that Radicofani – a town Paolo only mentioned in reference to the forty-five-minute lead Bordin had built up when he passed through – sat atop a massive and temptingly skirtable eminence.

Radicofani proved even loftier than it looked, a bleak and ancient village perched some two and a half Shards up in the grey heavens. Doing battle with a year-old cheese sandwich at its only bar, I gazed out at a tight little piazza and the hunkered alleys that radiated away from it. It was a town built for mean winters, the tough old houses hewn from heavy, dark stone. Having spent his post-war childhood in Rome, my father had shuddered when he spotted Radicofani on my itinerary: the place was such a notorious haven of violent criminality that his father, a famously bold adventurer who was then the *Daily Telegraph*'s Italian correspondent, afforded it a very wide berth on weekend family outings. No great stretch to imagine this hard-faced, lonely settlement harbouring a community of ruthless bandits.

On cue a leathery pair of ne'er-do-wells in big flat caps and donkey jackets pushed through the door and approached the bar with a proprietorial swagger, appraising me and a young German couple with gimlet eyes as they passed. On my way back from sprinkling the porcelain footprints – a sure sign I wasn't in Chiantishire any more – I caught a snatch of their conspiratorial mumblings: an extraordinary collision of alien sounds, many almost Welsh.

'My arse is on fire!' Luigi Ganna's memorable summary of his feelings as he stood atop the inaugural Giro podium silenced the Milan crowd. They weren't shocked; they simply hadn't understood a word he'd said. Though born and bred just 60km away in Lombardy, Ganna's dialect was an unfathomable mystery to the Milanese throng – not a regional accent, more an entirely separate language. In 1909 Italy had only existed as a nation for forty years, and was still at heart a conglomeration of disparate kingdoms and city states, all with distinctive customs, cultures and tongues.

The Giro was touted as a truly national event that might promote a sense of shared identity: its unifying potential attracted Mussolini's interest in the Twenties. It proved a slow-burning success. Only after the war would a Giro winner explain himself in words that made sense to everyone. The unintelligible lilt I was eavesdropping on is just one of the ten recognised dialects that still linger on today in Tuscany alone.

From my station at the back of the bar, I watched the old men order a bottle of red wine with no more than a vague nod in the barman's direction. How old *were* they? I'd recently read about some mountaintop 'village of eternity' in Italy that boasted a life expectancy of ninety-five, the highest on earth. Could this be it? Could that pair of gabbling, crinkled rogues be pushing three figures, old enough to have scared my granddad, old enough to have been gurgling in a cot when Lauro Bordin rattled through this square with a forty-five-minute lead? When I left eight minutes later I decided probably not, because in this time I watched them completely drain that bottle and make serious inroads into its successor.

The descent was a crazy plunge down a wet road veined with deep cracks, like a relief map of the Nile delta. At 60kmh my amplified rattle sent birds flapping out of trees and fields across a generous area, and panicked a little black-red squirrel into a trans-tarmac dash right in front of my wheel. If I'd had any brakes this might have lured me into a lethal skid; instead, I just braced for a pulping impact that miraculously didn't come. The more enduring miracle was that none of these lunatic downhill careens had delivered me at unstoppable velocity up to a busy junction or queue of stationary vehicles. Not yet, anyway: without wishing to spoil the suspense, I write these words from beyond the grave. (Yes, you can get Eurosport HD here.)

The rain died away and the road levelled out. A white parcel van overtook me on a bend at incautious speed, misjudging its exit in a fashion that filled the afternoon with the noise and smell of rubbery anguish and left a ten-foot streak of paint along a crash barrier. I watched him barrel carelessly off into Umbria, a lumpy land studded with ruined medieval turrets and hilltop towns. One sat imperiously above the rest, a lofty cluster of terracotta bell-towers that I wasn't at all surprised to find myself labouring up to an hour later.

Those familiar with the epoch-defining account of my Tour de France escapade may recall that I cycled through Switzerland accompanied by a guest pedaller, Paul Ruddle. I suspect, largely because he's repeatedly told me, that Paul wasn't entirely delighted with every published detail of our time together – on reflection, I perhaps might have downplayed our free-ranging, sweary rude-ness about Swiss people, at a time when one of us worked for a Swiss bank. Indeed, I might also have taken the time to consider how his wife – who had recently given birth to their second child – would react on learning that her husband had opted to look sharp rather than wear the helmet she had sent him out with. You may imagine my considerable surprise, then, when Paul expressed an interest in reprising our cyclo-partnership. Since my arrival in Milan this interest had matured into text-messaged commitment: Paul would, by appointment, be meeting me at Città della Pieve in the morning.

Over the years since elapsed, Paul has tirelessly applied himself in every arena of life, reaping rewards that us duller-witted idlers can but dream of: a completely flat stomach, children who take him seriously and – just a few Umbrian hilltops away – a big villa with a heated pool. In a frankly embarrassing bid to emulate his winner's lifestyle, I now checked into Città della Pieve's finest hotel, my virgin foray into three-digit room-rates. Facilities included a glass lift, private spa treatment rooms and a receptionist visibly resisting the urge to plunge a sack over my filthy wet head and bundle me down the garbage chute.

I left my kit marinating in a money's-worth bidet compote of perfumed unguents, and went out for the traditional aimless stroll. In moments I had forgiven Città della Pieve for being on top of an enormous hill. The town revealed itself as a becoming cluster of intricate old brickwork, with big red churches sprouting graceful towers and thin houses that supported each other with buttresses slung across narrow, winding cobbles. I turned every tight corner expecting to bump lens-first into a fellow sunburnt foreigner or ten, but the town had somehow escaped the fate its venerable beauty should have consigned it to. Instead of shops selling souvenir olive-wood bird baths and Sambuca-infused truffle oil there were hardware shops and haberdashers. Couples crossed exquisite little piazzas arm-in-arm; old men gathered outside bars in shrinking triangles of late sunlight; a boisterous young scene was taking hold around the football pitches across from my hotel. I lingered outside one or two restaurants, scanning the toothsome specialities being convivially forked up within, before a familiar voice – mine – reminded me how much I'd paid for my room. A while later the maître d' at my hotel handed me a spoon with the very thinnest of smiles; I took it in the fist that wasn't clutching a carrier bag full of supermarket pasta punnets and scurried into the glass lift.

CHAPTER 13

The blind man set his hands upon the young man's chest, then felt his legs, every muscle and tendon. 'A strong heart and the tendons of a buffalo. Fausto, you will be a great champion.'

The last time I'd thought about Fausto Coppi's masseur was the first time I'd put my goggles on: Biagio Cavanna lost his sight after getting dust lodged in his eyes on a bike ride. I thought of him now after encountering this account of his hands-on meeting with Coppi, in the e-book history of Italian cycling I'd been squinting at on my phone the night before. I imagined Biagio running those appraising digits of his over the torso in my hotel mirror, then turning his sightless eyes to the gaunt figure behind him. 'Hey, Fausto, check out the moobs on this fucker!'

Paul was putting his bike on a train that would arrive at midday, which allowed me a full morning to stare at my naked self through his eyes. (Calm down, Paul – all your friends do this.) Could these knobbly, two-tone legs keep up with a man who had finished several marathons in three hours flat? In the evenings I couldn't cross them without sending jolts of cramp all the way from groin to ankle. My right knee was on the blink again, and Gerard Lagrost had given me corns. Cavanna once compared massaging Coppi's legs to playing the guitar. Massage mine and he'd be smashing it against the speakers.

Everything further up looked damaged, icky or weird. My face was that of an alcoholic peasant at the end of a long harvest. The circular cut-outs in my gloves had left Japanese flags sun-branded into the back of my hands. My fingernails harboured unshiftable deposits of oily dreck: 'I see you are a man who works,' the receptionist at Sestriere had told me, staring hard at my cuticles. I'd lost all sensation in the tips of both little fingers and my loins were still dead to the world.

Weighed down by a breakfast blitzkrieg that left hardened buffet operatives cowering behind the bacon trough, I belched my leaden way up the road to the café that was our arranged meeting point. I spotted Paul at an outside table, delighting the barman with some lively anecdote – since acquiring his villa he has mastered the native language to a degree I'm fully authorised to describe as sickening. He bore a healthy burnish that compared well to my over-ripe fig-flesh, and a Lycra-sheathed physique honed by his 75-mile-a-week running habit.

In defiance of the middle-aged norm I looked considerably more stupid and less athletic with my clothes on, largely down to the practice of stuffing my roll-neck jersey's fore and aft marsupial pouches with a bulging profusion of accessibles: map, camera, hankie, phone, goggles case, breakfast leftovers and – not for the first time – a hotel room key I'd forgotten to give back, despite it being attached to a fob the size of the FA Cup. Paul's helmet – I feel obliged to emphasise its presence and full-time future usage – hung off the back of his chair; there wasn't a grey hair on the head it would shortly be protecting. It was at once both wonderful and slightly deflating to see him.

'Hello,' he said, flashing teeth as white as his fingernails. 'So where are the other Rubettes?'

With a rueful smile I passed on the bad news: they'd all been imprisoned for castrating a man who laughed at their hats.

Paul ordered more coffee, then turned his attention to the Hirondelle and its more manifest deficiencies. 'Are those *wine corks*? Unbelievable.' Another brilliant smile. 'Fancy swapping bikes?' This rhetorical taunt referenced a historical grievance: my shamefully petty refusal to grant Paul even a short turn on my Tour bike, a machine inestimably superior to the heavyweight clunker he'd turned up with in Switzerland. The mid-range hybrid leaning against our café table was a step up from his Swiss mount, but a stratospheric moon-shot above my current assemblage of failing pig-iron. It had twenty-four gears, an alloy frame and stop-on-a-sixpence V-brakes: facilitators of a type of safe and speedy progress with which I was no longer familiar.

Twelve years on the boot was on the other foot, the helmet on the other head, the better bike under the other arse. On the other hand, Paul would have to spend three days traversing the world's most image-conscious nation in the company of a colossal bell-end.

It was lunch by the time we'd finished poring over maps, and after I'd gone back to return my hotel key, having failed to interest Paul in tagging along to see what a high roller I was these days – 'Not even a quick look? It has private landscaped gardens and offers a spacious and air-conditioned Wellness Centre.' At his suggestion we dined outside one of the restaurants I'd regretfully spurned the night before, stuffing ourselves with wild boar pasta. When Paul asked if I fancied splitting a carafe of red, I rather stiffly informed him that I hadn't touched a lunchtime drop since day one. Then said: 'Go on then.'

Under restless, cloudy skies I led us off eastwards, to those unending ranks of dun-coloured hills. On the plunge down from Città della Pieve, a distant new sound inveigled itself into my creaks and rattles. When the gradient unwound I heard it more clearly: helpless laughter.

'Sorry,' shouted Paul, when he was able to form words. 'That back wheel's bouncing you all over the place. It's like you're on a runaway donkey or something.' I stopped pedalling to let him take the lead, a position I felt it best he retain for the duration of our partnership.

The balance of the afternoon took us up and down eminences topped by slumbering villages, their slopes studded with squat, gnarled olive trees of great antiquity. In the valleys beneath crouched Romanians harvested tomatoes under scurrying, rain-bruised clouds; we threaded the needle between hillsides blacked out by sheets of precipitation and somehow got through bone dry. I held Paul's wheel for an hour, then spent the next four watching him slowly shrink to a white-shirted speck up the road. Why can't I have his gears? I thought rather sourly, meaning: Why can't I have his legs, lungs and long-term commitment to intensive aerobic exercise?

Just before seven rain began to spot the tarmac; Paul stopped and at length I caught him up. We got the map out and somebody (clue: not Paul) raised the possibility of spending the night at Paul's villa, now just half an hour's ride away, on a route that had the advantage of passing through the village of Bastardo. But somebody else had an agenda that looked beyond a free bed, and we shortly found ourselves riding into the delightful if rather lofty town of Montefalco.

Paul had been there before and made a beeline towards the central piazza, a compact hexagon of arched loveliness. 'This place is supposed to be superb,' he said once we'd dismounted, and with something close to horror I saw that the square's fanciest palazzo was a hotel, towards which Paul was now striding. Flaming torches guarded an extravagantly proportioned entrance, and through the glazed loggia of its attached restaurant I could see sleekly groomed guests perched on the kind of stupid-looking designer chairs that never cost less than a grand a pop: this gaff made my Città della Pieve blowout hotel look like a condemned Travelodge.

Paul slipped through the panelled doors just as I was about to shout out my taxable income, and emerged moments before I enacted plan B: skipping inside with my jersey off and introducing myself to the reception staff through the medium of the power-yodel.

'Can you believe it? No rooms on a Wednesday night in September.'

'You're *kidding*,' I said, tucking my jersey back in.

We found a hotel down one of the steep little streets leading up to the square. Paul judged the rooms dismal and poky, and rather than tell him I'd slept in worse every night but the one before I tutted my world-weary assent. To be fair, it was good to be saved from myself for once: left to my own grimy devices I'd have rooted out yet another back-street pizzeria, instead of washing down inch-thick Fiorentina steaks with local reds from the wine list's deep end.

Paul toasted my achievement to date, I toasted his most welcome arrival, and together we toasted Lauro Bordin, who had slogged past Montefalco with his lead on the wane. Bordin had by then been out on his own for an extraordinary 280km, inspiring Paolo Facchinetti into a philosophical exploration of the loneliness of the long-distance cyclist.

'What thoughts sustain a rider in these moments?' declaimed Paul, after I asked him to translate the relevant passage in the bar we'd repaired to for after-dinner refreshment. 'His home, his family, the financial reward of this enterprise, his friends, personal pride . . .' Here Paul stopped to drain his beer and allow us both to dwell on this motivational roll-call. 'Lauro Bordin, a lively and, er, something or other young man of twenty-four let all these thoughts and more slide through his mind. When they'd passed, he was left with an empty head and heavy legs.'

Paul restrained a belch; I didn't. 'I don't want to spoil the suspense,' he said, 'but from that I'm guessing old Lauro doesn't make it.'

It was past midnight – a first – when I fumbled off my bedside light. Too soon afterwards I threw open my shutters with regrettable gusto: the skies had cleared in the night, and a faceful of blinding sun sent the hangover pixies scurrying about in my head, clashing their stupid little cymbals as they went. It was a relief of sorts to open the map over my breakfast table and learn that we would imminently be climbing a bona fide mountain: I knew from previous experience that no hangover is a match for drawn-out, shuddering exhaustion. I thoughtfully strove to communicate this phenomenon to Paul when he appeared looking unusually pallid. 'It's all about playing one pain off against the other,' I explained, running my finger up the cartographic contours of Monte Bibico. 'Like, I dunno, staving off hunger pangs by punching yourself in the face.'

Paul considered this briefly, then extracted a very large adjustable wrench from his panniers and slammed it down by my cappuccino.

'Ah!'

I bullied my features into an approximation of gratitude, abruptly remembering that I'd texted Paul a desperate request for such a tool some days previously. Recall was however far from total: I had absolutely no idea why.

By the time I was pushing the bike out of the hotel's store room I had decided it must surely be something to do with the bottom bracket, whose multi-layered sonic output had been entertaining Paul almost as much as my hopalong manner of progress. I put my face down to my *movimento centrale* and wondered how to usefully apply this great leaden implement to it. Of course! In homage to the sneering Luccan I brought its business end hard down on my cotters, dispatching a crescendo of blacksmith clangs that echoed away down Montefalco's narrow walls.

Paul reappeared as I dealt the final blow, swaying red-faced over Number 7 with a wrench in my whitened fist, every inch the recidivist bike-beater. He could have very reasonably asked me what the flaming arse I was doing, or suggested that I might more sensibly have asked him to bring a hammer along. Instead, he stooped down to the cobbles, picked up something extremely small and offered it to me in an open hand.

I recognised it at once: one of the five tiny bolts that secured my right-hand pedal crank to the chain wheel, evidently shaken free during the assault.

'Jesus shitting Krankies,' I gasped by way of thanks. 'That is an *extremely* vital component.'

The likelihood of sourcing replacements for century-old precision hardware had seemed so remote that I'd brought along a baby

7mm spanner expressly to keep this crucial quintet safely tightened. I retrieved it now from the ancient toolbag slung from my
crossbar, then crouched down to reinsert the errant bolt. An interesting revelation awaited: another two of his hex-headed friends
were already absent.

My commitment to routine maintenance, never exactly fanat-
ical, had over recent mornings ebbed away to a token squeeze of
the tyres. What a hopeless fanny I was. It seemed remarkable that
the Hirondelle remained rideable with this most fundamental
assemblage thus compromised, but Paul's prognosis was inargu-
able: lose one more of those bolts and I was shafted. I screwed
home the survivors as tight as I dared, and then a little tighter.

I followed Paul out of Montefalco at a distance, piloting the
Hirondelle with exaggerated caution, as if it was made of lolly
sticks. We stopped at Spoleto for elevenses, an appealing labyrinth
of twisty old streets. Dabbing focaccia crumbs off my face in the
shadow of a Romanesque church, I contemplated the bicycle's
clear superiority as a conveyance for urban sightseeing: no parking
woes, no mirror-scraping alleyway ordeals, and here in Italy no
obligation to obey one-way signs or traffic lights. It was only after
a second coffee, and a lingering survey of the medieval aqueduct
recalled by Paul from a previous visit, that I sensed the danger: we
were beginning to potter.

The following six hours yanked us brutally free from the embrace
of ruminative, point-and-click cyclo-tourism. Bordin's twenty-five-
minute lead at Spoleto was briskly diminished, and as soon as we
left the town we found out why. Long before the turn-off to Monte
Bibico we were working hard up a remorseless incline; the sun
was out and rumbling columns of HGVs strafed us with humid
diesel. Our appointed side-road offered smoke-free silence, at the
cost of baked perpendicular torment. The sun lasered down and

the gradient ramped up, swiftly reaching a pitch more monstrous than anything I'd tackled since Sestriere.

Looking back at me down the wandering, cracked tarmac, Paul captured my grovelling misery in a series of photographs: front wheel pointed this way then that, woollen shoulders rolling, wet red face caught in a rictus of slow-mo agony and half-formed Paul-centric verbal abuse. The rearing backdrop of pine and granite is probably magnificent, like I gave a shit.

So it went on, nothing but heat, pain and the odd derelict road-worker's house. Goal-oriented Paul was manifestly champing at the bit, the sprightly, multi-geared bastard, and in the end I rasped at him to go on ahead and orient his goal, or words to that effect. Watching him disappear at speed round the next hairpin I felt miserably defeated, like a team leader who cracks on a big climb and has to let his top *domestique*, in Giro-speak his *gregario de lusso*, off the leash to grab the glory.

Ruddle's away up the road and Moore is in all sorts of trouble, Sean – are we seeing a changing of the guard here? Sean?

Yes, um, well, he looks to be, uh, majorly suffering here.

After an hour spent mastering The Wobble in its purest, most ignoble form, I found Paul wandering amongst the clutch of slit-windowed farmhouse-forts that was the village of Montebibico. We were now at 840m, atop a big mountain girdled by even bigger ones. 'Are you sure we're supposed to be here?' he said. 'The road just seems to peter out.'

When I'd drained my least warm bidon and got my breath back I told him that couldn't be right: this section of the route was admittedly poorly detailed and abysmally charted, but as a result I'd spent an entire afternoon Google-mapping it back at home. There was definitely a way down the other side of the mountain, and we would find it.

Ten minutes of listless shambling turned up nothing more helpful than the only man in Montebibico, a vest-wearing ancient asleep in a camping chair by his back door. Needs must: I roused him with a furious reveille on my bell. He gripped the arms of his seat and looked at me in bleary panic, as if I was a ghost from his youth come to pay him back for Nazi collaboration or scrumping my olives.

'Terni?' I asked, the next big town along our route. The old man blinked himself properly awake, looked at our bicycles and pointed at the road we'd just come up. Paul explained to him that his friend here reckoned there was a way through down the other side of the mountain. Definitely.

'*Per bici?*' His prolonged cackle begat a phlegm-raising cough. After much waggling of raised palms and sucking through pursed lips, he jabbed a thumb at an unkempt garden path that to my mind – and more importantly to Paul's – seemed to head at least two full compass points away from the desired direction.

We thanked him and pushed our bikes towards the path. It was a scratchy *strada bianca* that sported a mohican of calf-high weeds, and wandered away through a desolate vista of sun-bleached crags topped with derelict, windowless hamlets.

'What does your sat-nav say?'

I wiped speckles of chin-sweat off the screen: the blue cursor showed our current position in the centre of a big, white roadless void. 'Er, "Don't look at me, mate, this was your stupid idea."'

It was gone two and scorching; we had no food and very little water. The only sensible option was to return to the main road, and follow that round to Terni as per the old man's initial suggestion. But a pathological abhorrence of retracing steps is a core male weakness, and after a mutual shrug, we wordlessly remounted and scrunched away down the threadbare, fallow gravel.

I am unlikely to forget the afternoon that now unfolded. Given the choice I'd restrict my memories to the wonderful first half-hour, during which I exploited my recent white-road experience to leave Paul eating beige dust. Then the trees closed in and the path began to disappear under crispy drifts of last autumn's leaves, and presently we found ourselves inching cautiously through long-forgotten highlands. Wheel to trembling wheel we passed listing, rust-streaked signs to dead villages, a Chernobyl playground reclaimed by nature, the flyblown corpse of a porcupine. It was a relief of sorts to round a corner and encounter a large brown dog standing by the path. But in place of the habitual bark-fest and rabid pursuit, it just tilted its head curiously at us, as if thinking: What strange furless creatures are these?

Hunger, heatstroke and reedy panic were all well entrenched by the time the track rounded a further mountain and at last began to head in an approximation of the right way. Then there was a house with a roof, another with a front door, and an actual moving car with an actual living man in it. Gravel turned to patchy asphalt, pointed downhill at a valley joyously alive with traffic and the evidence of human cultivation: I aimed a parched roar at the cloudless sky and tipped my entire water supply over my head.

It was a straight descent, and I rattled down it very much faster than my surviving chain-ring bolts would probably have wanted me to. When the road flattened out Paul and I trundled along side by side, compiling a joint wishlist of the condensation-beaded refreshments we would shortly be enjoying. But events then took a very regrettable turn for the worse; indeed several of them, each one uphill and away from the developed world.

We weren't side by side for much longer. Rivulets of sweat gathered along the brim of my cap and dripped onto my cramp-shot thighs. Active settlements gave way to abandoned hovels and pre-war commercial vehicles with trees growing through their roofs. With the brow in sight I made a last stand in the saddle, a creaking tangle of shiny limbs.

And Moore is all over his machine now, yammered my inner Paul Sherwen. *He's turning himself inside out here, Phil, just hoping to drag his body up to the summit.*

I got there and found it was merely a starter summit, the warm-up act for a much loftier crest that the distant figure of Paul was steadily ascending. *Biddle-ip!* Once more I suffered the taunting bleat my sat-nav issued whenever I got off to push: the sound of failure, rubbed in with a dread on-screen legend, 'Movement not detected'. *What a disgraceful, repulsive spectacle this is, Phil. We're watching professional road-race cycling die right here before our very eyes.*

An eternity of shrivelled shuffling took me back up to 800m, almost as high as we'd been at Monte Bibico. At least when I caught up with Paul I was back on the bike, kind of: not so much in the saddle as draped over it, like a dead cowboy brought into town across the back of a horse. It took me a while to register that the scabrous whitewashed structure sheltering Paul from the sun was an ancient communal laundry, servicing the shuttered hamlet behind. There was a packet of Omo next to its mossy trough, and a brass faucet decorously styled as a dragon's head, which was soon vomiting cold water all over my scalp. Then I drank and drank and burped and drank and hoped Paul couldn't distinguish dragon-water from tears of relief.

On any other day, the 40km that followed would have seemed a terrifying ordeal. As it was we breezed gaily from one near disaster to the next, feeding off the immortal insouciance that is the legacy of miraculous survival. Ha, ha: look at us, skittering down a strip of vertical gravel with barbed wire an inch from our elbows! Who's this heaving their bikes over a railway fence, then shouldering them across the main-line tracks behind? That's right: it's us! Hey – and here we are again, racing teenage drivers at 50kmh along the rim of a bottomless gorge! Oooh: they're overtaking us on a blind corner! And now we're going at 60 and – wheee! – edging helplessly over onto the wrong side of the bends and buddying up to Mr Oncoming Traffic.

We'd intended to call it a day at Terni, but it proved an undistinguished and surprisingly industrial place, with a steelworks and everything. Not a fitting location, we agreed, for what was to be (gulp, sigh) our final night together. After a rather irresponsible slalom through Terni's busy pedestrian zone – oops, *scusi, signora* – we were swept out of town into the early-evening traffic. Paul shouted a suggestion as we sped along the hard shoulder of a long, flat road full of Fiats: 'Not far to Narni. Every time I drive past on the motorway it looks so lovely, perched up there on its cliff.' Up there on its *what*, now? But with my brain no longer up to formulating an argument I pedalled automatically on.

I'd been in my ladies' gear for days now, and trying to hang on in Paul's slipstream meant spinning the pedals like a pilled-up dervish. After a while he looked round, so briskly I didn't have time to slip on a mask of effortless nonchalance. 'Everything OK?'

Taking a loud oxygen break between syllables, I suggested that perhaps we might take the pace down a notch or two. 'Got to, you know, marshal my reserves.' Paul nodded, slowed, and let me slip past to set my own speed.

I settled into an easy rhythm, watching Narni take gradual shape atop a rearing promontory ahead of us. After a while I looked down and saw Paul's shadow looming right behind me, indeed overlapping my rear wheel. I suddenly thought: Marshal my reserves for what? The sodding afterlife? And with that I gripped the bars and turned my legs so fast, and for so long, it was a surprise to arrive at the foot of Narni's cliff with only one of them churned to butter. I survived the climb up to the town's four-square old gates through an old ruse: yes, Paul, I *am* captivated by that distant view of Terni's factory chimneys, and I *will* keep stopping to photograph it.

We found a pleasingly odd hotel in the heart of the old town, a mismatched trio of tall, thin medieval houses internally connected with bits of left-over Pompidou Centre. Locating my room meant a dilatory blunder up and down cavernous ventilation shafts and corridors carpeted with rubber polka dots, though in fairness locating my arse would have seemed a tall order: we had celebrated survival by pouring two enormous Baffo d'Oro beers into our empty bodies.

I fell into the shower, almost literally legless, then sat on the tiles for fifteen minutes gurgling random profanities with a tepid dribble breaking over my head. In Paul's company I had covered 170km in two days – a fair bit less than I'd been averaging alone of late, yet I was utterly, messily shattered. No real mystery: in trying to keep up with a fitter man on a better bike, I'd been drawn into sustained bursts of red-zone effort. Not many of us can muster the will-power to drive ourselves that hard solo, without a colleague or rival to dangle a carrot or brandish a stick. And that's why not many of us have villas with heated pools, or embark on record-breaking Grand Tour breakaways.

I took Paolo Facchinetti out to dinner with us – a wise move, as Paul and I would otherwise have had an entire fancy restaurant and three ingratiating waiters all to ourselves. As a pair of these presented us with jus-swirled steaks on square plates, I established the accidental import of our stopover choice: after 350km out on his own, Lauro Bordin had been finally reeled in at Narni.

'He moved over to let his pursuers by,' Paul translated as I savoured my farewell experience of premium wine, 'smiling as they went past, confiding that he was relieved to be caught: he couldn't stand it out there on his own any more, the torture of solitude had, um, done his head in. Thank you, he said to each one. And then they all rode away and left him.'

'That's nice of them,' I said, unfolding the map over my sautéed rosemary potatoes. With Rome barely 80km off, the four who caught Bordin might at least have let the protagonist of this historic accomplishment enjoy the long-lost succour of human company to the stage finish. But that's cycling for you: riders stoutly uphold the chivalric code of fraternal honour right up to the point where doing so might exert the tiniest adverse impact on their chances of victory. The Bordin they rode by did a very good impression of a hollowed-out shell of a man – but he also had a bit of a rep as a sprinter, so best just leave him behind to enjoy the old torture of solitude.

I shook my head and crumpled the map back to the start of what Paolo called 'the impossible escape'. It seemed like days and days since I'd passed the point where Bordin set out on his own, largely because it was. Since leaving Lucca I'd been through a great compendium of tribulation: painful ascents and their terrifying follow-ups, hunger, thirst, wilting heat and clattering rainstorms. Bordin had condensed all that and more into fifteen unbroken hours of triple-distilled solo suffering. At least, as Paul noted, we both now knew what Bordin and friends had faced on the loose-surfaced mountain tracks of 1914. I nodded, mixing a manful sniff with a silent prayer that my wheels would never again darken a *strada bianca*.

That would have been a fair deal, in the light of what I've just gleaned from a belatedly un-stupid analysis of that day's route. When Paolo wrote of the post-Spoleto climb to '*il passo della somma*', I had taken that to mean 'the pass over the summit': by default a clear reference to Monte Bibico, the only nearby peak with a road up to it. On closer examination Paolo didn't write of that at all, but of '*il passo della Somma*', which it transpires is but a modest pimple on the smoothly tarmacked main road from Spoleto to Terni. That's right – we didn't need to go up any part of that mountain, or flirt with dehydrated death in its ghostly hinterland, or tackle a single one of the ordeals that piled up in our wandering route back to earth. There's no easy way to say this, Paul: it's all your fault for not questioning more rigorously the judgement of a known idiot.

In ignorance of this monolithic cock-up we drank to our achievement, a two-bottle task that would add an edge of hungover melancholy to my impending re-entry into the Paul-free world.

How very cruel this world began to look in the morning, when we went to retrieve our bikes from the hotel's medieval lock-up. 'I don't know how you've been putting up with all that squeaky clanking,' said Paul, as an introduction to doing something about it. Calling upon many adolescent weekends spent working in his local bike shop, and several subsequent decades of grown-up practicality, he smote out my right-hand cotter pin with a hammer some Victorian janitor had thoughtfully left on a cobwebbed shelf. *THUNG-tink*, onto the lock-up tiles it dropped, still wrapped in Fabio's tinfoil. Further shelf-rooting sourced three thin nails and a twist of copper wire; Paul bound these together around the pin and battered the ensemble home.

'Shouldn't be any play in that for a bit,' he said as I sat beside him forlornly toting the adjustable wrench, like a kid with a set of plastic play-tools trying to help Daddy.

'Can I still bang them in every morning with this?'

'If you like.'

It proved an effective running repair that ferried me in near silence up to the top of the gorge behind Narni. Beneath us lay a grander version of the prospect I'd gazed listlessly at from my hotel balcony the night before: a logjam of bell-towers and tiny-windowed old houses poised to hurl themselves down at the ant-like autostrada traffic inching across the valley floor. 'A view always looks better when you've earned it,' said Paul, though this one was principally improved by not having cycling clothes dripping diluted hotel shampoo all over it.

We stopped for a coffee and a brioche, which allowed me to savour two imminently absent blessings: companionship, and being able to go for a pee without having to lug all my stealable belongings into the cubicle with me. Then it was a long downhill drag to Borghetto, where Paul was turning off north to get his homeward train.

'You know what,' he said, waiting for a gap in the oncoming traffic, 'I'm actually really knackered.'

Yes! I thought. Then Paul politely but firmly unclasped my hands from his ankles and pedalled out of my life.

CHAPTER 14

I rode disconsolately down the Via Flaminia, another of those ancient thoroughfares that led to where all roads did back them. It took an undulating route through increasingly warm countryside; I pushed hard, trying to keep up with a slipstream that wasn't there any more. When a dog threw itself at a farm gate, I automatically *ding-ding-dinged* my bell to wind it up to a delirium of spittled barking: one of Paul's rare weaknesses is a mild phobia of canine attack, and stimulating this fear had become an unedifying reflex.

The world around began to curl up and fray: the road surface, the jerry-built, half-finished farmhouses, even the scabby fields, unabundantly dotted with scrawny goats and sheep nibbling brown weeds in pockets of shade. It was as if Paul had taken everything nice away with him. Repulsive wodges of tissue paper festooned every verge, and the crumbling tarmac was bejewelled with glinting shards of discarded bottle. Lorries roared by, the sun blazed pitilessly and *pttth-ber-dum-ber-dum-plap-plap-plap-plap*. Oh. I looked down, praying for a front-wheel puncture, though my arse was telling me otherwise.

As ever, my arse knew best. To spare myself an audience I dragged the Hirondelle through a roadside gate and leaned it against an oak tree in the crispy wheat-stubble beyond. A little commuter train trundled past on the line behind, hailing me with an asthmatic toot of its horn. Light-headed with potent, neat dismay I effortfully removed the back wheel and yanked the tube-less flattie off it. Then I retrieved a tiny bottle of thinners and an old sock from one saddlebag side-pocket, a roll of double-sided tubular tape from another, and stood there with my last spare tyre trying to summon up the spirit of Suneil, who in a previous life-time had shown me what to do with all this stuff.

He came to me in the form of a small, grey cricket – an enig-matic presence who hopped into my hat, upturned on the brown bristles, and sat there twitching slowly. 'What's that, Suneil?' I asked him. 'Rub the old glue off the rim with a sock soaked in thinners? Stretch the shit out of the new tyre by standing on it and pulling up hard? Apply the tape in two sections either side of the valve, remembering to leave a bit sticking out so you have some-where to start peeling when you roll the tyre on? Thanks, Suneil! Here's a shiny new acorn for your trouble.'

It took me an hour and a quarter, a delay that would have cost Alfonso Calzolari the race lead but with which I was very pleased indeed. The new tyre had gone on much straighter than its prede-cessor, and that rearward wobble was no more. Look, Daddy Paul, I done it all by my own! For a final flourish I got the tiny spanner out to tighten my remaining chainring bolts. One, two . . . *sweeee*. The last bolt span loose; I'd stripped its thread. 'You daft cock,' chirped Suneil, and hopped away into the hot afternoon.

I rolled carefully on towards Rome, watching the villages coalesce into satellite towns and the roadside rubbish pile up into astonishing, waist-high drifts. It was hardly the route I'd have chosen, but I stuck with it, knowing that this age-old thoroughfare was unquestionably the road that the 1914 boys took into Rome. There were eight of them together up front by now, powering past that church, swooping under this railway bridge, narrowly missing those cypress trees.

A tail wind picked up, and once I'd established that my knackered chain-ring bolt wasn't about to fall out – I'd brutally cross-threaded it into its hole – I let myself be blown along at a rare old lick. With my chin right down to the bidon lids I swept through the excitable Friday traffic, scattering bony stray cats and sun-dulled plastic detritus.

For a long while I meandered through villas that tumbled down some of Rome's more considerable hills; then the Tiber was at my side, the traffic unravelled into a lunatic free-for-all and vaguely familiar postcard scenes began to take shape around me. *Biddle-ip!* For once Paolo had supplied the precise stage finish, and a couple of miles north of the city centre the sat-nav told me I'd reached it: the viale di Tor di Quinto, where just before 6 p.m. the eight front-runners had launched their sprint for the line.

Girardengo, the champion of Italy, broke the tape and moved up to second overall; Calzolari finished seventh in the same time, retaining his fifty-five-minute lead in the general classification. I looked at my watch: it was just before 6 p.m. I'd finished the longest stage in Giro history in sync with the original riders, but had taken a while extra to do it. The kind of while you'd measure with a calendar rather than a stopwatch.

Feeling much more pleased with myself than this data implied, I gaily pushed the Hirondelle through pavements massed with boisterous, sparsely clad weekend-welcomers. Make way, little people: conqueror of ultimate sporting challenge coming through!

My legs glowed and so did my heart. I'd changed a tyre, and Number 7 was riding sweet and true; together we'd given Marathon Paul and his brand-new bike a run for their money. For a man who could do no wrong, it was no surprise to swiftly run across a cheap and friendly hotel, a little family-run job on the Via della Farnesina. 'You have luck not to be on your *bici* here two days before,' said the wife-receptionist. 'We have some terrible rain!'

'I know,' I said, having kept up to speed with the progression of national weather fronts courtesy of the breakfast-telly generals. 'It reached me in Siena.'

'And today, so hot for *Roma* in *settembre!*'

'Yes,' I nodded, picking bits of wheat-field off my jersey. 'But not like Milan in August. It was forty-one degrees when I started there.'

She looked at me, at the dusty wooden wheel poking through her front door, then back at me.

'You start on *that* in *Milano?*'

'You better believe it, sweet-cheeks,' said my odious smile.

I dumped the bike in the basement, my kit in the bidet and hit the streets. It was an almost tropical night out in Rome's inner suburbs, the air thick and blood-warm and the pavement vibe muted from frisky to mellow. Bats flitted across a midnight-blue sky, every other tree was a palm, and the whole city seemed lightly infused with that equatorial miasma of ripe garbage and cannabis. I ambled along with the slow-mo flow, lazily coveting roof terraces and Lambrettas, then marked my return to a pre-Paul lifestyle by dining early at a restaurant selected on a calories-per-euro basis. Rome looked even better through chianti-tinted spectacles, but it proved a struggle to sustain the mood throughout my after-dinner mission.

Back in Lucca, at the start of this monstrous stage, I had rather intemperately filled one of my bidons with pear nectar. Five long, hot days later it wasn't hard to tell which one: the other didn't stink of fizzy vomit. My son had recently told me about pruno, an intoxicant produced illicitly in prisons by leaving cartons of fruit juice mixed with tomato ketchup and milk to ferment behind a radiator. I have yet to taste this refreshing summer drink, but I do now have a good idea what it smells like.

During my Tour ride, a related bidon-blend of folly, fruit and filth had brought on a debilitating stomach condition that laid grim waste to lay-bys right across Provence. I still have the chlorine-purifying tablets that a chemist near Avignon had sold me to tackle this issue at source, but didn't bring them along, having vowed to never again be so very stupid as to fill a bidon with anything but water. Sadly, this vow took no account of finding pear nectar on special offer.

Anyway, something had to be done, and it wasn't something I'd fancied doing in Paul's fastidious company. I wish I had, though, as the task demanded rather too much of my Italian. For an hour I flitted between North African-run cornershops, squinting cluelessly at the labels of potential sterilising agents. Could dishwasher sanitiser do the job without dissolving my innards? Might a cheeky drop of Toilet Duck be an option? I found a small pink packet decorated with a happily living baby and the word *sterilizzazione*, but doubted its potency: these were man-germs I needed to kill. In the end I ransacked my vocabulary, and went up to a counter.

'Good evening,' I said to the bearded grandfather behind it. 'I have a dirty bottle.'

As midnight approached I was in my en suite, administering Granddad's solution: two iridescent orange litres of 90 per cent industrial alcohol, a fluid I had last employed to burn a housemate's eyebrows off during a student-era fire-eating experiment. The faltering half-sentences with which I'd explained myself to the shopkeeper – at one point I think I offered to sterilise him – had been reciprocated with an elaborate one-man public-information mime when he handed over his recommended fluids: as far as I could tell, the cautionary tale of a desperate alcoholic who pretended he had a dirty bottle, then went blind and died. I took his point once I'd filled both bidons and every hole in my head with tramp fumes, and fled choking from the bathroom. Then I took a deep breath, burst back in and ripped the labels off those most shameful of empties.

In the morning it still smelt like Oliver Reed's autopsy in there, and twenty full rinses of fresh water did nothing to diminish the dreadful influence of industrial booze on my bidons' contents. Somehow both were now infused with the gagging taint of export-strength rum and raisin: I would henceforth be refreshing myself with Pruno Gold Label.

The breakfast room was on the top floor, and I absorbed Paolo's 1914 update with another scorcher brewing up on the hazy skyline before me. Poor Lauro Bordin crossed the line tenth, 16 minutes 50' back; I was suddenly certain that some improbable tragedy lay ahead for this ultimate nearly man, and darted over to the adjacent Internet terminal expecting to find that he'd copped a fatal fire-work in the face during the 1918 armistice celebrations, or similar. In fact, he was still riding ten years later, and in retirement made a name for himself on TV panel shows. Four hours after Bordin, the final finishers reached Rome, with our friend Mario Marangoni last once more: he was now a spectacular seventeen hours off the pace. But the longest Giro stage of all time claimed just one retire-ment, and twenty-six riders would turn up on the stage-four start line.

Paolo located this at porta San Lorenzo, which required me to cycle right through the heart of old Rome. On a hot Saturday, the downtown traffic was wonderfully sparse and the pavements annexed by foreign pedestrians with better things to do than play chicken with brakeless cyclists. Other things, anyway. As a self-styled visiting sportsman, I felt entitled to nurture an ugly superiority over tourists and the inanity of their hateful ways – just as everyone always does, in fact, even while they're waving a camera at some overseas attraction with ice cream all over their sunburnt faces.

The principal revelation that emerged during two full laps of the Forum was just how few visitors seemed glad to be there. Not just the French: it wasn't yet eleven and everybody looked grumpy and tired, weighed down by the overbearing entreaties of the plastic-sworded centurions, by their own distracted, foot-dragging children, by the language barrier and the dread prospect of all that hot trudging to come. How wonderful it felt not to be on holiday! In an hour-long ride around Rome's most fabled sights I saw only a dozen foreigners who were certifiably enjoying themselves. They were gathered beneath Trajan's Column, exuding the voluble, ruddy good cheer of people who had breakfasted on Pruno smoothies, and in loudly guttural voices that suggested some of the thicker lumps were still finding their way down. Calling on my extensive exposure to BBC4 drama, I identified them as Danes – the all-drinking, all-smoking, gabble-mouthed good-time Italians of northern Europe.

The porta San Lorenzo lay just behind the main station, and was the go-to bathroom destination for this area's many tramps. As I set up my traditional stage-start self-timer shot, four stood behind me tipping drinking-fountain water down the inside of their grime-waxed jumpers and trackie bottoms, while another groomed his colossal beard in the wing mirror of a graffiti-plastered van. All around us reared monumental hunks of ancient masonry, arched remains of the three Roman aqueducts that once converged here and a mighty section of the third-century city walls, the capital's primary defence right up to Victorian times. No doubt ancient Rome was well-stocked with homeless derelicts, but the contrast between this nation's supreme imperial past and its scraggy, low-rent present was unavoidably compelling. It also made me feel suddenly homesick.

My road out of town was a crazy-paved horror, full of potholes and rubbish and weekend drivers looking for two-wheeled target practice. Roman motorists are serial nudger-outers, incapable of toeing the line at any junction, taking that big red octagon to mean 'vaguely slow down if you can be arsed'. Flouting the rules of the road chimes with the national hatred of authority: when a driver edges out a metre beyond those give-way lines, he hasn't just scared the piss out of a cyclist – he's stolen back a metre from The Man.

Like most Britons, I do not ascribe sentient qualities to my fellow road users. Other drivers, all of them, are to me automatons incapable of independent, reactive response to any unfolding situation. As such I assume that if I pull out directly in front of a vehicle, it will continue along its path in a robotically mechanical fashion, thereby running me over and causing me to die. Roman driving, though, is an interactive multiplayer game for actual living people. When a Roman driver pulls straight out of a side-road, he does so on the understanding that as an adaptive and free-spirited human individual, you will take spontaneous and ideally stylish evasive action. 'I know,' they say, 'it's crazy, but it works!' Except when it doesn't, which the bodywork of every single car in Rome suggests is almost all the time.

Anyway, that morning I developed a defensive maxim that would do me proud for the rest of my journey: imagine the most selfish and irresponsible thing that any given road-user might feasibly do next, then watch him do it.

On and on I went, through an endless, grubby hinterland of flooring superstores and near-death experience. It was so hard to get my speed right: going below 18kmh or so was a sign of weakness that saw me bullied into the gutter, above 24 and I had absolutely no hope of avoiding the next Franco Big Bollocks who pulled straight out in front of me. *Ding-ding-ding-ding!* In two hours I thumbed the bell more than I had over the previous two weeks, but it seemed such a feeble reproach for attempted murder that I then gave up.

The road surface decayed further, now strewn with so much glass it was as if someone had spent the night throwing chandeliers out of an airship. And all the while those dunes of roadside rubbish grew ever taller, an encroaching moraine of cans and fag packets topped with the stained hulks of discarded furniture, domestic appliances and sanitary-ware. Also: shoes. How does that happen?

'Know what, Carlo, I've gone right off your trainers. Do us a favour and chuck them out the window.'

'Can't it wait until we get home? I don't fancy braking in bare feet.'

'You don't fancy *what*?'

The scale was so far beyond casual littering that I began to wonder if the locals made a day of it: 'OK, kids, we're going fly-tipping today – last one in the car with a massive load of broken crap is a cissy!' I suppose it's just another of those unfortunate retro pastimes that some Italians cling on to, like racism and animal circuses.

The sat-nav beeped me up a side turning and Rome suddenly

ended: no cars or shops, and no people once I'd gone through the prostitute belt, an unusually tragic straggle of black girls who vacantly raised their tiny skirts at me as I toiled past. Two hours of hot and increasingly famished loneliness ensued, just me and my booze-water, crawling up hillsides laid waste by a recent wildfire. Half-melted plastic reflector posts sagged over the charred verges like some hellish Dali landscape, and the whiff of barbecued wild-life hung heavy in the air. I was so desperate for calories it made my stomach growl.

In a world that my under-nourished brain was ceasing to make much sense of, it didn't seem entirely surprising to pass a completely naked lady beckoning me from the shadows at the back of a lay-by. I gave her a sleepy wave and creaked on, then noticed a familiar cityscape taking unwelcome shape ahead of me: that was Rome, and I'd just gone back in through its tart belt. An addled whimper escaped my cracked lips, followed by a groan of sickening enlightenment. After the sat-nav directed me into Rome on a six-lane motorway the previous day, I had clicked an option that told it to 'avoid highways'. Its interpretation of this order, now that I troubled myself to look at the map, was an evidently phobic aversion to anything busy, and thus direct. I had been led away into the untrafficked wilds at the earliest opportunity, and kept there without any concern for the wandering build-up of excess mileage.

The cliff-top imperial resort of Tivoli, when at last I lurched blankly up to it, should have been a 29km ride from my start point; I had covered well over double that. Happily by this time I was deep in a land beyond caring. In a robotic quest for the stuff of life I dropped my bike onto the pavement outside the first open grocery, bought three bars of Milka Extra Cacao and slid down against a wheelie bin in the full glare of the afternoon sun. I fed one sticky slab into my pallid food-hole, then another. At once I felt markedly better; at twice, markedly worse.

If I'd done what I now did in a Swiss gutter, I'd be writing these words in a secure unit for the criminally repulsive. As it was, the Saturday strollers squeezed past my doubled, retching form without comment. No one even intervened when, after a brisk sluice with diluted industrial alcohol, I sat back down again and ingested the third bar.

For three strange hours I pedalled beyond nausea and fatigue and into a state of fallow, druggy detachment. The road snaked ever upwards into whatever stretch of the Appenines this was, but instead of working on my hatred for Italy's horrible, pointy spine I gave a mental shrug and carried on. There was a railway above and a river beneath; in days gone by I'd have desperately willed my road to bind itself to one or the other, the lazy cyclists' friends with their promise of modest gradient. That afternoon I just didn't care. Things were so bad that when I came up to a sign welcoming visitors to the town of Arsoli, my brain had to activate its emergency puerility reflex to save me from going past without taking a photo.

Onwards and upwards I went, through the villages sprinkled atop every big green hill, creaking in and out of the lives of few-toothed rustics keeping their impassive doorstep vigils. Then the landscape opened out into a lofty plateau, and a dramatic cooling of the air began to rouse me from my waking coma. Very gradually, mind: after I stopped at Carsoli, it would be twelve full hours before I appreciated it as the Italian motorist's spiritual home.

It was a curious town, a mile-long strip mall of tyre fitters and snack bars that made no sense up here in the mountain-flanked middle of nowhere. Fine by me: at the moment, nothing made sense. Finessing the transatlantic commercial vibe, Carsoli's final establishment was some kind of budget country-club hotel. I freewheeled to a halt by the empty tennis courts, and stood astride the Hirondelle while my head slowly refilled, mesmerised by the bright yellow balls strewn across the orange clay. I must have looked like Frankenstein's monster gazing in wonder at his first daisy, just before he drowns that little girl. As I pushed the bike through the reception doors somebody let out a single yowl of drunken laughter: it was me.

An Alsatian standing guard by the threshold backed silently away at my approach, and before I'd even said anything, the woman at the desk pushed a room key across the Formica with studied deliberation, as if to counteract the urgency with which her other hand was battering a hidden panic button. Having temporarily mislaid my entire Italian vocabulary, I gestured at the Hirondelle and arranged my mouth into what even I could tell was the wrong sort of smile – not so much asking where I might store a bicycle as introducing my teenage mistress. The receptionist's steady gaze said: 'Whatever floats your boat, mate. We don't want any trouble.' I winked at her and walked the bike straight into the lift.

Even the generally reliable restorative powers of *pizza diavola* didn't make me normal. The restaurant back up the road was another Americanised establishment with bowls of condiment sachets on every table, and surgically overbearing strip-lights that bent me down into a muttering hunch. What a miserable figure I cut amongst the lively Saturday-night families, sagging like a punctured love-doll as I ferried torn wodges of stonebaked dough across the diminishing gap between plate and mouth. When I tried to dress my side salad, the little plastic pillow of olive oil exploded in my clumsy fists. My reaction to this disappointing development caused the family who had just sat down beside me to rise as one and move three tables away.

What was happening to me? It seemed a week since I'd left Rome that morning: so many sweeping changes of mood and scenery, grumpy tourists, bathing tramps, tarts on a burnt hillside, a gutter of chocolate chunder. I shut my eyes and for a tiny moment sped through every single inch and second of the day in Google StreetView HD, every shard of glass on the blistered tarmac, every death-dealing Fiat, every rasp and squeak and grunt and creak. I blinked my lids open and saw a dozen faces quickly turn away. That and the bead of drool poised to drop from my bottom lip suggested I had just been fast asleep. Had exhaustion and under-nourishment driven me into the feral, dead-eyed realm of Fonso la Mort? If so I wanted to get the fuck out of that realm pronto. Definitely out of here, in any case. I slapped an oily hand to my back pocket in search for my wallet. It wasn't there. And nor indeed was my pocket, because as I now established, looking down at my olive-oiled, chocolate-speckled chest, I had somehow neglected to change out of my kit.

Eat before you are hungry. It wasn't the first time I'd fallen foul of Paul de Vivie's golden rule of distance cycling, but might have been the most dramatic. The cowboy-shirted restaurant owner was very good about my predicament, nodding sympathetically as I strove to articulate it in the voice of Scooby Doo emerging from general anaesthetic. I stumbled back down the road, lurched into my hotel room and yanked open the Calzolari-embossed frame-bag where my wallet lived. But now didn't. A deep breath and a systematic search weren't options that interested me; with unhinged Godzilla abandon, I bestrewed the room with worldly goods and a ticker-tape parade of receipts. I was about to thrash the Hirondelle until it talked when a shapeless snatch of semi-memory caused me to pull open the front pocket of my jersey. The wallet had been there all along. Having returned to the restaurant to pay, I strode back through the sharp night with calm purpose: I was going to punch myself to death.

GENERAL CLASSIFICATION – STAGE 3
(Lucca-Rome, 430.3km)

1. Alfonso CALZOLARI 49:33:01
2. Constante GIRARDENGO + 55:07
3. Enrico SALA +1:34:49
   Timothy MOORE +23:12:50
   Stage starters: 27
   Stage finishers: 26

CHAPTER 15

Stage four rolled out of Rome before a larger crowd than one might reasonably expect at 2.24 a.m.: the citizenry had a local hero to cheer, Calzolari's Stucchi teammate Dario Beni. In other circumstances Beni wouldn't have turned up at the start, after suffering multiple fractures in a horrible fall towards the end of the previous stage. As it was, he acknowledged the cheers, pedalled grittily round the corner and promptly retired. There were now just twenty-five riders left, with the Stucchi squad down to its last two: in Paolo's words, 'one half-crippled and the other visibly shattered'. Fonso was the invalid, forcing that shrieking knee through every revolution, and Clemente Canepari the frail ghost. Paolo describes Canepari as 'a tiny man with long limbs, like a spider on a bike', who had started the Giro as Stucchi's de facto number one, but was now two hours off the pace, struggling grimly on in support of the unlikely race leader.

It was a comfort of sorts to discover that Alfonso had suffered his own blighting misfortunes at Tivoli. Halfway up Choc-Vom Hill, pitch darkness and a huge logjam of Rome-bound horse-wagons caused such havoc that Fonso and the other leaders blundered off the road to outflank it, shouldering their bikes through steep undergrowth. With the race almost half-run, the bigger teams were now ready to try anything to reel in the upstart Stucchi rider, and after staggering back out onto the route, Calzolari had to watch his rivals pedal away: at some point in their off-piste diversion, he now discovered, one of the riders behind had stuck a tack in his rear tyre. As Fonso later told Paolo Facchinetti, the one thing you didn't expect with your bike on your back was a puncture.

The faithful Canepari helped him with the tyre change, but it was eight long minutes before he got back on the road. Profiting from a race leader's mechanical misfortune is frowned upon today, but having caused that misfortune Calzolari's rivals were hardly about to take pity. At once the Bianchi boys steamed off into the night. The box of dirty tricks was open, and from now on Fonso would be having his head slammed in its lid for day after bitter day.

I pushed the Hirondelle out into a gorgeous country-club morning: the taut *ber-dung* of yellow ball on fat man's racquet, a sliced drive launched across the crisp, azure sky. A mile up the sunny road I passed through Carsoli proper, a pleasant stack of old buildings with plenty of spare room for all the tyre-fitters and pizza restaurants laid along its hideous introductory drag. My thoughts on this and the many similar mysteries of urban planning I encountered as I continued southwards are collated in a companion publication, *The Hopelessly Corrupt Application of Regional Development Grants*.

A cock crowed, a bike creaked, the road turned a corner and

squared up to the squat green bulk of Monte Bove. It was a whopper, a climb that nearly did for Calzolari: he succumbed to 'a crisis of cold' that saw him crawl over the summit twenty minutes behind the Bianchis. Even in embarrassingly superior weather it made a stiff challenge, or should have. My eyes kept trying to tell my brain that these winding curves were steep beyond reason, but my legs would have none of it: objection overruled. Instead, I busted out the hotel biscuits, took a throat-bobbing glug of tepid alco-bilge and powered on up the silent Sunday tarmac, taking the high-line through the hairpins and breathing smoothly. *Moore's found something special here, Phil. He's back in the game!* Oh, the enduring enigma of good form. Or perhaps there was no great secret after all: I simply had to spend every afternoon starving myself and doing big brown yawns in the gutter.

In an hour I climbed almost 2,000ft, and when I did get off it was only to take a snap of the blue-misted valleys beneath. The village of Montebove, clinging to a precipice below the head of the pass, was the most stubbornly ancient timewarp yet, a corridor of cockeyed masonry so narrow that the balconies on one side almost grazed the eaves on the other. A radio-broadcast Sunday mass droned through shutters that had kept out the odd couple of hundred winters, and the only face in town belonged to an extremely old man in Harold Macmillan pinstripes, watching me from his doorstep in the standard inscrutable manner. How was this place less than 50 miles outside the capital city of the world's eighth largest economy?

I crested the col – 1,220m, suckers – then plunged into Tagliacozzo, a busy little place full of multicoloured Sunday bikers in both flavours: leather and Lycra. On the pan-flat plateau outside town a steady stream of club pelotons filed past, hailing me with a 50/50 blend of jeers and cheers. The most enthusiastic of the latter was issued by the last rider in a line of six, who then shouted something to his Bike Sport Fortunato colleagues and dropped back to join me.

He gave the Hirondelle an appreciative once-over through his orange wraparounds, nodding all the while and finishing off with a huge grin and a thumbs-up.

'Giuseppe,' he said, patting his chest.

'Tim.'

'OK, Jim – andiamo!'

Let's go! My new friend stood up in the saddle and beckoned me into his slipstream, then slowly built speed. Soon he was pulling me across the plateau at one hell of a lick, absorbing a fierce headwind that flapped at his jersey sleeves. I inched as close as I dared to Giuseppe's rear wheel, my face indecently near to those rolling buttocks. For a glorious half-hour the world before me was filled by this tremendous man's hot lycra and incredibly hairy forearms, which he periodically flapped down to warn me of potholes and draincovers. It felt just like being in a real breakaway – in fact, even better than that, because the one arm-signal I never received was that elbow-flicked command to take my turn at the front.

Giuseppe sucked me hard into Avezzano, swishing slickly through the busy junctions and roundabouts. What an enjoyable revelation to witness his furious response to motoring negligence: it wasn't just me, then, things really *were* that awful. Then he turned his tanned face to mine, said a lot of things in an encouraging tone, and with a final wave swept away down a side-road. I shouted out a heartfelt *grazie* for those 20 free kilometres, then unerringly steered myself out of Avezzano and onto the one road I'd been trying to avoid, a dual carriageway that pierced a lofty mountain ridge with the busiest, darkest, most petrifying tunnel to date. Part of me died in that deafening, glass-strewn hell, and I could only hope it was the part in charge of navigation.

Even the right road, when I found it, went wrong: freewheeling down the Liri valley with a gut full of crisps, I almost Starsky & Hutched it straight through a substantial barrier laid across the tarmac. In any other European country, I'd have stopped, booted that no-entry sign right in its fat white slot, shouted terrible things at the cloudless sky and pedalled back up the way I'd come. That's because in any other European country, round the corner the road would have been blocked by several hundred cubic metres of collapsed hillside, or a smouldering diesel locomotive, or a dozen escaped leopards. But in Italy I figured there was at least an even chance of encountering nothing worse than some knocked-over traffic cones and a long-idle steamroller. I squeezed the Hirondelle through the barrier, slalomed past the drifts of leaves and ran plumb into a pack of shuffling zombies. I'm one of them now, but it's actually a lot more fun than you might think: we're off to a water-park next weekend. I'm joking, of course! It's actually a petting zoo.

Having negotiated the predicted scatter of recumbent cones I rattled up to 60kmh, using the full width of the vacant downhill tarmac and restricting myself to snatched glances of the heat-hazed valley beside. I should have known better than to expect a matching barrier at the other end of the closed section: I only gathered the road was now an open one when I leaned through a left-hander on the British side of the white line and found myself sharing five foot of road with an oncoming coach. In a reflexive act of perverse brilliance I leaned further left and swept past him on the inside; the driver didn't even have time to blast his horn, which must have upset him for the rest of the day. I had cheated death,

but careering through flyblown villages the episode swiftly faded: it was as if sheer speed was fast-tracking the flash-frame present into a distant past.

I stopped at Sora for my first *gelato* of the trip – I had been denying myself the world's finest ice cream as a stand against The Holiday Tendency – then enjoyed a steady and uneventful ride through an almost continuous straggle of low-density towns. Boredom set in amongst the mid-rise apartment blocks, and how I savoured it: the luxury of an empty mind no longer crammed with pain and hunger. For the first time, now that it could make itself heard above more strident complaints, my bottom started to make a bit of a fuss. Extraordinary to think it had held out this far, having straddled a leather house-brick for 1,600km. Why couldn't my legs and lungs take a leaf out of my arse's book? It's quite the page-turner.

Frosinone was my destination, and after the usual hill-top finale I made it just before 6 p.m. A good day: 125km, my overall average speed up from 16.4kmh to 16.7, and just the one dalliance with instant death – OK, just the nine if we include that tunnel. I was well off the tourist track now, wheeling the Hirondelle through empty squares crammed with church towers and carpeted in the day's confetti, up steepling alleys bridged by archways, past a massive municipal building of Fascist aspect, sneering down at the villages sprawled across the plain beneath. So sharply pitched was old Frosinone that my hotel's rear-facing basement garage, the Hirondelle's overnight home, opened onto a street 50ft below the one that passed its front door.

After remembering to change, I hit the empty Sunday streets, and round on the southwestern face of Frosinone's rearing hilltop located what appeared to be its only restaurant. The outside tables had upside-down chairs on them and all the lights were off, but the door was open and I sidled tentatively in. Calorific desperation lured me towards a dim pool of light at the foot of a staircase; I pushed open a door and found myself sharing a basement with an elderly chef in bottle-bottom glasses, a roaring wood-fired pizza furnace and a tiny, flour-dusted baby asleep in a travel cot beneath a marble work-slab. The old boy was working dough with the showy air of a street-juggler, rolling it, spinning it skywards, slapping it back down on the marble. A shelf by the oven's chimney was stacked with trophies and with a surge of glee I knew I was now truly in the south of Italy, where the pizza was born and where the pursuit of its perfection is a competitive culinary sport.

A waitress appeared, ushered me back up into the street, switched the lights on and readied a table. She disappeared without taking my order, then briskly reappeared with a carafe of red, a plate of bruschetta and a smile. This was shortly supplemented with the most toothsome roundel I have folded into my gob: never has an old man's blistered crust tasted so good.

I imagined I was having as great a time as you could on a Sunday night in Frosinone, but I was wrong, because in fifteen mad minutes the whole town burst into life like one of those fast-forward, stop-motion film sequences. Three jolly couples commandeered the table next to mine, followed almost at once by a dozen more. The sun went down and a billion lights came on, strung in rows between the palm trees that lined the promenade before me, pulsing in gaudy neon above previously dormant gelaterias and bars, winking out in great constellations across the darkening plain below. The road was abruptly filled with youthmobiles pumping out endearingly improbable tunes – *The Lion King*'s 'Circle of Life' fed through an earth-shaking subwoofer – and in a blink the pavements were aswarm with loud and happy people. I drained my carafe, paid the trifling bill and inveigled myself into the throng, in thrall once more to Italy's wonderful civic togetherness, its irrepressible urge to do everything en masse and in sync. For an Englishman it was a heady spectacle. For a Londoner, an almost bewilderingly alien one.

I filed along with the gesticulating *gelato*-lickers, window-shopping in the land that made it an art. On a Sunday night, the only shop open was the only one I needed: a pharmacy, which I walked into to buy a new deodorant and hone that fantasy of my future life as a small-town Italian chemist. It would certainly be a well-remunerated career: I came out with a roll-on that fulfilled my only stated requirement – saddlebag-ready tininess – at the armpit-watering cost of €14, a euro more than I'd just paid for a huge meal and slightly too much wine. The senior white-coat explained in commendable English that this revolutionary product was to be applied before going to bed, once every four days. Sadly he failed to explain that it didn't work, at all. It would have been cheaper just to pay off people who complained about the smell.

While getting pleasantly lost on the way back to the hotel I paused above a public space that at 10.15 p.m. was still crowded with Frosinonians of every age. Unsupervised toddlers were climbing all over the war memorial at one end, cheerfully ignored by elder siblings playing twenty-eight-a-side unisex football, and parents gathered convivially outside the distant opposite bar. The twinkling flatness beyond Frosinone was now fringed with moonlit hillsides, and as I stood there a garish firework display burst forth from some distant settlement. I leaned on the low wall before me, breathing in the scene and lungfuls of warm dusk, feeling very good about what I'd done, where I was and my future progress southwards to the insole of that Italian boot. Then I levered myself upright and found that some joker had switched my legs for concrete bollards. What a strange state I'd ridden myself into, nonchalantly racking up 120 big ones in the saddle, then reduced to a knee-less cripple by half a mile of urban ambling.

Two riders, Giuseppe Azzini of Bianchi and Globo's Pierino Albini, were way out in front when the 1914 Giro crawled up to Frosinone. Calzolari was now almost half an hour back, behind another pair of Bianchis, having suffered a further act of sabotage while signing in at the Avezzano checkpoint: a pin-jabber amongst the crowd of fans, mechanics and journalists dealt him another sly puncture. 'Someone with large interests at stake did not want Calzolari to win the Giro!' was Paolo's uncontroversial conclusion. That someone can only have been Bianchi, as no other team had a rider in reach of the lead; Maino's Girardengo, having started the day second, cracked horribly on the way up Monte Bove and would end the stage almost three hours in arrears.

Still, this compared favourably with the four days that was my standard deficit by the end of each stage. I had of late developed a keen interest in covering a full leg of the 1914 Giro in a day less: the Hirondelle and I were hitting our stride, and 400km over three days now seemed within our compass. I laid out my map across yet another deserted breakfast room and realised it wouldn't be this stage. Frosinone sat almost smack in the centre-fold of a region I'd been inching across for half a week, but the next town Paolo referenced – not even the stage finish – was nowhere to be seen.

Going south gave summer a new lease of life. It was 34 degrees by 10.30, so cloyingly hot that even the lizards grew sluggish: I saw a wiry ginger cat trap one under its paws, looking a little freaked out by this unexpected triumph – crap, now what? The terrain was manageable, but keeping cool meant keeping the speed up. When I slowed down, the breeze died away and a fat blanket of heat was thrown over my shoulders. When I stopped, sweat pooled into every cleft. Only my deceased privates were immune to the conditions, and trundling between the palm-studded vineyards I hummed my way through their funeral playlist: 'Uncomfortably Numb'; 'Where Did You Go To, My Lovelies?'; 'Cock 'n' Balls Suicide'; 'Eunuch City Blues'. These days I contemplated their demise with no more than wistful stoicism. I had three kids; maybe their work here was done. Sorry, boys. Let's remember the good times.

I stopped to refuel at a small-town grocery, run by another of those motherly signoras. When I put a litre of Coke on the counter and pointed at her pastry cabinet, she waggled a chubby finger and gave me an 'oh, *honestly*' look. The Coke was wordlessly returned to the fridge and replaced by two bottles of beige vegetable juice, along with a packet of quarry tiles. *'Biscotti biologici,'* she clucked, making a strongman gesture and ringing up €6.45 on the till. I laughed helplessly, paid up and ingested the cardboard slurry on the bench outside. Why couldn't I have puked up this pointless rubbish instead of all those lovely chocolate calories?

The afternoon heat was crushing, and my surroundings sombre to the point of eeriness. Villages were full of neglected shacks and every other farmhouse was roofless. I even passed the odd ruined church, which seemed pretty hardcore for rural Catholics. Full-blown, huddled-masses emigration from these parts – to the north of Italy, to the north of Europe, to the States and beyond – continued into the 1960s, and the region remains mired in terrible poverty. If southern Italy was a separate country, it would be by some distance the poorest in Europe.

Almost inevitably, no other part of the nation suffered more brutally in the war. Passing below Monte Cassino in the dog-day sun, I stopped at a military cemetery, one of many honouring the 55,000 Allied troops who died along the eponymous brown ridge above. As a wide-eyed twelve-year-old, my father witnessed the lingering aftermath from the back seat of the US Army Jeep that was his family's runabout; two years after the war ended, the roads here were still lined with dead Germans, buried under mounds of earth topped with their battered helmets. I wandered leadenly through the cemetery's display of period military hardware; the tanks and field guns were too hot to touch, though I stopped trying after reading a multi-lingual warning about 'the eventual presence of deathly serpents'. Instead, I cooled my brain under a gardener's standpipe, mustering lethargic sympathy for the attritional slaughter, and for those in the 1914 Giro who would never ride another race, laid to rest in places like this all over Europe.

I find I'm unable to recall in detail my ensuing ride through the drooping scrub. The photographs I took suggest a wandering mind: amongst the usual shots of risible garden statuary and derelict buildings are a dozen blurred studies of snails ascending the leg of a signpost. Perhaps I saw them as kindred spirits, single-mindedly committed to the slow but steady accumulation of distance. In truth, I embraced the onset of auto-pilot oblivion: with my journey almost half done, cycling all day had at last become routine, no more than a mindless duty. I could slip both feet into the toe-clips at the first attempt, hold my rhythm into a headwind or up a hill, grind out the kilometres with my brain on standby. Sometimes whole hours would pass without me asking aloud whose stupid bloody idea this was.

After 128km I pedalled up to an enormous building of recent construction, marooned amongst the olive groves and lumber yards. A sign identified it as 'Hotel The Queen'; I swept in past a moss-rimed water feature and dismounted by the dusty glass doors. After a while they parted with a gritty hiss, and a yawning male receptionist beckoned at me across a vast acreage of white tiling studded with excruciating contemporary artworks. '*Congressi – Sale Meeting – Business Seminar*' read the banner over his desk, detailing some of the many events that had not and would never take place here. This wasn't so much a white elephant as a high-gloss, vanilla-lacquered albino mammoth, and as such is included in the previously cited reference work on regional aid (see also: *Organised-Crime Tax Losses and Why I'm Too Scared to Do More Than Hint at Them in Print*).

The novelty of having a guest to process aroused the receptionist to great feats of hospitality. He insisted on leading the Hirondelle to its overnight quarters, an unfinished ballroom shared with a cement mixer and a dozen scuttling lizards, and then very splendidly presented me with a large glass of chilled lager. I drained it along the parade of echoing corridors that took me to my room. Once inside I pulled up the blind and beheld the giant cone of Vesuvius, nosing up from the smoggy horizon. How very glad I was that my route would now take me away from that smog, and the horn-happy Neapolitan bike-squashers who were whipping it up. Then I opened the minibar, intending to put my bidons inside overnight as was my recent habit, but not doing so after discovering that it had been left unplugged for some time while full of drinking yoghurt.

I ate at a truck-stop restaurant up the road, just me and a shifty degenerate who drank a litre of Fanta straight from the bottle (also me). On the way back into The Queen, I stopped to take a snarky photo of its mouldy fountains; suddenly the hotel's façade was bathed in multicoloured light, and jets of stagnant water shot up into the black sky. Peering towards the entrance, I spotted the excited receptionist waving at me with one hand and working a bank of wall switches with the other. And so I trooped to my distant bed feeling like a bit of a wanker.

CHAPTER 16

Getting out of bed in the morning always felt worse after a good day, as if to redress the pain deficit. The trick, I'd discovered, was to hit the road before brain and body had time to compare notes and demand an end to this lunatic endeavour. My legs began to stiffen and throb during the receptionist's one-man *business congresso* on farewell paperwork, involving more forms than you might expect to fill in while applying to euthanise a relative. I slapped my credit card on the counter, then stifled many yells of cramped frustration while he explained an obligation to pay the separate €1.50 tourist tax in cash. Handwritten receipts were prepared for each charge, and at length I pushed the Hirondelle out past the fountains in a foot-dragging Igor hunch.

I headed out onto the SS7 and into a blue-skied, blue-aired night-mare. Lorries crossed each other when there was no room to do so, shunting me into the roadside brush with bow-waves of hot fumes and a dragon-like hiss of hydraulics. I bellowed vitriol into their stinking wake, not caring that at any minute I might attract the interest of a lorry driver who had returned from an English run with an understanding of our potty-mouthed vernacular, and that this minute would therefore be rounded off with an efficient beating.

Just an hour in the company of this undersized road's oversized regulars brought on something close to shell shock. The swelling rumble of diesel thunder caused me to twitch and whimper, and the point-blank blast of air-horns melted my very marrow. In the brief gaps of secure silence I cobbled together a detailed revenge fantasy. I would find out where one of these twelve-wheel klaxon-lovers lived, then climb in through an open window in the dead of night. Creeping up to his bedside I would feel for the gas-canister fog horn nestling in its bespoke shoulder-holster, then have a better idea and decapitate him with a hand-axe.

Presently, as Liverpudlians like to say, my arse went; every time an HGV approached, I wobbled into the undergrowth and waited for it to pass. I counted my blessings as they screamed by: that one might have killed me, or that one, or that one. Finally I cracked completely, and with a craven, juddering finger ordered the sat-nav to Avoid Highways. *Biddle-iddle-ip!* 'Route recalculated'. I darted through a gap in the traffic and bounced away up a rustic footpath.

The enormity of my relief made everything in the very different Italy I now entered seem wonderful, even the bits that definitely weren't. Between the gnarled olives and plump, dark grapes, my path was overhung by sheaves of bamboo and steer-clear cascades of prickly pears – a tropical vibe enhanced by the sun-bleached shanty towns I passed through, full of unruly dogs and barefoot, bare-headed children bucking over potholes on ancient mopeds. Briquettes of horse-crap scattered the dusty track; there was a marked absence of four-wheeled traffic and roadside litter, presumably because the locals couldn't afford to buy a car or throw anything away. Presently there weren't any locals, and I was into a great swathe of moribund cultivation, all haunted farm-houses and overgrown orchards hung with rotten fruit.

Approaching Caserta, tarmac and acceptably small vehicles returned; as the road began to haul itself upwards I heard the rear-ward approach of whirring chains. Cyclo-chums! I turned to hail a mini-peloton of four senior clubmen: as with everything else in Italy there's a north–south bike divide, and these were the first fellow *rouleurs* I'd seen since Giuseppe. When the leader pedalled up to my side I helplessly blurted out my entire repertoire: brakes of cork, wheels of wood, the 1914 Giro d'Italia, Milan to Milan, 3,162km.

Having blankly absorbed this information as his colleagues filed past us, he fixed me with a challenging look and said, in Italian: 'Right. How old are you?'

Oh, OK. I told him.

An unappealing smile. 'Forty-eight, eh? So how old do you think I am?'

I gave him a shufti: grizzled Super Mario 'tache, plenty of crin-kles, probably sixty-five. 'Fifty-five?'

'Ha! I'm sixty-five. *Ciao!*'

With a huge grin he levered his bony brown frame up in the saddle and set off after his friends. I watched them disappear into the trees round the next steep bend, then thought: Bollocks, I'm not having that. And I didn't. I got my head down and my dander up, mashing the pedals until the bottom bracket shrieked for mercy. Two bends later I wordlessly dispatched the paunchy strug-gler, then with the crest in sight picked off the rest one by one. Super Mario was back in the lead and I caught him just as the road flattened out.

'*Ciao!*' I trilled, looking straight ahead, then hurtling down into Caserta without any respect for my well-being. It was a lively old town with much to detain the visitor, including a 1,200-room Bourbon palace and several red lights. I resisted them all and steamed out the other side without slowing down or looking round, waiting in vain to be overtaken by old cyclists or the sense of shame my antics merited. When I finally freewheeled to a halt at Maddaloni, my legs were basted in shiny pain and the Hirondelle sounded like a honeymoon can-dragger.

Coke, carbs, coffee: after the usual bar-raid splash-and-dash I went back out to do battle with the swelling hills and the midday sun. Horse-carts trundled through fields of tobacco, and every cottage garden seemed blessed with a tree full of cricket-ball pomegranates and another of ripening figs (bleargh – give them another couple of weeks). Stinking bin-bags were slung high over railings awaiting collection, out of reach of the rats whose flattened husks lined the gutters.

The towns grew steadily more traditional. High streets were lined with butchers, bakers and candlestick makers, along with the 'I Buy Gold' pawnbroker's shops that seemed a ubiquitous expression of Italy's micro-level economic plight. Long gone were the pet-grooming salons I'd encountered in even the tiniest settlements up north, always given English names like My Good Snoopy or Super-Smart Dog Town or some other incitement to arson. Down here almost every commercial concern seemed principally interested in deterring potential customers:

'Pepe Pizza – CLOSED EVERY THURSDAY AND THROUGHOUT AUGUST.'

'Electrical appliance spares – NO GERMAN MACHINES, NO SERVICE 12–4 p.m. OR ALL DAY FRIDAY.'

On the outskirts of one town I passed an old chap in a boiler suit tinkering with an upside-down kid's bike on the pavement. 'BICYCLE AND SCOOTER REPAIRS' read the sign above the roller-shuttered entrance behind him. 'NO CREDIT CARDS' read a larger one beside it. After a wobbly U-turn, I squeaked up to him and dismounted, raising the back wheel and rotating the pedals to showcase my predicament. I watched his casual nodding morph into an open-faced shake of the head: Yep, I know *exactly* what to do about that, mate, but – pfff – I just don't fancy doing it. With a private smile he returned his attention to the little pink bicycle before him; with a mirthless laugh I remounted and rode away.

Beginning – at last – to regret my unsightly and draining granddad showdown, I laboured up a steepening valley with a motorway over my head. A robust odour hung around, and at length I established it came from the unfortunately marinated brim of my cap. 'KIT WASHED DAILY' – another message I needed to have embroidered on the back of my jersey, along with 'BLOWA YOUR HORN I SMASHA YOUR FACE' and 'I SLOW DOWN FOR CATS'.

Four hundred metres, 500, 600: the air freshened, especially once I'd stuffed my cap in my back pocket, and the settlements seemed progressively better groomed. Avellino had the look of a prosperous town in the French Alps, ringed with trim new corporate headquarters and landscaped apartment blocks. A rearing meander through its older streets led me to the well-scrubbed Piazza della Libertà , a showpiece space bordered by public buildings faced in the many shades of ochre that nineteenth-century Continentals were so partial to. This was it: the finish line of the leg from Rome, four down and four left. Would you just look at me go, ladies, like some kind of Four-Stage Johnny Halfway.

I pushed the Hirondelle through the piazza's ageless lawns and fountains, finding it quite easy to picture Giuseppe Azzini working his Bianchi over the line here. It would be half an hour before the rest of the field began to toil in, delayed by a convoy of carts and carriages en route to a religious shrine. Calzolari lost forty-four minutes, though he retained the overall lead by a country mile; Azzini moved up to second, but was still over an hour behind. Marvellously, though probably not for him, Mario Marangoni once again brought up the very rearest of rears, five hours down on the stage and almost a full day behind Calzolari in the general classification.

It was gone five, and with some very lumpy scenery to traverse I was sorely tempted to call it a day. But sitting on a bench in the clear, bright sun with Paolo in my lap I was rashly galvanised by the tale of Riccardo Palea, one of the surviving trio of rank-amateur *aspiranti*. On the run-in to Avellino, one of those shrine-bound carriages ran Palea over, inflicting terrible head injuries that saw him rushed to hospital after he had somehow made it over the line. Despite working on him throughout the rest day, the doctors were unable to save the sight in one of his eyes; yet when stage five started out at 4 a.m., there he was on his bike, just his mouth, nostrils and functioning peeper visible through a hefty swaddle of bandage. Palea retired after a few dozen miles, but even so I felt honour bound to crack on. And as it turned out, to crack up.

The celebration of unlikely local foods had been a feature of recent days: south of Frosinone I'd just missed out on a local Day of Dumplings, and now I passed under several banners advertising the Avellino and district hazelnut festival. It was difficult to avoid the townspeople's enthusiasm for these diminutive hard-shelled fruits – every other household had at least a couple of hazel trees in the garden, and with school and work done for the day these were now being energetically relieved of their ripe bounty. At the same time I couldn't begin to imagine how one might fill an entire weekend with hazelnut-themed celebrations, though I gave it a go as the road left Avellino behind. As it also left the town very distantly below, oxygen debt took a toll on these imaginings. 'Smear your nuts in Nutella,' I rasped bitterly at the empty tarmac. 'Stick a Topic up your arse.'

Stage five, Avellino to Bari, was comfortably the shortest of the race. It was also, in the estimation of the *Gazzetta dello Sport's* correspondent, uncomfortably the most debilitating: 'At least 200 of the 328km are painfully steep, the road always up and down, without a moment's respite.' Had my Italian been better I'd have understood enough of this to have regrouped overnight in Avellino. As it was, in failing light I progressed ever more agonisingly up the Campanian Alps, through the hazelnuts, then the chestnuts, and at horrid length into the lonesome mountain pines.

Skree-eenk, skreeee-eee-eeenk. That becalmed slave-ship sidled back into my head as the pedals groaned round, full weight on left leg, full weight on right. Piles of leaves and twigs were heaped across a road that didn't see much action these days, as further evidenced by the derelict holiday chalets leering creepily at me through the dark conifers. Occasionally the suffocating greenery parted and a yawning, untamed vista of rocky stacks and clefts tolled out.

The sat-nav told a tale of falling heat and rising height, 10km of uphill shit-eating, now 15, now 20. At 900m the temperature had sunk to 12 degrees, but I was frothing death-sweat like it had gone out of fashion, which I'm told it may have. How I longed to rip that hateful woollen jersey off and hurl it into the plunging abyss of my choice, followed by these hateful woollen shorts; with the elastic gone and the safety pin bent, they spent the day working their way down my hips, leading to unseemly and sometimes illegal scenes by late afternoon.

After a finale of wildly flailing switchbacks, the road topped out by a desolate clearing strewn with a museum of litter. I was beyond hate now; a toneless, reedy lament creaked unbidden from my throat, the sound of Harvey Keitel's whimpering nude meltdown in *Bad Lieutenant*. Too bollocksed to manage a dismount, I slid my arse forward off the saddle and planted both feet on the gravel, a procedure that simultaneously slammed my testes against the crossbar. A pallid smile: a month ago, that would have really hurt. Then two shiny squares bounced the last rays of sunset into my hooded eyes, and I shuffled the Hirondelle across the gravel towards them.

Embedded in the wall of rock at the clearing's edge: a pair of small hand-decorated tiles, each portraying a cyclist in traditional kit astride his machine. The blue-glazed words beneath were in a cursive, old-school hand, and the iron frames around them bore rusty witness to the passing of many hard winters. 'Ad Angelo,' began the first, '*continua pure la tua scalata, noi ti staremo sempre a ruota.*' The second: '*A Benedetto Corrado, indimenticabile compagno di tante scalate. Gli amici del G.S. ciclo run.*'

As my brain stumbled through the translation, I realised my Bad Lieutenant had turned sad, so sad that a fluid other than sweat was now dripping off his chin.

'To Angelo – carry on with your climb, we will always be at your wheel.'

'To Benedetto Corrado, unforgettable companion of so many climbs. The friends of the G.S. ciclo run.'

I stood there in the gathering gloom and let my face leak. No one does poetic eulogy and pathos better than the Italians. I wept because I was only halfway through and already running on empty. Because I could see no end. Because I didn't want to die, and because if I did I'd wind up on that unbearably poignant memorial wall and Angelo and Benedetto might not like that and their ghosts would draw a nob on my plaque.

And I wept because riding a bike up a big hill makes heroes of us all. It was impossible to imagine Angelo and Benedetto being so affectingly immortalised had they occupied their leisure hours with any other recreational activity. Nobody waxes lyrical about the Convicts of the Baize, or publishes lump-throated retrospectives entitled, *The 1914 Mixed Doubles Final – The Toughest of All Time*. Footballers don't play on after losing an eye, and no darts player will emulate Tom Simpson by checking out with the croaked words, 'Put me back on the oche.'

But when Angelo and Benedetto toiled up here, and when I followed them, we'd all starred in our own one-man epics of tribulation and triumph. In conquering this forsaken mountain road we had suffered like Merckx suffered, like Coppi, like Alfonso Calzolari; for 24 brutal kilometres, we were one of them. Yet the two old boys on those tiles had died many years ago, and it now struck me that it was some time since I'd seen any young cyclists. A wave of nostalgic regret for the passing of an age of everyman two-wheeled heroics swept over me and I wept some more.

The tear-smeared view from the other side of the summit was both wonderful and appalling: a shadowed eternity of plunging green valleys and peak after mist-wreathed peak, more like the bastard Andes. Emptied of human needs and emotions, I succumbed to gravity, and after eight missing minutes registered that chilly mountain isolation had given way to balmy civic hubbub. Having freewheeled through a number of vibrant, messy towns I grasped that it was now completely dark, and came to a halt outside the large mirrored-glass hotel that welcomed visitors to Montecorvino Rovella.

I propped the Hirondelle against an upside-down chair by the brackish outdoor pool and stumbled woodenly inside, greeted by a wave of stale heat and the smell of cupboard and Dettol. The fading red carpet was lavishly soiled and the lights flickered; that soaring glazed façade seemed distantly at odds with what it concealed. There was something funny about this place, but, swaying Weeble-like at the reception desk, I was in no fit state to put my finger on precisely what.

Presently an unprofessional character sauntered out of a back room and assessed me while blotting his brow with a crumpled hankie. He considered my rasped request for a room by repeatedly flicking his tongue across a stubbled lip, and at length asked for €60. I fumbled out three sweaty twenties and he snatched them with a chancer's glee: Done – you have been.

Every town in Italy boasts at least some small pocket of loveliness, but if Montecorvino had one it had hidden it even better than La Spezia. The total absence of municipal illumination didn't help: I almost had to feel my way into town, guided by passing headlights and the cluster of orange glows emitted by groups of aimless young smokers. If my mirror-fronted hotel exuded the tatty, Western-knock-off vibe of Brezhnev Communism, then the town centre went the full Ceauşescu. Because they were Italian, people were gamely out in droves along the dingy promenade, but because they were here, there was nothing for them to see or do: no well-dressed shop windows to linger before, no neon-fronted gelaterias to gather outside, nothing in fact but a kid-show puppeteer packing his stall away by torchlight.

This was by no means a small place, but hunting down calories necessitated a twenty-minute trudge. Still, just as it was when I drove through Romania in 1990, when I did find food it was almost free. 'Solo bottiglie,' said the pizzeria waitress after I asked for a carafe of red. I didn't think I was up to a whole bottle, but nearly asked for two when I learned they were €3.

Replete with dough and plonk, on the way back I viewed Montecorvino through more forgiving eyes. Look: there's a rather delightful old doorway. Hey, love the war memorial! And what's this fetching townhouse with its softly lit façade and hand-painted hallway murals and promise of free wifi and . . . oh, it's the hotel I should have stayed at.

Approaching the very strange one I was staying at, a cheery little scene played itself out before me. Three young men were trying to hitch a lift on the main road out of town, employing an age-old ruse: the most presentable stood at the roadside with his thumb out, while his vest-wearing friends crouched behind a wall. Almost at once an old Fiat Uno pulled over, already crowded with heads. Thumb-man jogged up to the driver's window, followed by his emergent chums; after an exchange of companionable noises, two of the three somehow bundled inside and the overladen Fiat laboured away. Their remaining friend was bereft for no more than twenty seconds, at which point a ponytailed girl pulled her scooter to a halt just past his outstretched thumb. After a brief and jolly chat he swung his leg over the pillion seat – no helmet, no problem – and off they buzzed into the darkness, down towards the clusters of light spread distantly along the valley.

It was at once a heart-warming vignette of the kindness of Italian strangers, and an appalling tragedy: to think that young people from across a generous area had to congregate in a dump like this in search of fun. But two minutes later, pulling back my red nylon bedspread with a dramatic crackle of static, I accepted that Montecorvino Rovella was no worse than a good 70 per cent of British towns, in fact better than half, and that if you tried to hitchhike home from any of them you'd be walking in at 4 a.m. wreathed in flob.

GENERAL CLASSIFICATION – STAGE 4
(Rome–Avellino, 385.4km)

1. Alfonso CALZOLARI 63:35:18
2. Giuseppe AZZINI + 1:03:15
3. Clemente CANEPARI +1:57:07
   Timothy MOORE +31:50:10
   Stage starters: 26
   Stage finishers: 23

CHAPTER 17

'That gentleman is doing a historic tour, I saw his antique bicycle in the games hall.'

The great thing about very old Italian men, other than sometimes being slower than me on a bike, is the loud and measured clarity of their speech. A couple of granddads were in conversation at the breakfast salon's dim fundament, yet I could hear and understand their every stentorian word.

'Why is he here?'

'In Montercorvino?'

'No, in our hotel.'

'Ha! I have no idea. Hungry, isn't he?'

'Very.'

The TV hall outside the basement games room was dotted with geriatrics paying homage to the breakfast-show weather-general. At last the pre-decimal penny dropped: this was an old-people's home. Or, to quote the homepage I've just consulted, 'The largest hotel for pensioners in southern Italy.' Suddenly I understood why my en suite had been carpeted in non-slip mats, and why I'd woken up in the sweaty small hours to yank off a heavy plastic undersheet. The games room, I now noted, was a bingo hall, with a tombola on the stage before many ranks of chairs with faded, balding red-plush seat cushions.

Having lugged the Hirondelle into the TV room I paused before the scattered audience, with the general over my shoulder. This was surely my crowd, an unmissable show-and-tell opportunity for nostalgic reminiscence. I recalled how Paolo Facchinetti had tracked down Alfonso Calzolari to an old-people's home up near Genoa, and now scanned the crinkle-eyed faces: he might be Calzolari's nephew, she might be Benedetto Corrado's widow. But fiddling with the moist brim of my freshly sink-laundered cap I realised they were just too far gone, not looking at the general or me but straight through us, two dozen studies in crumb-mouthed vacancy. These people had been born into the almost medieval world of Calzolari-era southern Italy, and had since lived through some of the most profound changes any human is ever likely to experience: so much locked up in those heads, with the key now thrown away. I'd have smothered them all with a pillow, but it was pushing nine and I had a long ride ahead.

Morning kilometres come cheap, two-for-one, get 'em while you can. I'll have twenty of those big hilly ones, a couple of dozen flatties – oh, and five straight into a gale past these wind turbines. I piled on the miles before lunch, up and down sweaty valleys threaded with skeins of smoke: this was still hazelnut country, and the after-harvest leaf-burning left a not displeasing tang in the hot air. Coke and a sack of crisps were taken on board at Zurpino, and I was still chewing when the road abruptly threw itself at the scrubby plain beneath the village. It was a straight descent sign-posted at 15 per cent: I tucked down and went for it, hitting 64kmh amid a tumult of rattles, creaks and howling wind. Near the bottom, with the Hirondelle under no overall control, a big blue school bus passed me with an inch to spare and the usual colon-draining horn blast. You should have heard what I called the driver. If you live within 30km of Zurpino, you would have.

As the sun went down, the price of a kilometre went up. It always did, though the rate of inflation seemed particularly harsh that afternoon. I began to understand why the 1914 pundits had decreed this stage the most forbidding: there were five ups for every down, and the threadbare semi-desert made every horizon seem a hundred miles away. The few towns I passed through were cursed with dauntingly steep high streets that I would gladly have pushed the bike up. But never did, because every one of them was dotted with witnesses, groups of locals idling in the shade with their arms folded, watching the world go by. And paying especially close attention when that world was one hundred years old, squeaking past on wooden wheels wearing a funny hat and Child Catcher goggles.

Vietri di Potenza was pencilled in as my overnight stop, after a lunchtime map session revealed it as the southernmost point on the route: every turn of the pedals from here on would take me closer to home. A flick through Paolo sealed the deal. 'After Vietri, the road became worse: riders faced a terrible ascent of many kilometres on a surface of big stones.' The gradient would still be there, and the way things had been going so might the big stones. It was a prospect that begged for fresh legs.

I emptied myself up the fearsome hairpins that snaked down from Vietri di Potenza's rocky pinnacle, then wound through its quiet, narrow streets in a state of weary dismay. If I'd learned one thing in the last few days, it was not to count on finding a bed in even quite sizeable towns down here. But I clearly hadn't learned that thing at all. Vietri was big enough to merit boldface typography on my Touring Editore map, yet had nothing to offer the visitor but fags and alcohol, plus fresh bread and shoes if he came back in the morning.

After two difficult day-ends on the trot, the unthinkable thought of a third yanked me in through the swing doors of the last-chance saloon: I was going to ask strangers for help. The people of Vietri could certainly boast a promising record of assisting cyclists in need. When the 1914 frontrunners rode up to the dreaded post-Vietri section, they were astonished to find townspeople crouched by the roadside with hammers and chisels, making those big stones smaller. It proved no great challenge to connect the current inhabitants with this distant act of dedication: everyone I saw could quite plausibly have participated in it. I have seen the face of death: it lives in Vietri di Potenza and wears a black headscarf.

Having failed to find a single Vietrian who looked likely to have a handle on the postwar guest-accommodation scene, at the exit to the town I stopped by a horseshoe bench tightly packed with half a dozen silent elders.

'*Scusi, signore. Hotel?*' Nothing.

'*Pensione? Albergo?*' It was the morning TV room all over again: a deadpan wall of corrugated leather.

'Greyhound stadium? Chandlery? Noose and chair?'

As I rammed a weary foot into the toe-clips a cracked whisper rose from the far end of the bench. '*Hotel in Potenza.*'

I issued a general thank-you, then rode around the corner to stifle my screams with a bunched fist. Potenza, I knew, was a bona fide city – but I also knew that Vietri's big brother lived miles away, beyond what was left of daylight and my own physical reserves.

Every kilometre that followed was acquired at ruinous cost. As the road petered out into gravel through the brown-shrubbed cowboy hills, I began rooting about down the back of my meta-phorical sofa for loose change, scrimping up enough to take me to the next brow. Pretty soon I was digging into reserves I didn't have, buying miles on the never-never, dabbling in the future-calories market. Sorry, this is a bit embarrassing, but I don't have enough for this climb – would you be prepared to accept the extra break-fast roll I'll eat tomorrow morning?

'Twelve, fifteen kilometres of ascent up the gravel, without moral support, without a word of comfort, three or four kilometres down, then back up . . . so slow, so painful, so insidious.'

Tell me about it, *Gazzetta dello Sport* 1914 Giro correspondent. The sunset was protracted and doubtlessly exquisite, but then it was over, and I found myself crawling across a bleak monochrome highland. Higher than the headlights moving smoothly across a distant motorway viaduct, higher even than the TV masts atop more modest surrounding hills. The sat-nav told me we were at 950m, and then it told me no more. A blank screen; the battery had gone. As I'd been off-map for some time this was a most exciting turn of events.

A sharp wind began to whip through the twilit thistles and the track reared up once more. Wrapped in my orange jacket I got off and pushed, shoes scrabbling on loose stone. A group of figures took shape in the gloom, and not in a good way; I presently found my path blocked by half a dozen stocky, beetle-browed men. They were shepherds, I decided, having seen a few sheep dotted lumin-ously about, and preferring to imagine these men employing the six-foot staves they toted to prod ruminants rather than cripple foreigners.

'Potenza?' I said, sounding like Oliver asking for seconds.

'Po-ten-za?' came the mocking, trilled echo. Sour, gruff laughter broke out, giving way to a garlic-scented chant as I forced my way through a corridor of dark and dirty faces.

'Po-TEN-za! Po-TEN-za! Po-TEN-za!'

Suddenly the hill seemed much less steep than it had, and I crested it at some speed.

With daylight down to a two-watt glimmer and that *Bad Lieutenant* bleat of ultimate despair seeping through my lips, the under-wheel crunch gave way to a slick swish and the grey landscape fell away. Downhill tarmac! Sweet bosoms of mercy. I slalomed madly through the bends, squinting at every sign that flashed by. This road must surely be taking me to Potenza, I reasoned, but speeding into the darkness, unease began to nibble away at relief: no other European nation has such a cat-slappingly capricious approach to the business of keeping the traveller usefully informed.

Good evening, unfamiliar road-user! So – what do you need to

*know about the Strada Provinciale 51? Let's kick off with the basics:
no tractors after 4 p.m., keep an eye on those deformed sagomas, this
next bridge is 18m long. Please – no horns in built-up areas! Yeah,
thought you'd like that one. Road narrows. Rocks roll off cliff. Red
car overtakes black one. Tree burns. Priority over oncoming handcarts. You want to know what? All right, calm down:* POTENZA 14.
What is it now? I just told you: POTENZA 17. *Can't you read?*
POTENZA 9. *This pass is* carrabile. *Absolutely* no sosta. *Look, for
the last time:* POTENZA 21.

I'd never previously understood why so many rustics go out and
shoot road signs in the face.

It was now past eight and entirely black, my senses tuned into
nothing but distant barks and the chirrup of nocturnal insects. I'd
already tried out a bus-shelter bench for size when a roadside light
drew me onwards. A moment later, Gerard Lagrost's filthy, clacking
shoes were disrupting the solemn gentility of the Bouganville Hill
Resort & Wellness Space. It would be thirty-six hours before they
clacked back out.

A bale of plump towels in a wenge-wood en suite the size of my
garden, veal strips with rocket and parmesan, a full day of heavy
rain: just some of the reasons for my extended stay. As an irrelevant aside, the nightly charge was precisely €6 more than I had
paid to sleep on incontinence sheets in a careworn rest home. The
receptionist had to confirm the price three times before I believed
it. She was handing me the registration form when her manager
walked out of a side-office and froze in his tracks at the sight of the
soiled weirdo slumped against the front desk. He shot her an
urgent look and she replied with a tiny, helpless shrug: too late,
boss, he's just signed in.

That first dinner in the Bouganville's crystal-chinking, heavy-
linen restaurant was a proper head-melter. Sitting there with a

bottle of prosecco in the glistening ice bucket beside me, I gazed around at the well-groomed clientele, simply unable to accept that less than two hours before I'd been lost on a dark hilltop, pushing my bike through a gauntlet of cudgel-bearing peasants.

My fellow guests took a pleasingly traditional approach to the business of spa living, following a wellness regime that crowded every table with expensive carbohydrates and dark green bottles. In this convivial company I savoured an exquisite meal that employed every one of the dozen pieces of cutlery laid before me, then went up and flumped down on my enormous bed with outstretched limbs and a huge dopey smile: the cat who got the cream, then found a tenner under the cream bowl.

I spent most of the next day holed up in my room, having begun to fear that the Bouganville's absurdly modest rack-rate must be a loss-leader, and that as soon as I stepped into the corridor two white-coated orderlies would pin me to the floor and mete out an unbidden €400 foot massage. There was plenty to do in there. I watched weather-generals point at animated rain-clouds in 51-inch enormovision, then gazed at the real thing smudging out the world beyond my vast balcony. I scrubbed at least four of the seven shades of shit out of my jersey, carved two pairs of prosecco brake blocks, and opened a new front in the war against bidon-dwelling bacteria with a packet of bicarbonate of soda I'd bought the day before. 'A thousand uses for a thousand occasions,' read the label, and I idled away some more time imagining the lower 900s: alchemy, belch roulette, stage dandruff, 'Jacob paste'.

And I enjoyed an unusually contemplative Paolo session, soaking up the full awfulness of the 1914 Giro's fifth stage. Only now did I note that it had taken place in driving rain, which sluiced away all but the heaviest, sharpest stones from the road, and embedded these in a river of mud. The shrunken peloton left Avellino with twice the usual number of spare tyres wrapped round their torsos, but several riders used their last before the first service point, and had to push for miles. Riccardo 'Cyclops' Palea didn't survive long, and nor did Costante Girardengo. The future *campionissimo* would be Italy's first cycling superstar, but at twenty-one 'the relentless effort was just too much for his young body'. He'd never really recovered after winning that epic 430km stage to Rome, and sobbing apologies for letting everyone down, after 35km he crawled into the team car.

Calzolari was having quite a night of it. At Eboli, just past my old-people's home, he skidded into a ditch so slippery with mud that he couldn't haul himself out. The other frontrunners ignored his cries and rode by – anyone left in this race was by default a nasty bastard – and he'd lost long minutes before Clemente Canepari stopped to pull him out. Fonso's last remaining teammate was dressing his leader's muddy wounds in the road when one of the press cars came steaming round the corner. As it fishtailed towards them, Calzolari recalled the words of that holy prophetess he'd visited near Bologna the week before the race began: 'You will win the Giro, *signore*, but must endure much suffering and face death.' After a great slithering screech, Death stopped with his muddy front wheels resting against Alfonso Calzolari's left leg.

Having beasted the previous stage, Bianchi's Giuseppe Azzini was again tearing it up off the front, taking insane risks on every lethal descent. Fortune favoured the berserk: by Potenza he had taken half an hour out of Calzolari's overall lead, while back down the road his more cautious rivals repeatedly crashed and punctured. Giovanni Gerbi, warming up for his forthcoming assault on the customs officer, kicked his bike into a buckled mess after

suffering six blowouts in short order. He wound up walking it over the stage finish, six hours behind the winner.

The rain clattered my balcony windows as I read, a complementary soundtrack that the generals reckoned would be tapping out its rhythm on my skull for much of the following day. That should have given me pause for thought, but instead I found myself more interested in nurturing the spoiled pickiness that comes with prolonged exposure to luxury. Is anyone *seriously* expected to blow-dry their bidet laundry with a one-speed Remington? What does a guy have to do round here to get his complimentary fruit bowl replenished? And really, how am I going to enjoy my third siesta of the day with that smoke-alarm LED blinking away on the ceiling? It's like club night on the flight deck of the Starship sodding Enterprise.

It was dark when the phone call I'd been expecting came through. Afterwards I walked out of my room, keeping the waiting gang of wellness therapists at bay with a stool, and went down to the Bouganville's restaurant. Here I dispatched two courses of wondrous fare in a state of ratcheting anticipation. The third – a cannonball stack of truffle ice-cream boules – had just been placed before me when I saw two familiar figures walk up to the reception desk and receive a rather warmer welcome than I had twenty-four hours earlier. This was the moment that sustains every endurance athlete throughout those hours and days of long and lonely toil: my mummy and my daddy had come to make everything all better.

CHAPTER 18

As soon as I'd booked my flight to Milan, my father had expressed an interest in turning up at some point to see how I was getting along: any excuse, frankly, for a hopeless Italoholic. My mother's agenda was framed during our weekly phone calls, the most recent of which I had enlivened with many pithy appraisals of Italian driving and geography, and their exciting interface with hundred-year-old bicycle braking systems.

'I'm just so, so happy to see you alive,' she said, embracing me in a way that made me feel every one of my nine years. My parents were both seventy-seven and had just driven from Naples airport; I resisted an impulse to reply with the same words. They had texted an intention to accompany me for a few days just forty-eight hours before, and I may now disclose that their impending arrival offered further justification for staying an extra night at the Bouganville Hill Resort & Wellness Space. Better safe than sorry in this region: how awkward if I'd 'accidentally' checked them into an old-people's home.

Irresponsible flights of young-hearted fancy appear to be rather a tradition amongst Moores of a certain age. When my grandfather was seventy-two he went all the way to India and back in a Land Rover, before rolling it over coming home through France. When my parents were seventy they paid £280 for a Transit van without a starter motor and drove it across a swathe of western Europe, before dumping it in the passenger drop-off zone at Genoa airport. When I was forty-eight I rode a hundred-year-old bike all round Italy, before dying of embarrassment in my mother's arms at a wellness space in Basilicata.

But as weird as it felt to greet my parents under such improbable circumstances, it was also utterly wonderful, and I made an especial effort to prolong our damp-eyed embraces just long enough to oblige the watching manager to upgrade me from filth-faced, cheapskate scum of the earth to honorary Italian mummy's boy. Any lingering fears that my quest might henceforth seem a little less flinty-eyed were soon banished by the welcome discovery that Alfonso Calzolari's mother rode beside him on a penny-farthing for lengthy sections of the 1914 Giro, beating hostile fans with an umbrella and feeding her grateful son spoonfuls of his favourite cinnamon porridge. 'No sporting spectacle was more noble or impressively masculine,' declared the *Gazzetta dello Sport*. It's all there in the appendix to Paolo Facchinetti's book that I just wrote in my head.

Other than Paul, no one I knew had yet seen me in my 'welding pervert' get-up. The last time I felt so self-consciously costumed before my parents was probably at the 1977 Silver Jubilee Swerford Flower Show Fancy Dress parade, just after the judges asked me to go and stand with all the other little girls. 'Oh dear,' said my father when I turned up fully goggled at the breakfast table. 'No wonder they keep trying to run you over.'

And yet my parents hadn't just come to dispense emotional succour. On a purely practical level, my father spoke fluent Italian, and could call on much youthful experience of rubbish old bikes – (his initial assessment of mine: 'Does it always sound like that?'). Their hired Fiat Punto would, gloriously, be accommodating the anti-matter deadweight of my saddlebag for the next four days. I also rather enjoyed setting off each morning with a no-nonsense and irreversible commitment to a stage finish. My father had booked us into a pair of apartments in Matera, and before they drove off we agreed to meet in this town's main square at 8 p.m.

Pedalling the de-bagged Hirondelle around the hotel car park felt like a taste of zero gravity, a magical floaty weightlessness. For almost 2,000km I'd been giving a plump toddler a backie, and now my parents had bundled him into the boot of their car and sped away. So long, Fatty! I swished down the rain-blotted valley road from the Bouganville with a liberated whoop, flying feather-footed up the other side with almost laughable ease. We'd made a late start and Matera was 120km off, but at this rate I'd be there in . . . ow. Ooh. No, please, not that. Not now. OW!

All men of my age and above have a duty to carry at least one chronic, long-term malaise, and mine is syphilis. No, hang on – it's kidney stones. These cheeky little renal calcifications have visited me half a dozen times over the last couple of decades, though I hadn't experienced that ominous, preludial lower-back twinge for some years. OW, SHIT OW OW OW. No mistaking those vicious clamps of agony: self-diagnosis complete. I stumbled off the bike and bent double over the crossbar, pressing my right hand to the offside small of my back like some parody of a stricken ancient.

The intense sensations associated with passing a kidney stone are supposedly the closest a man can get to empathising with the joy of giving birth, and extruding this devil spawn through my man-pipes generally involves forty-eight hours of blanched writhing. If I acted at once, though, there was at least hope of sluicing myself clear sooner. And so, still hunched at 45 degrees, I unenthusiastically took aboard two full litres of bidon grog-water.

The morning congealed into a fog of sloth and torment. Hill begat hill begat hill and I pushed up most, treating the tarmac to my Christ-on-the-cross face. Martyred forbearance was a tough look to pull off in this outfit: I caught my reflection in a bus shelter and saw some whinging oaf in a flat cap. Just a twat and his will to survive.

A headwind picked up and the sullen sky spat at me. I weaved horribly, too distracted by those blinding pulses of neat pain to focus on such trifles as oncoming heavy-goods traffic. At length I laboured through Potenza, an appalling wasteland of abandoned factories and kidney-battering potholes, each one another step on the road to dialysis. On the way out of town I hobbled into a grocery, bought three more litres of *acqua minerale* and water-boarded myself on the pavement outside. Then it was back up into the sturdy, rolling highlands that defined this whole ghastly stage.

MATERA 93

At 1.30 p.m., what a potent mettle-drainer that fingerpost was. I had sometimes managed less over a whole day, in good health and on flat terrain. Gigantic carrion birds circled overhead. Knowing I'd never make it I phoned my father's mobile; knowing he has only twice in his life successfully answered it I heard it ring and ring before a computerised Italian lady told me I was wasting my time. By now I'd brimmed myself, and was pulling over every half-hour to flush my kidneys out across Basilicata, into a glove-speckling, bike-spattering wind. On the map, the town of Tolve looked like mankind's last stand before a chasm of nothing; I stopped at a bar there to arduously wash down a pizza slice with a further half-hogshead of water. My only fellow customers were a middle-aged Asian couple, feeding the fruit machine with parallel enthusiasm.

Those after-lunch hours fulfilled the map's empty promise, delivering me through an eerie void of sandy humps and hollows. I crawled for long kilometres alongside a narrow-gauge railway decorated with ruined stations, their platforms sprouting water gantries and other rusted trappings of the steam age. Ghost farms; bare, mustard-coloured hills; a wind so fierce it blew every half-formed thought clean out of my head. When the rain came back I gazed along the weed-decked tracks beside me, understanding how very hard it would have been for the 1914 riders to resist cadging a crafty locomotive lift through this miserable landscape. Only now did I remember that Paolo had twice cited kidney pain as the cause of a weeping abandonment. At once my heart soared. Look, Mum: I'm placing personal experience in a historical context! I'm contemplating my surroundings! My brain is no longer completely preoccupied with physical agony!

The pain had indeed receded to no more than a bruised throb; I had evidently expelled one or more mineral granules somewhere into the dun emptiness behind, though once again without the satisfying pop-gun report I always hope for. Praise be to those frothing roadside gallons! It was 4.20 and I had 61km to go: I belted out the cat-piss tarp song and pedalled madly on through the bald hills.

Moore's getting his head down, Phil. If he can treat this like an individual time trial he might just have a chance. I honestly don't think I could have made it without Paul Sherwen. When a mighty side-wind blew up: *These are always dangerous moments, but Moore's got the race-face on and he's pumping those two big pistons he calls legs.* When this same wind shot-blasted my left-hand side with pellets of big, fat summer rain: *What an incredible job of work this is in these conditions, Phil. This man has a rendezvous with destiny and I do believe he's kicking again!*

What an almighty slog it was, though, a great, long wet and windy grind. I wrung out the last drops of pizza-fuel up a final ridge topped with wind turbines, then wobbled through Matera's busy outskirts as the streetlights blinked on. *He's under the red kite and now he can enjoy this, Phil, there'll be no more pain in those legs.* And there wasn't, nor any blood in my head or sweat on my brow. As Matera's many clocks struck eight I lowered my brittle, ruined husk of a body onto the steps of a sombre old bank at the edge of the Piazza Vittorio Veneto. My support crew arrived just in time to stop me taking furtive fortifying bites of limestone out of its threshold.

After a hard day – and of late there seemed to have been nothing but – I was never much fun to be with. At least I assume so: until full-blown schizophrenia kicked in I was poorly qualified to assess my own solitary company. But slumped at the restaurant table I found it hard to muster any show of enthusiasm as my darling aged parents clicked through their photos of a day they'd spent sightseeing, and which I'd spent flogging myself through renal purgatory. (Brainlessly failing to realise it would upset her tremendously, I'd already treated my mother to a mumbled rundown of my brush with organ failure.)

A more awful truth suggested itself once I'd been reanimated with house red and *linguine alle vongole.* I just generally wasn't much fun at all, yammering tonelessly on about the 1914 Giro d'Italia, and how my 1914 Hirondelle No 7 Course sur Route and 1964 legs were coping with its reproduction. I had no interest in anything else, obsessed to a point beyond rationality: had I not been their son, the two gentlefolk learning all about Alfonso Calzolari's knee problems would have long since stopped smiling indulgently. I had apparently forgotten that in common with almost everybody I've ever shared a home with, my parents have absolutely no interest in watching or playing sport, and therefore less than none in hearing somebody else drone on about it. When my father expresses astonishment at my Tour de France endeavour – as he still does, regularly – it's not because he's impressed that I cycled 3,000km, just enduringly and utterly bewildered that anybody should ever want to attempt such a thing.

In the morning I saw what darkness and hollowed exhaustion had deprived me of. My apartment was a delightful vaulted capsule hewn into the living rock; I opened the shutters and blinked out at a tumbling panorama of bleached walls and windowless grottoes under a deep blue sky, unavoidably suggestive of Jerusalem in the *Life of Brian* era. Matera's Sassi district is an extraordinary ancient netherworld, home to the planet's oldest continuously inhabited houses – at the seat of that compaction of ancient white masonry lay caves that have been lived in for over nine thousand years. It was the sort of view that cried out for an extended wander, which I could be sure my parents would be taking care of on my behalf. I left them to it after an alfresco breakfast and a deep drink from my father's well of cotter-pin knowledge – 'Oh dear. Have you tried banging them in with that wrench?'

It was Saturday and I rattled northwest on a supine and deliciously unpopular dual carriageway. This swiftly delivered me into Puglia, which seemed very keen to showcase its credentials as the hottest, driest and most ancient region in Italy. The sat-nav

thermometer hit 34, and the tawny, barren landscape had a savagely desiccated look to it. I couldn't begin to understand what had been attracting living creatures here since the dawn of time: I rode past a quarry that is home to 30,000 dinosaur footprints, and a cave where archaeologists recently found the fossilised skeleton of a 400,000-year-old hominid. Near Altamura I rolled through a hillside piled with pre-Roman remains and bronze-age tumuli, and then into a shocking demonstration of the barbaric inhumanity to which its long-civilised townspeople have now sunk. The towering wrongness of Saturday-morning school has enraged me ever since I first encountered this odious Continental practice during my French exchange, and watching children of all ages dash out through gates right across town I felt an urge to hug every one of them to my hot chest. Happily I resisted this urge, even though it went down pretty well on the French exchange.

The fifth stage ended at Bari, and I knew I was nearing the city when two cheery blonde street ladies hailed me from a tatty road-side sofa: '*Signore! Ménage à trois?*' Then careworn outskirts, a grid of grimy old boulevards and – *skreeeeeeeeek-k-k-k* – up to a halt by the esplanade railings.

More than two weeks before, just past La Spezia, I'd turned my back on the Mediterranean; now here I was looking out at the sun-jewelled Adriatic. Coast to coast, north to south, west to east. How extraordinary to have made it this far. From the saddle-snap on that first morning to the previous afternoon's organ malfunction, almost every day had featured some potentially terminal, sceptic-pleasing calamity. 'Into the home straight,' I said, giving Number 7 a matey slap on the down-tube, and deciding not to tell him that straight was 1,300km long. Then I sat down heavily on the pave-ment, took a commemorative selfie of the two of us, and at least thought about terrifying the afternoon rollerbladers and pram-pushers with a mighty, spittled roar of hard-won achievement.

True to the 1914 Giro's curse, it was bucketing down in the capital of Italy's driest region when Giuseppe Azzini crossed the line at just after 5 p.m. A large crowd stood waiting in the rain, drawn by the news that Alfonso Calzolari had passed through Matera forty-seven minutes down on his rival. Azzini had started the stage over an hour in arrears, but anticipation built as the clock ticked on and the rain beat down from a darkening sky. The hour was up by the time Calzolari finally ploughed doggedly into view; he stopped the clock 3 minutes 15 seconds later. Over to you, Paolo: 'Incredibly, after 2,000 kilometres and a thousand adventures, our two heroes were separated by the blink of an eye.' Bianchi's Giuseppe Azzini had snatched the race lead, by six seconds.

I felt I should have lingered in Bari to pay tribute to this extraor-dinary turn of events, but away from the seafront it seemed a tire-lessly drab and disordered city, with great sprawls of brownfield wasteland and a general air of almost war-torn neglect. Stray dogs roamed the dusty, quiet pavements and a feisty grey-brown example hastened my exit by pursuing me at full, slavering pelt through a derelict industrial estate. This was no bark-heavy warding-off: all I could hear was insistent, purposeful panting and the fast-closing scatter of gravel. I have no doubt that my flesh would have been multiply pierced had he caught me, and ensuring he narrowly did not meant reaching speeds I would never again equal on a flat road.

To avoid another ugly collision between the forces of sightseeing and Sisyphean toil, I'd arranged to meet my parents at Giovinazzo: a 94km ride seemed about 15 shy of the daily distance beyond which I started hating everyone. Courtesy of his abrupt mastery of the SMS, I met my father outside the extremely wonderful hotel he'd found for us, a former monastery overlooking the sea. I glanced around my room and sighed: just two more nights of four-poster beds and complimentary mineral water, then it was back to the stained hovels.

It had been an immeasurably better day, which sired an evening to match. We dined outdoors beneath moonlit baroque façades; I cheerfully perused their daily harvest of digital images and discreetly jabbed a fork in my leg every time I felt the urge to discuss the history of competitive cycling. The balmy Puglian night and a second bottle brought on an expansive mood: I nominated Lucera as our next rendezvous, an ambitious 120km foray deep into my red zone of Vacant Contempt.

Sunday morning was establishing itself as my favourite slice of the Italian week. The towns were vibrantly abuzz; the roads between them wonderfully moribund. Old men in caps like mine shouted cheery abuse at each other across outdoor café tables, hailing me with cries of 'Forza Girardengo!' and 'Eh, il campionissimo!' Every *pasticceria* was full of jolly cake-faced families soiling their Sunday best, and I picked my way through downtown traffic jams amusingly athrob with amplified Disney hits.

When the 1914 boys sped through the port of Molfetta at 1.15 a.m. they wouldn't have been missing much. On any other day, those gusts of rancid seaweed would have sent me smartly out the other side, but with the town seeing out the week in such style under a bright blue sky I slowed to a wobbly dawdle. A police marching band trumpeted round a palm-lined harbour, and the street outside the big white cathedral was packed with a funeral parade jauntier than most English weddings. The main square was thronged with one of those endearingly hopeless street markets: shoes made from leather-look cardboard, luminous net-curtain lingerie, acrylic vests emblazoned with thoughtful messages like 'Sweet Fashion Years' and 'Funky Dance Trend'. Every town in Italy seems to host one of these weekend craporiums. No one ever buys anything but they're always teeming with locals, drawn by force of ancient habit and that unstoppable urge to congregate.

As utterly clueless businessmen, Italian market stallholders are certainly in good company. Any settlement you pass through will be bookended by boarded-up, half-built or burned-down commercial ventures, all of them shriekingly ill-considered. How I'd love to have heard these wrong-trepreneurs explain themselves to their bank managers.

'What are you on about? There's no such thing as too many roller discos.'

'Come on, you show me one other cutlery warehouse in Bari that offered regular customers access to an indoor adventure playground.'

'Puglia's largest range of coloured gravels . . . if I'm guilty of anything, it was daring to dream too big.'

My favourite was a bricked-up retail unit I'd passed in the countryside outside Potenza.

'Franco: you like guitar effect pedals, right?'

'Are you kidding? I love those little guys! *Vreeooommm-om-om-wowwwww!*'

'Me too. Wonder if anyone else round here does?'

'Hmm. I think that friend of Gianluca's might, you know, the foot masseur at the wellness space.'

'I suppose there's only one way to find out.'

'Ask him?'

'Don't be stupid. Let's build an absolutely enormous shop on a hill miles outside town, and call it Guitar Pedal Valley.'

'Excellent! You design the logo and order a load of pedals and stuff, and I'll book the bailiffs in for next year.'

After Barletta – where Giovanni Gerbi went all stampy on that customs officer – the route turned inland, and the blustery crosswind realigned itself to my disadvantage. For the next four hours I reeled in a prostrate enormity of industrial-scale Europlonk vineyards, now being energetically harvested. Romanian cries echoed out from the mile-long vine corridors, and tipper lorries rumbled gingerly past, brimful of dusty grapes. Since starting out in the north, I'd watched the roadside produce slowly swell and ripen around me: mine was a season-bridging, nation-spanning accomplishment. This stirring thought kept the forces of tedium and wind-faced lassitude at bay for up to thirteen minutes.

I tried very hard to appreciate the dead-straight horizontality, aware that from Lucera onwards I would be spending several hundred kilometres cresting the perpendicular granite vertebrae of Italy's spine. But there was just far too much of it, a geometric infinity of tarmac and parallel vine-lines that stripped away any sense of progress, as if I was back in the training loft on my exercise bike. Reading Paolo the night before, I couldn't understand why dear old Mario Marangoni, the perennially hapless table-propper who had been last over every line, had finally bailed out on this undemanding plain. Now I completely did.

With Alfonso Calzolari currently 500km up the road in our sat-nav showdown, over recent days I'd been working on an undercard battle with Marangoni, who seemed much more like my kind of guy. Here, the action was hotting up. Mario had ended the stage from Rome 22hrs 16' 56" in arrears, having covered the race to date at an average speed of 18.3kmh; my own at that point was 16.8. After a typically disastrous performance on the following stage to Bari – last again, seven hours behind the winner – Mario's AVS slumped to 17.79kmh. Mine was currently 17.0. Poor Mario had now fallen by the wayside – Paolo describes him lying flat out in the road, not caring if he was picked up or run over – but his AVS lived on, as my target. Me v Mario, *mano*-a-long-dead-*mano*. Yes, I was doing this race in bite-sized chunks, not massive, raw 400km slabs. But I would finish it, and I would do so with a faster average speed than its slowest competitor. Reach for the sky! Well, you've got to pick your battles down my end of the sporting spectrum.

The headwind was blowing like a bastard now: two steps forward, one step back. Every time I opened the map it wound up wrapped round my head. Presently I battled it off and saw a sign ahead: FOGGIA 40.

OK, I thought, I can do that: Foggia was a large town just shy of my destination. Then, five flat and blustery kilometres later: FOGGIA 53.

You hopeless, filthy goat-botherers! I lowered my nose to the bars and cursed this horizontal gust-factory with the very worst words the English language has to offer, and then, after my food ran out and hypoglycaemia began to erode cognitive function, in a tongue known to no man.

As dementia kicked in I sang into the wind – an hour of gasp-along-a-Beatles – then roared at it, proper iron-throated bellows that I sustained until a huge black airborne insect of some sort ricocheted off my front teeth. When something that wasn't a big straight road or a grapeless vine wandered into view I wished it hadn't: a derelict shack with a hollow-cheeked Romanian child burning pallets on the doorstep, a warning sign with all the red sun-bleached out of it, encouraging right-turns it had once prohibited.

The rash of roadside memorials suggested boredom-related recklessness was endemic round here, and more than once I emerged from an a cappella Motown anthology or extended kneecap survey to find myself in the middle of the tarmac. Full attention was thoughtfully restored by a pick-up truck, which approached me from behind at enormous speed before violently slamming its brakes on. A screeching, slithering halt left a gap of perhaps four inches between my rear wheel and a front bumper that had visibly played this game many times before, and lost. When this vehicle then sped past trailing a jolly gale of male laughter from its opened windows, I found I was too stimulated to articulate an objection.

A text from my father pinged in as I nosed out of the Plain of Terminal Disheartenment and into the outskirts of Foggia. The hotel he directed me to was just shy of Lucera, a forty-minute ride down a dual carriageway; I wound the cadence up and saw my AVS nudge to 17.1. After a late start and a day of dilatory tourism, my parents pulled into the car park just in front of me. We'd contrived a finish from that famous fable: 'The Tortoise and the Other Two Tortoises'.

GENERAL CLASSIFICATION – STAGE 5
(Avellino-Bari, 328.7km)

1. Giuseppe AZZINI 77:22:00
2. Alfonso CALZOLARI +6
3. Clemente CANEPARI +2:47:30
   Timothy MOORE +40:41:30
   Stage starters: 23
   Stage finishers: 21

CHAPTER 19

The Misadventure of F. H. Grubb set an unfortunate precedent for his countrymen. After Freddie's capitulation in the 1914 Giro's opening stage, it would be more than fifty years before another Brit dared enter the Giro, and Vin Denson's experiences in 1966 failed to open the floodgates. 'People were chucking their leftovers at us from the balconies,' Denson recalled, his punishment for joining a group of foreigners chasing down the national favourite, Gianni Motta. 'Tomatoes, spaghetti, anything. When I walked into the hotel that night, someone dumped a full dustbin on me. Bastards!'

Heroically, Denson won the following stage: something no other British rider would manage for twenty-one years. That rider was Scotland's Robert Millar, who in the 1987 Giro completed a full emulation of Denson's experience when he found himself in the compost crossfire. A week before winning the penultimate stage – securing himself the King of the

Mountains title and second place overall – Millar nobly placed himself and his bike between the Giro's perennially combustible roadside patriots and Stephen Roche. The Irishman, having rashly taken the race lead from an Italian teammate, was the target of a rolling food-fight that saw both him and his Scottish defender pelted with vegetables and 'some kind of grain', drenched by oral expulsions of red wine and – most compellingly – slapped in the face with a raw steak. More traditional shoves and punches accompanied the buffet punishment, and after the post-stage press conference, Roche's deposed teammate Roberto Visentini was fined three million lire for threatening to knock him out. 'The behaviour of the people was bad,' recalled Roche, with the indulgent understatement afforded by eventual victory. (Roche went on to claim that year's Tour de France and the world road-race championship, a treble shared only with Eddy Merckx. Visentini never won another race.)

Robert Millar's achievement hardly got the Brit-ball rolling: another twenty-one years had elapsed before Mark Cavendish brought home a stage win. In fairness, Cavendish has since claimed more Giro stages than anyone else, and in recent years David Millar, Lord Wiggo and Alex Dowsett have doubled the tally of British stage winners. But no compatriot has come even close to matching Millar's podium finish: the best any British rider has managed since was Charlie Wegelius, who came home twenty-ninth overall in 2010. The Giro is horribly, uniquely gruelling, and soft-cheeked, milksop Britain has yet to produce a glutton primed for three weeks of punishment in all its forms: the endless climbs, the blizzards, the flobbed wine and steak-slaps.

Bloody, bowed and plastered with leftovers, Vin Denson hung on to finish the 1966 Giro in fortieth place – a feat that ranks him alongside Lord Wiggo in the all-time British top five. Riding in a humbler professional age, Denson received his modest wages only at the end of the season. By then he was always flat broke, reduced to sustaining himself on training rides with stolen carrots yanked straight out of the field. Vin would have understood what the ever-ravenous, salami-swiping desperadoes of 1914 endured, and by the time the sun went down so did I.

'Let's be honest, no cyclist wins on bread and water.' Five-time Tour winner Jacques Anquetil's famously oblique reference to doping was later adapted by the Lance Armstrong generation, in pitying reference to those sorry no-hopers who rode clean: *pane e agua*, in the translation appropriate to Spain's durable status as dopemeisters general. Anyway, that day I purified these cynical maxims and rode 101km to Campobasso on nothing but H_2O and dough: seven requisitioned breakfast rolls and bidon after bidon of village pump-water.

Twenty-one riders had rolled out of Bari back in 1914; only twelve would make it to the stage finish at L'Aquila. Dear old Mario Marangoni was first to fall by the wayside, soon followed by his fellow privateer *isolato* Michele Robotti, who shattered a wheel rim in a crash just past Foggia. Ahead lay a day of brutal reckoning for the amateurs, one survived by just two *isolati* and a single *aspiranto*: the miracle of teenage pluck that was Umberto Ripamonti, the youngest rider in the race, who had entered at the last minute simply because he fancied an adventure and happened to live near the Milan start line.

The pros hardly giggled their way to L'Aquila. Giovanni Gerbi gave up just past Lucera, suffering from 'a swollen and turgid right leg'. As this affliction hadn't prevented him from meting out a sound kicking a few hours earlier, I preferred to imagine Gerbi being terminally demoralised by the looming sight of the terrain I was now ascending.

When the turbine-topped hills hoved into view I'd felt no fear or loathing. Indeed, when the moment came I stood on the pedals with something like enthusiasm, or at the very least relief to have left that accursed wind-faced flatness behind. Towing a heavy cloud of sweaty wool stench, I hauled myself up the tilted slopes of hot scrub, arriving presently at a big hole full of headlights and engine roar. A sign outside identified this as Wolf Tunnel, which at a declared length of 1,372m was well beyond my nervous system's shrivelled subterranean capability. With the nonchalance afforded by a merciful absence of saddlebag, I shouldered the Hirondelle and strode up the hill over the hole.

This interesting decision deposited me, an hour later, by a service track linking the wind turbines that marched along the hilltops in both directions. My legs glistened with perspiration and bloody bramble scratches; embedded burrs, furzes and other pointy plant-parts mingled with melting chips of tar accumulated from a newly-resurfaced road. The sat-nav was treating me to its Screen of Blankest Disapproval: You've really done it this time, goggle-boy.

Midway through my steepening and ever-blinder scramble, I had stumbled heavily out of some head-high brambles and almost fallen on top of a gummy, nut-brown rustic, scrattling away at a small patch of maize and melons. Everything about his appearance and environment suggested he had been living there undisturbed for months, for years, for ever: at the edge of his little clearing stood a corrugated-roof shed he evidently called home, with two vests drying on the back of a stool outside its door, alongside a tin bucket piled with old pots and plates. I staggered to my feet fully prepared to be furiously grunted at in some incomprehensible dialect, or maybe eaten. Instead, he interrupted his labours only to aim me a lugubrious nod. I think this meant, 'You are about to enter Molise, young man, Italy's loneliest and emptiest region, a forgotten land where the afternoon cyclist always goes hungry. Next time, buy a melon off me.'

I topped the hill, hit an approximation of tarmac and settled into many hours of undernourished undulation. The biggest enemy, not for the first time in my journey, was overbearing isolation: Molise's populace, never more than modest, has shrunk by nearly a third since the Fifties, and it showed. Barren hillsides rolled into every houseless valley, and the only other road-users were school buses delivering children to far-flung homes. Following the established pattern, every one of these vehicles tried very hard to sever my left ear with its right wing mirror as it sped by. Harassed and taunted by his passengers, a road-blocking resentment to motorists and an object of outright derision for the drivers of heavier and more masculine conveyances, the school-bus driver's lot is not a happy one. In all honesty I hardly begrudged their murderous glee at finally getting a chance to take it out on someone further down the road-going food-chain.

This time I narrowly beat my parents to our nominated rendezvous in Campobasso, a town that owed its startling unloveliness to a prolonged disagreement between Canadian and German troops in 1943. My father had presciently chosen a hotel out in the hills, though it lay some way beyond the off-duty distance I was prepared to cycle on an empty stomach. There was only one thing for it. Reducing the Hirondelle to the dimensions of a Fiat Punto's boot was a challenge my parents confidently decreed unfeasible, so they watched with some interest as the bike more or less fell to bits in my hands. Quite how it had thus far failed to do so of its own accord while in violent motion remained a mystery.

In the morning my parents returned me to the outskirts of Campobasso. An aptly morose drizzle speckled the tarmac as I put the Hirondelle back together in a lay-by, before an inquisitive audience of yellow-jacketed road-workers. One came up and asked if I was heading for Naples. I told him I wasn't. That's good, he said, miming one of the shifty antiquarian bicycle thieves I had thereby avoided. L'Aquila? Not so good: I watched his right hand impersonate the Loch Ness monster in motion.

As a farewell present my father summoned his latent powers of mechanical improvisation, stabilising the bidon rack with a length of anti-pigeon spiking he had obscurely salvaged in Matera, then pinging out my bothersome right-hand cotter pin with three taps of the big wrench. We surveyed it in wonder: a tormented stub of rusty gouges, embedded with the flattened remnants of those wire-wrapped nails Paul had wedged round it a thousand kilometres before. It looked more like some crude Iron Age artefact than a vital component from the most successful machine in history. The pin was forced back into its burrow along with a bracing pair of pigeon spikes; the anvil-carrier saddlebag strapped on. Having handed my parents a now superfluous map of southern Italy I embraced them, then briskly pedalled away before I could disgrace myself in a manner inconsistent with my age and mission.

Alfonso Calzolari was already twenty minutes behind the leaders at Isernia, but then he'd been fending off attacks before the stage had even begun. Dozing in his Bari hotel room on the rest day, Calzolari woke to find a sinister stranger bent over his bed.

'Want to make fifteen thousand lire?' the shadow whispered. 'Just finish second in this race.'

Again this could only have been the work of Bianchi, the standout Dick Dastardlys in this hardcore wacky race. They were by a distance the wealthiest team in the Giro, and as the nation's dominant bicycle manufacturer had the most to gain from the promotional windfall of victory. Their rider Giuseppe Azzini now held the lead by a sliver, but insurance never hurts.

The inducement proposed to the bleary Fonso was five times the prize for winning the Giro, but he resisted grubby temptation and its attendant opportunity to take the remainder of this appalling challenge rather less seriously. Recounting the story to Paolo Facchinetti in an old-people's home fifty-eight years later, Calzolari vividly described his furious pride as he bundled the interloper out of the hotel-room door. 'I am winning this race for my hometown Bologna, not losing it for money!'

Afterwards he did what Italians do: he went and told a monk. 'Fifteen thousand lire's a packet, you melon,' the holy man forgot to say as he pressed a lucky crucifix into Fonso's hand. 'Calzolari could not yet know how vital this gift would be,' wrote Paolo. Mapping the SS17's Parkinsonian progress over lunch in an Isernia bar, I understood why: between me and L'Aquila lay 150km of writhing mountain road, with another 150 afterwards.

The valico del Macerone was lofty enough to merit one of those 'pass open/closed' signs, and a name-check in Paolo's roll-call of stage-six infamy. It was 684m and I pissed it. That smug little face in the selfie I took at the summit sign says: What mountain? Its white-lipped counterpart taken ninety minutes later atop the passo del Rionero says: Oh, this one. Proceeding to 1,052m – the highest I'd been since the day after Rome – had required extensive emulation of 1914 methods, as described in Paolo's account of the Rionero climb: 'With the riders now suffering a crisis of exertion, most walked on foot.'

Recrimination took hold during a foolhardy descent. That's it, I thought, crashing bitterly through potholes as I overtook a dawdling Fiat Panda: no more pushing. It was a question of pride. Or would have been if I had any. In fact, this determination to go less slowly up mountains was closely related to my new policy of going much too fast down them: whatever it took to better the average race speed of Mario Marangoni.

With my expression set to Hungover Withnail, I somehow kept both legs over the crossbar and rotating; by the time I reached the ski-centric village of Roccaraso, a sharp and nippy mountain twilight was setting in. The sat-nav told me I'd managed 100km in the day – just – and was now up at 1,256m, a post-Alpine high. However, it also told me that my average speed had dropped by 0.1kmh. Such are the margins at the bleeding edge of gladiatorial contest: it was enough to downgrade my evening from celebration to wake.

CHAPTER 20

I woke at dawn with stomach cramp and the shivers. In bleary alarm I feared a dose of bidon poisoning; imagine my relief to discover it was nothing more than malnutrition and first-stage hypothermia.

Both were my due as Roccaraso's only guest. The hotelier had quite understandably elected not to turn on the heating for my sole benefit, especially as he'd only charged me €25 for a room, and the lone waiter/chef at the one open restaurant had been able to offer nothing more than two lamb cutlets and a grilled courgette. '*Carboidrati?*' I'd wheedled, drawing deep from those roadside-litter vocabulary lessons; after a helpless shrug he returned with a three-inch baguette knob-end. I burned that off relocating my hotel amongst the snowboard rental shops and shuttered chalets in Roccaraso's funereal, ambitiously pitched streets.

I did what I could to address this deficit in the pine-clad

breakfast room, just me and a table of plastic-sheathed, long-life comestibles. As ever these were dominated by the plastic-wrapped, long-life, jam-filled brioche that was such an unfortunate fixture of my Italian mornings: sickly gel entombed in claggy wool, like biting into a dead Clanger. I downed four between practised sighs, gazing out beyond the window-boxed geraniums. A fox trotted across a disused railway viaduct below the town; above it, muscular pinnacles and a cold, grey sky. In the typically demoralising manner of mountain stages, I would be going down before I went back up. All the way down: the map promised a forthcoming descent of some magnitude, all squiggled hairpins and those double-chevrons of sternest gradient.

As my route also passed through expanses of foodless nothing, I filled my front jersey pouch from the brioche pile – my brain and legs might be grateful later, even if my mouth wouldn't be. Bent over my saddlebag by the reception desk, this swag disgorged itself en masse across the lino before the proprietor's disappointed eyes.

'*Carboidrati*,' I mumbled, gathering it all up and making the slowest quick getaway in history.

Eight o'clock: I'd never have been on the road this early if my parents had still been here. For most of the previous day I'd been trying to find upsides to their departure, offsetting the downsides of a return to crappy hotels and muttering, solitary madness. One thing I certainly wouldn't miss was my nightly failure to evolve from hard-bitten endurance athlete to cheekily lovable youngest son. In fact, it had become clear during our time together that after-hours I was entirely unfit for public consumption, and should for the benefit of society be left in some dark corner with a wet towel over my head, hooked up to a drip of slurried wine and pizza. Nor would I be rueing the absence of my mother's standard day-end greeting, which managed to cram embarrassment and disheartening intimations of mortality into five brief words: 'Timbers darling, you're not dead!' And how very crushing it always was, having once more flogged myself halfway to that death, to learn that their hire car had covered the same daily distance in a carefree hour. However irrelevant, this disparity never failed to cast a great shadow of pointlessness over my whole endeavour.

I even managed to extract a positive from the reappearance of my saddlebag, now adding its considerable heft to the momentum I was building in the early stages of the promised descent. Is this a tunnel coming up? *Swoooosh!* So it was. *Sweeeesh!* There goes another. The map had promised many unavoidable black holes, and I'd started the day with my little head torch lashed round the bidon rack. A wise move: I shot past a roadside warning of inoperative interior lighting in all tunnels ahead.

The road was broad and smooth; I let it come to me. Out of the next tunnel a dramatic Imax-scale preview of my immediate future opened up. I was tearing around the rim of a gigantic, sheer-sided bowl of grey and green, connected to the very distant valley floor by a wandering tarmac stripe that periodically launched itself across an eternity of dead air with some prodigious viaduct. The short word that now passed through my gritted teeth was the last coherent sound I would issue for fifteen minutes and as many kilometres.

The Hirondelle had, by accident or design (OK, accident), been looking after itself very well of late. Other than supervising my father's farewell remedial work, I had for many days felt no need to disturb Number 7's slickly run regime of self-maintenance. When things fell off (sometimes a brake block; at least once a day one of those caliper-return springs) I put them back on, but those mornings of preventative and precautionary tightening and tinkering lay in the distant past.

I think you can guess where this is leading: that's right, a golden eagle now swoops down and flies away with my scalp in its talons. Either that or my front wheel develops a petrifying lateral shimmy above 40kmh, when I'm no longer in a position to go below 40kmh.

One moment I sensed a certain wobbly vagueness beneath my clenched fists; the next the handlebars were a juddery blur. A Vulcan death grip on the brake levers merely delayed the attainment of awful, cheek-rippling speed, and suddenly the road didn't seem quite so broad, or so smooth. I entered the most horrifically exposed viaduct on the wrong side of the white line, and literally screamed out of it with arcs of verge-gravel flying from under my tilted wheels. This was it, the big wipeout, the coconut clonk of skull on asphalt, the little roadside epitaph: 'He died doing what he loved most – hospital morphine.'

In the middle of the longest, darkest tunnel the head torch bounced round and shone its beam directly into my eyes. It hardly mattered: instead of contributing usefully to the emergency, my senses were now just blaring like klaxons. Soon they began to shut down. The roar of frozen wind faded to a muffled, womb-like whoosh, my vision magically purged itself of those ghastly peripheral voids, and I only noticed that some sort of dragonfly had spread itself terminally across my Adam's apple three hours later, when one of its wings fell into my lunch.

By the final bends I was letting the road steer the bike for me, submitting to its banks and cambers like a corpse thrown down the Cresta Run. It took me a while to notice the SS17 had pulled itself straight and was now trundling along the valley floor. A petrol station with an attached bar appeared and I pulled over. It was a struggle to make myself understood to the young barmaid, and not just because wind-chill and post-traumatic stress were causing my jaw to shiver along with my limbs. She seemed like a nice girl, who was simply reluctant to accept that hers was a world where men might demand brandy at 9.40 a.m. And do so again at 9.42.

Even half-cut and whimpering, it didn't take me long to find out what was up with Number 7's front wheel. The nuts holding the front axle to its hub were finger-loose, a daring set-up for an 800m drop. I spannered them tight, forced two dead Clangers between my protesting lips and freewheeled away down the valley. Through Sulmona, where Calzolari signed in at the control half an hour behind the frontrunners but twelve minutes ahead of race leader Giuseppe Azzini, then into Popoli, where I garnished my *panino* with dragonfly wings.

You could describe the 48 remaining kilometres of the Giro's sixth stage as incident-packed, in the same way you could describe Hitler as naughty. It all kicked off on the Svolte, a vicious eminence that hosts an annual motoring hill climb – I rode over its chequered start line in Popoli's outskirts. Halfway up this ascent, a red car overtook the group containing Calzolari, his teammate Canepari and Carlo 'The 'Tache' Durando. What happened next was encapsulated by a headline on the front page of the following day's *Gazzetta dello Sport*: 'Drama and intrigue at the Giro'.

The *Gazzetta's* report revealed that official complaints against the Calzolari group had been lodged by two teams, Bianchi (no, really) and Globo, alleging that the mysterious red car had towed the trio up a section of the Svolte. More detailed, and much more serious, allegations were published in *Il Resto del Carlino* – a paper printed in Calzolari's hometown Bologna, would you believe. The Svolte Three hadn't just enjoyed a quick tug, as it were, but had climbed inside the car and been driven all the way up the climb.

(By way of a tension-sapping interlude, let us take a moment to enjoy the charming history of *Il Resto del Carlino*. Founded in 1885, its name means 'the change from a Carlino', this being the smallest denomination of a papal currency that was then legal tender in Bologna. Unable to offer change to customers who paid with a Carlino, shopkeepers would instead offer a sheet of local news. The paper remains in print today, one of the most venerable in Italy.)

Clinging to a vehicle's door pillar is the oldest trick in the book (*How to Cheat in Professional Cycling*, vols 1–412). First trialled in the inaugural 1903 Tour de France, it still thrives today: I was lucky enough to spend a day in a team car at the 2004 Tour, and witnessed the practice at stirring close quarters. As an act of mercy for riders in distress, it's broadly tolerated: it's a fair bet that almost everyone in the 1914 field held on to bits of passing car at some point on their way up Sestriere, though only three were penalised. (The unfortunate rider our car towed along the 2004 route for a good 5km was grovelling miserably in no man's land, having been spat out the back of a long breakaway. It was his first and only Tour.)

But in scale and import, the allegations carried in *Il Resto del Carlino* were of a rather taller order. Calzolari was well aware of his predicament: if the race jury agreed that a rider six seconds off the lead had tackled a decisive swathe of the Giro d'Italia in the back seat of a car, he would be instantly disqualified ('and made to pay back all the bonus money I'd won so far', as he later told Paolo). In truth, Fonso and friends already knew they had some explaining to do. The next car to overhaul them on the Svolte was driven by a race official, who caught the three riders and the mystery red motor in a compromising position.

A century of sporting precedent teaches us that those accused of cheating plump for one of three initial responses: denial, bluster or blustering denial. Having been witnessed by an official, Calzolari and Co. couldn't quite go the full Armstrong, but they did what they could. A bit of collusion would have helped, though, as their tales were severely compromised by a conspicuous lack of consistency.

Clemente Canepari, Calzolari's lieutenant, spoke first to the jury. In his version, the trio had literally just that very second grabbed on to the red car – 'we held on to it for no more than 100 metres' – when the official caught them. 'Obviously we let go then, because we didn't want to be disqualified.' So who drove the mystery motor? Canepari's extraordinary response must have made for a very awkward team dinner that night: 'Oh, some friend of Alfonso's.'

Calzolari's riposte was a triumph of bare-faced self-exoneration. 'I'm riding up the climb with the others when this red car goes past. One of the passengers tells us to grab on, and the other riders do just that. "Shame on you!" I shout at them, at which point the driver swerves and pins me against the wall. It was then that the official's car came past.' It might have looked to that official as if Calzolari was taking a tow along with the others, but nothing – *nothing* – could have been further from the truth. The driver? Never seen him before in my life. By way of a final flourish, Alfonso reported that the repellent dishonesty of his fellow riders – teammate Canepari amongst them – had upset him so much he 'cried like a baby'.

Asked for his side of the story, 'Tache Durando jumped over a wall and ran away. (Just a theory, but he looks the type.)

I suppose Calzolari's shamelessly implausible tale should have put me off him. It certainly encouraged a more sceptical assessment of other self-reported incidents, notably the sinister stranger's bribe and its haughty rejection. But as a man whose love of professional cycling has survived the rolling scandals of the last two decades, I've learned to cut my heroes an awful lot of slack (I don't hate Lance Armstrong because he was a drugs cheat, but because he's just so thoroughly unpleasant).

Yes, Calzolari cheated and told a gigantic and ridiculous lie about it. Yet in the circumstances I could easily forgive him. For one, he'd just been inexplicably landed in it by his own teammate. (Neither Paolo nor I could imagine Calzolari persuading some car-owning chum to drive all the way from Bologna to tow him up a hill. I've no idea why Canepari said what he did, but wonder if he was just a bit dim and naïve, and thought the jury might think he was really cool if he told them his mate's mate had a red car.)

More compellingly, in a no-holds-barred contest that had already lobbed its moral compass down a well, Calzolari was a man more sinned against than sinning. The entire Svolte episode, right down to the convenient appearance of the official's car, carries the haddocky whiff of a brazen stitch-up. It is Paolo's belief that Bianchi was once more the *éminence grise*, plotting the entrapment to secure Fonso's disqualification, and by default victory for its man Giuseppe Azzini.

The six-second advantage Azzini held at the start of the stage looked rather tiny when set beside the time penalty now imposed on Calzolari and his fellow car-clingers. In one of those arcane punitive compromises that cycling authorities so effortlessly pull out, the jury found the trio guilty of 'a serious infraction', and decreed they should all be given the same time as the stage's final finisher, plus – why not? – an additional minute. Calzolari's team stared in horror at the published stage rankings: the teenage amateur Ripamonti had rolled last into L'Aquila, 3 hours 22 minutes behind the winner, Durando's teammate Luigi Lucotti. A penalty of over two hundred minutes seemed almost too huge to make sense of, though I like to imagine Canepari expressing gormless relief. 'Get in! If that Marangoni character was still running we'd have been stung for, like, twelve days or something!'

A cursory map-glance at what lay in wait for me between here and Milan suggested the Svolte – a gain of 500m in 8km – might well be the 1914 Giro's final properly massive climb. If that explained why so many of the surviving riders tried to bunk it, then it's also why I was determined not to. At Sestriere I'd miserably flunked my first mountain examination, metaphorically doodling nobs and swastikas all over the question paper, then screwing it into a ball and eating it. This could not and would not happen at my last.

When the first bead of sweat trickled from temple to chin it felt like a tear, an expression of my body's deep sadness at what I was asking it to do. For the next forty-five minutes it cried its hot pink eyes out. Ragged breaths, bidon sun-glints, the treacled passage of tarmac beneath the front wheel's fraying grey rubber: I was locked in my own private world, until some idiot unlocked it and let four thousand flies in. Perhaps I should have imagined Calzolari being driven against one of these retaining walls, except he never had been, and in any case there was no room in a mind purged of all thought but the primitive will to pedal. In the latter stages I felt myself – indeed heard myself – possessed by that circus train in *Dumbo*, steaming effortfully towards the crest of a giant hill. 'I-think-I-can, I think I can, I . . . think . . . I . . . can . . .' This commentary went rather off message when at last the hill-climb's chequerboard finish passed beneath me. 'I thought I could, I thought I fucking could, stick that up your fucking cartoon funnel!'

The run-in to L'Aquila was undemanding, a straight road up a gently tilted plateau. Race leader Azzini inched over the Svolte half an hour behind Calzolari and in a bit of a state – a reporter described his 'pitiful, feverish appearance, his teeth chattering though it wasn't cold'. Poor Azzini wasn't to know that his rival would shortly be hit with a swingeing time penalty – so swingeing that the Bianchi rider could probably have walked to L'Aquila and still kept the lead. Instead, he pedalled fraily on across the plateau, running on fumes and a stubborn desperation to limit his losses.

Lucotti's average speed in winning the stage, 22.1kmh, ranks amongst the slowest on record for any grand tour. But as an expression of the draining demands of the Bari–L'Aquila leg, this statistic was eclipsed by the unfolding fate of Giuseppe Azzini. When Ripamonti crossed the line just before midnight, the race leader had yet to appear. Nor had he when the papers went to press. 'At the time of writing, nothing is known of Giuseppe Azzini's whereabouts,' noted the *Gazzetta dello Sport* in a poignant postscript to its stage report. Journalists and officials drove up and down the plateau all through the night. 'We wandered in vain through the surrounding countryside,' wrote one reporter the day after, 'searching every village and unnecessarily awakening many locals.'

At 10 a.m., Alfredo Cavara – the same journalist who'd almost run Calzolari over when he crawled out of a muddy ditch on the previous stage – stuck his head into a ramshackle barn and saw a man slumped in the straw, hugging a bike. He had his scoop, and the headline spooled through his mind: 'Locals wakened unnecessarily in search for missing cyclist.'

Shivering and semi-conscious, Azzini had lain there for twelve hours. The barn's location was an eloquent indicator of his condition: it lay halfway up a mountainside, miles off the route. 'He had spent the night there burning with fever, without help or human comfort,' wrote Cavara. Azzini was rushed to hospital in L'Aquila, where he quickly rallied – so quickly, that by the time the riders started the next stage he was already on a train home. In truth, the Bianchi rider would hardly have wished to linger. I have a feeling he might have found himself rather haunted by recollections of the 1913 Giro, a race he had thrown away while in the lead on the penultimate stage. You will simply never guess how, so here it comes: he stumbled into a barn and fell asleep.

Broncho-pneumonia, said the papers, dutifully accepting Azzini's own diagnosis. There were rumours that Azzini had been found clutching an empty brandy bottle, but cycling's rich heritage of mystery meltdowns invites us to explore the shadier end of the substance spectrum. In his introduction, Paolo pertinently quotes a pre-Giro report in *La Stampa Sportiva*: 'Certain riders are in the habit of drugging themselves, but do so without measure or caution. Hence their erratic performances: brief periods of utter brilliance, sudden collapses, the inevitable withdrawals.'You could hardly improve upon this as an encapsulation of Azzini's last week at the Giro. Astonishing performances in the two preceding stages – he averaged 29kmh from Rome to Avellino, the fastest of the race by some margin – had catapulted him from a distant sixth to the top of the general classification. Then that addled freak-out with the stage finish almost in sight.

Paolo seems in little doubt that dope, *la dinamite,* was Azzini's undoing, almost certainly in the form of strychnine. Strange as it is to imagine intelligent grown men dosing themselves up with what we primarily think of as a murder-enhancing drug, the amphetamine-like boost of strychnine in small doses made it the pick-me-up of choice in those merrily unregulated early days of endurance sport. The winner of the 1904 Olympic marathon, Thomas J. Hicks, was kept topped up all the way around the St Louis course with the precise cocktail of stimulants that went into cyclo-surrealist Albert Jarry's fictional Perpetual Motion Food. 'I injected him with a milligram of sulphate of strychnine,' boasted Hicks's trainer afterwards, 'and made him drink a large glass brim-ming with brandy. Towards the end I gave him another shot to get him to the finish.' Hicks collapsed shortly after and never ran again. (He won gold after the original winner was disqualified for taking a lift in a car – come on, pioneering sport cheats, where's the imagination?)

Paolo Facchinetti blames the same drug for Dorando Pietri's stumbling indignity on the 1908 marathon finishing straight. 'A granule of strychnine taken 4km from the end of a race makes you a flying machine,' he writes. 'Taken at 5km, it makes you a vege-table.' Azzini's barn lay 18km from the finish.

Was Fonso on the naughty sauce? Hard to believe otherwise. Paolo trots out the ageless line that 'only a superman could manage those terrible, enormous stages without "help"'. Dope was then legal and almost universal; dosing yourself along that fine line between flying machine and sprout was considered a skill, much like taking a descent fast, but not too fast. In any event, with his only rival now dramatically removed from the race, Calzolari could probably have ridden to Milan on bread and water and still won. Having woken up on the rest day at L'Aquila thinking he'd blown it, he went to bed savouring an extraordinary truth: with the field culled to twelve riders and Azzini staring dully out of a train window, even with that penalty Fonso now held a two-hour lead.

In sympathy with Giuseppe Azzini, my own ride to L'Aquila unravelled messily at the death. An awful lot of roads were closed, and the sat-nav's alternative routes led me an unmerry dance through far-flung, dog-ruled suburbs. It started raining, hugely, and when at last I found my way up to the hill-topping old town the sky was as dark as my mood, and my arse as damp as my spirits. And what an unsettling city it was, deserted and unlit, half the houses boarded up and entire streets barred off with scaffold and gantries. Every dusty shop door was either chained shut or crowbarred open, offering a shadowy glimpse of its ransacked interior. Signs everywhere warned of rat infestation. L'Aquila means The Eagle; it had flown.

The only noise that wasn't rain drew me to the cathedral square. In the corner of this grand but utterly desolate civic space, a solitary bar was playing the radio at thunderous, distorting volume through a monumental outside speaker. A morose accordion ballad boomed raggedly out across the acreage of wet and empty cobbles; a yellowy light glowed from the bar's uncustomered interior. The door was locked and I propped the Hirondelle against it, looking out at the square through a curtain of awning drips and feeling like the subject of an Impressionist painting, *Le Peloton Traqique*.

A fresh sound suddenly caught my attention, the rumble of heavyweight internal combustion. I squinted through the rain and saw a troop carrier disgorging its helmeted occupants by the cathedral's white steps. My knuckles whitened around the bars: I prepared to be frogmarched into quarantine, hosed down with antidote or riddled with silver-tipped bullets. What in the name of Jeremy D. Heck was going down in this place?

'Is like this since 2009,' said the receptionist, as her hotel's lift juddered us down to the underground garage. It had taken me half an hour to find somewhere to sleep, and she was the first unarmed person I'd met. 'Everybody from here now stay in some new houses many kilometres from L'Aquila.' She shook her head as the doors opened. 'They are so bad places, small room like, ah, *penitenziario*.' I nodded sympathetically at this sad but unenlightening tale, while locking the Hirondelle to the handle of a fire extinguisher.

'But why?' I asked. 'Why is that?'

A huff of Latin exasperation. '*Il governo*, is why. We wait and we wait for decision, for money, for *assistenza*.'

Shamefully behind schedule, revelation came to call as I rinsed my shorts in the bidet. *Since 2009* . . . L'Aquila had rung a bell, but only now could I name the mournful tune. News reports flashed through my mind: rubbled buildings, a gymnasium full of sheet-covered casualties, Silvio Berlusconi touching up a rescue worker. The town had been shattered by a catastrophic earthquake, and three years on was still picking up the pieces.

Three hundred and eight people had died, I later learned, in the city and all along the plateau I'd crossed before it. Over thirty thousand Aquilans lost their homes; the entire old town was evacuated and remained unoccupied by order. If the authorities had been struggling to muster the cash and enthusiasm for its reconstruction, I could understand why. I later read that in the seven hundred years since it was founded, L'Aquila has suffered eleven devastating earthquakes. Three of these completely flattened the city, killing over ten thousand. Six months after the 1914 Giro passed through, a quake that brought down a couple of churches in L'Aquila did rather more damage in nearby Avezzano, the town I'd been towed through twelve days before by the cheerful Giuseppe: a dumbfounding 96 per cent of its citizens were killed.

Outer Rome's smouldering hillsides and the ominous cone of Vesuvius, that devastated ghost town laid out beneath my hotel window: it struck me again what a cruel and untamed place Italy can be to call home. Medieval, almost. Which perhaps explains why a month after I came home, half a dozen Italian seismologists were metaphorically strapped into ducking stools, each given six years for failing to predict the L'Aquila earthquake.

It didn't take too long to find somewhere to eat: the pizzeria is the apocalypse-resistant cockroach of catering. Afterwards I wandered about in the drippy dark, emoting with L'Aquila's awful plight and failing to suppress a guilty thrill at all this dishevelled abandonment. L'Aquila apparently does pretty well out of ruin-porn tourism, but that night my rain jacket was the only dirty mac in town. I peered saucer-eyed down shored-up ancient alleys strung with faded, wind-torn washing, and gawped at boutique-mannequins sporting the shop-soiled fashions of 2009. I nodded at soldiers and shouted at rats. I imagined how very upsetting it must have been for a boisterous and convivial Italian to be torn away from his beloved civic rituals, and am therefore very pleased to have learned that he hasn't. Had I been there in sunny daylight, I would have seen those silent, shuttered streets crowded with well-dressed old couples and families: the former residents of downtown L'Aquila, drawn from their far-flung new homes by that irresistible urge to stroll and natter and pose en masse. What a sad but very wonderful spectacle that must be.

GENERAL CLASSIFICATION - STAGE 6
(Bari-L'Aquila, 428km)

1. Alfonso CALZOLARI 100:28:39
2. Pierino ALBINI +1:55:31
3. Luigi LUCOTTI +2:04:26
   Timothy MOORE +48:23:20
   Stage starters: 21
   Stage finishers: 12

CHAPTER 21

BANG!

I had eggs for breakfast. It was about time: the 1914 riders ate almost nothing but. Raw eggs, somewhat improbably, were the energy-gels of a whole generation. As late as the 1940s, Gino Bartali was fuelling his contests with Coppi on a dozen a day. My boys set off every morning with their front pockets abulge with up to twenty eggs, whose contents were liberated throughout the stage with a practised knock against a knee or the handlebars. The white was flicked aside, the yolk swallowed, and then the best bit: pelting the journalist's motorcade with the empty shells. 'Such behaviour is below expectations,' noted one po-faced, egg-faced writer in his report.

Twenty raw eggs seemed overly bold at this stage of my game – with three-quarters of the 1914 Giro retraced, this was not the moment to welcome salmonella into my life. I took five boiled eggs from a basket in the corner of the breakfast buffet, leaving as many as none left in it, ate four and a half and checked out, burping uncontrollably and pelting onlookers with shells.

I rode out of L'Aquila under cloudless skies, those messily bisected houses and piles of bulldozed masonry telling an incontrovertible tale in the light of a pin-sharp morning. The hills beyond were plumply swathed in chlorophyll, with none of the jagged browns and greys of weeks gone by, as long as I didn't look too closely at the distant hulk of snow and rock that was the 2,912m Gran Sasso d'Italia. It was days since I'd seen a squashed snake, and though the heavens blazed, it was chilly enough to reverse my recent habit, by steering into patches of sun rather than shade. Conclusion: I was back in the north, and heading norther.

During one of the idle contemplations that while away those in-saddle hours, I realised I'd now touched every compass point. Sestriere was as far west as I'd go, Vietri di Potenza as far south, Bari as far east and Arona, where in some faraway previous life my saddle had broken in half, as far north. That morning I'd christened my last disposable razor, number four of four: almost 900km still remained, but I was past third base and on the run for home.

A return to Italy's top half meant roads filled once more with keen and elderly cyclists. The climb up to Montereale – no pimple at 950m – proved a particular granddad-magnet, thronged with wrinkles and Lycra. Aware that the mountains were running out, I went for it, powering past group after wiry, nut-brown group. I hadn't slipped into my ladies' gear for two weeks – now there's a bold admission – and on days like this felt ready for a hairier-chested sprocket than the twenty-two-toother spinning my rear wheel.

Approaching the summit I cut rather dismissively past a Spike Milligan beard-alike in yellow and black on a matching bike. Ten minutes later he eased to a halt by my table as I sipped a celebratory espresso outside a bar in the hilltop town. *'Piano, piano,'* he said rather sternly, gently plumping an imaginary pillow with both hands. Slowly, slowly. Cool your boots. Easy there, sport. I gave him a wide berth when I shot back past him two descents later, but he still wailed theatrically. Sorry, Gramps: I'd just hauled my AVS back to 17.1, and was bent on doing stage seven – 429km from L'Aquila to Lugo – in three days. This was no time to soft pedal.

I'd lately deduced that I began each day with one good climb in my legs. Invariably it would be the first; sometimes I'd also make a decent fist of the last, which allowed me to forget all the uphill humiliations in between. This, however, was a different sort of day. I motored on with relentless purpose, up thousand-metre hills and down tumbling dales, dispatching impatient sandwiches and bars of cocoa fat in the sleepy towns between. As the afternoon rolled forth the challenges piled up: a twisting gorge full of unlit tunnels and heavy-goods traffic, a swarm of bees, a couple of assassination attempts by a school bus and a farmer's wife in a Fiat Panda. It was as if the bike-hating gods were laying a trail of hazard and tribulation before me, a ride-through Room 101 of known weaknesses. I flicked them the Vs and pedalled placidly through it all. Or most of it: no point pretending those bees were negotiated with panache or in silence.

With the sun still high above the hills behind, the road broadened out and coiled lazily downwards. In moments I was freewheeling into Ascoli Piceno, a town I hadn't expected to reach before dark. It was only 4.20 p.m., but surveying the map on the cathedral steps I saw the route ahead squiggle away into miles and miles of lumpy, town-less nothing. Then I looked up to appraise the scene before me, and accepted how incredibly stupid it was to even consider staying the night somewhere else.

I had no expectations of a place I'd never even heard of, marooned in the hills and 40km from the sea. Had Ascoli been full of open-cast bauxite mines and brawling derelicts, I couldn't have felt let down. As it was, the private smile of sporting fulfilment that had embellished my face when I rode into the town broadened all night, ending up as a wet-lipped, slack-jawed gurn of boozy awe.

I booked into a hotel just behind the cathedral square, confident that nothing in Ascoli could trump the marbled magnificence of this piazza's fountains and loggias. A pre-dinner saunter proved me gloriously wrong. Every street and citizen was a study in well-scrubbed grace, testament to many and ongoing centuries of unbroken prosperity. For an hour I ambled past elegant public edifices and arcades agleam with well-presented merchandise, admiring once more the showmanship that urban Italians bring to everything they do: the shampoo-ad girl laughing into her phone as she cycled by hands-free, the white-coated barber wafting hair from a customer's shoulder with a deft flourish of his badger brush. Have you ever seen a grandfather suavely manoeuvring a push-chair down a flight of steps? That night I saw two.

In the event it was a challenge to decide which of the town's embarrassment of winsome piazzas I should dine in. The one with the palm trees and the statues? The one girdled by Renaissance palazzos? Or – yes, yes and thrice yes – the Piazza del Popolo, a civic space of almost outrageous beauty, laid in travertine marble and edged with period Italian architecture in all its most venerable and appealing forms: the dome, the tower, the crenellation, the arch. So captivating was its splendour that I shed all pretence of haughty ennui and just touristed out big-style, snapping dozens of beaming self-timer shots from all angles and taking up station at an outside table of a corner restaurant with its menu printed in four languages. In mind of the view, I hardly cared that previous experience of such establishments guaranteed dull fare at daft prices, served by dead-eyed sycophants who would coerce me into an oversized tip by asking how I like Ascoli, is pretty town, no?

But as this was a place that could do me no ill, everything from my bruschetta onwards proved delightful and unexorbitant and was placed before me by a shy young man whose commitment to gouging customers was so slack that he forgot to put my second carafe of bianco on the bill. Until I pointed it out to him. Yes, that's how much I loved this town. One day, I thought, swaying back to my hotel through the gay crowds, I shall return here and put right everything that was wrong in my life and in Ascoli Piceno's, by opening and running a pharmacy on the Piazza del Popolo.

I woke in a blue-skied morning that smelled of basil and Vespas: the scent of summer was back. The last four days had ended with the water in my bidons cold enough to hurt my teeth, but looking at the map I sensed those days were over. If all went to plan, by evening I'd have put the mountains behind me.

They didn't go down without a fight. Straight out of Ascoli I was launched up an extortionate incline that would, in the sweaty fullness of time, deliver me from under 200m to over 800. It seemed very poor manners to issue such a demand when I still had bits of breakfast brioche stuck in my teeth. Exhausted delirium of the type that didn't usually kick in until sundown began to take hold: when I looked deep inside myself for reserves of fortitude, all that turned up were the full lyrics to 'Down in the Tube Station at Midnight'. I also managed to ride for some time on a truly terrible section of road before realising it was in fact beautifully smooth. I had punctured my front – and final – tyre; it was time for Stan's Sticky White Fluid to come into its own.

Suneil had given me the bottle of what is more properly known to grown-ups as Stan's Sealant. He spoke glowingly of its miraculous properties of puncture cure and prevention; in pursuit of the latter I had squirted both replacement tyres full of this liquid latex, the front at Fabio's place in the Alps, the rear just after Paul left, near Rome. My dismay that Stan had literally let me down abated now that I examined the airless front tyre in detail: its rim was scarred with gashes and gouges, each one a puncture magically sealed at source. And those in addition to a pair of finger-long open sores in the centre of the tread, fringed with tufts of bare fabric, the consequence of asking a grass-track cyclo-cross tubular tyre to cover more than 2,000 gravelly, potholed and heavily-laden kilometres.

The sun was fierce, the hillside empty and I'd just passed a sign banning handcarts from the road: this environment was not one pregnant with the possibilities of expert outside assistance. In what may have looked like a panicked fenzy to the casual observer, and indeed his professional counterpart, I pulled out the front wheel, ripped its tyre off, and yanked the least shit of my two used and pre-punctured spares gluelessly onto the rim. (I could perhaps be forgiven for not sourcing new tyres – as it had taken weeks to hunt down the last four Vittoria Cross Evo XNs in the UK, it hardly seemed worth trying – but the failure to replenish my stock of readily available sticky tyre tape or glue was one of unfathomable stupidity.)

Having squeezed Stan's final dribbles into the valve hole, I span the rim and pumped. No hissing: it held air. God bless you, Stan. Trying hard to ignore the eccentric gyrations of that unaffixed front tyre – my bidons were now being stirred, not shaken – I nursed the Hirondelle onwards.

In the hours before the bare handful of 1914 survivors pedalled away from L'Aquila, 'waves of strong emotion' splashed through every team hotel. Some of these lapped sympathetically around Giuseppe Azzini's calamitous race-losing sequel, *Barn Coma II*,

but the serious storm was being whipped up by those push-me-pull-you shenanigans on the Svolte. A red-eyed Alfonso Calzolari spent the entire day visiting journalists to promote his frankly laughable version of events, explaining in a cracked voice that the slights upon his integrity had suffered him to weep through the night. You've got to hand it to the guy. In what looks very much like a masterstroke of PR deflection, in the afternoon he ran out of his hotel room waving an anonymous letter that someone had supposedly just pushed under his door. Within minutes, every journalist in L'Aquila had read its succinct contents: 'YOU WILL NEVER WIN THE GIRO!'

Calzolari's desperation was understandable: word had got out that the Italian Cycling Union, outraged by the reports of wholesale cheating, was telegramming an order to invalidate the entire race should the next stage begin with the Svolte Three still in the field. This telegram was duly dispatched, but before it arrived –

so they would claim – the race committee rushed forward the start, hurrying the riders out of L'Aquila with that traditional pistol shot into the air. (In the fierce power struggle that inevitably then erupted, the Giro's chief financier and effective owner – the newspaper group that published the *Gazzetta dello Sport* – emerged triumphant: the president of the ICU was forced to resign, and his governing body effectively reduced to a puppet institution run by pro cycling's commercial paymasters. *Plus ça change!*)

With their main man Azzini out, the two remaining Bianchi racers figured they had nothing left to ride for, and withdrew before the stage start. That left just ten competitors, a field so startlingly denuded that the organisers now sent home half the motorcade of journalists and officials, to make for a less embarrassing balance. It was – no, really – pissing down, and these 'ten anguished souls' pedalled through the sodden night in close company.

Given the ratcheting traumas and Calzolari's prodigious two-hour lead, no one had the stomach for a fight – literally so in the case of 'Tache Durando, who began throwing up almost at once. At the Ascoli Piceno feeding-station, he locked himself in a lavatory and didn't emerge for an hour. Durando had started the stage a distant fifth overall, and to finish it now faced riding alone for another 300km, leaking egg from both ends. The temptation to retire must have seemed irresistible; he resisted it. *Who were those guys?* My AVS had just clicked up to 17.2kmh: way to cast my celebrations into unflattering perspective, Signore Durando.

After Amandola, where I rode through a well-attended Festival of Lovely Cakes, the hills shrank and the road straightened. Was that really it for the mountains? As I scanned the horizon for signs of life, the long-forgotten sound of a better cyclist on a faster bike hoved once more into rearward earshot.

'You are crazy English, yes?'

For some kilometres I now rolled alongside Silvio, a gladsome geologist in a Spiderman cycling jersey, who had acquired his knowledge of English, and the ability to spot a crazy native, while spending five months of his masters course studying in, um, Cardiff. 'Fantastic adventure, *bici incredibile*,' he said after I had explained myself in return. 'You must show to my father, he will fucking love it.' (I gathered later that Silvio had picked up the bulk of his vocabulary in Cardiff's pubs.) And so, having succumbed to the cheerful insistence of an Italian host-to-be, a short while afterwards I found myself sharing a trough of *spaghetti vongole* with three generations of Silvians.

In the lonely mountains of post-parental Italy, I had rather lost touch with my fellow man. How good it was to rediscover him in his most affable indigenous habitat: the family-packed dining table. I was welcomed into a seat between Silvio's mother and his twelve-year-old son, with no hint of the suspicious *froideur* that would have underscored this scene in a more northerly European country. I looked around at the smiling faces and thought: So this is why I've never, ever managed to find a restaurant open at lunchtime.

Nobody but Silvio spoke any English, and my Italian curled up into a ball once I'd furred my brain with sweet white wine. Before it did I learned that his son was called Leonardo, that his wife was a fire fighter, and that lunch breaks in this country really are something else (Silvio's applied understanding of earth materials was interrupted by our leisurely repast and the long bike ride that preceded it, and if you ever find yourself engulfed by Italian flames, pray to God it's not between 1 p.m. and 3.30).

When the coffee pot came out, Silvio disappeared onto the

balcony to take a phone call. Cross-table communication in this phase leaned heavily on the exchange of Harpo Marx smiles, which did the job until Silvio's wife and mother hauled me aloft and began to barge me cheerfully down a corridor towards the bathroom. 'Don't worry,' he said when he returned to rescue me. 'They just ask if you like to have a fucking shower.' I'd like to dedicate this highlight of my career as a guest to the pharmacist who sold me that very expensive miniature odorant.

I befouled Casa Silvio a while longer, finishing with a tour of the shed housing Granddad's pride: a vintage town bicycle ingeniously powered by a little petrol engine, which released brown fluid all over my shoes in response to a witless prod. As the clan gathered to see me off, Silvio's dad – who had been smiling slightly too much since the witless prod – fixed me with a beckoning wink. I wheeled the Hirondelle over to him and he palmed me two orange sachets marked 'Sustenium Plus Intensive'. This name and its encirclement of thrusting upward arrows suggested a cure for chronic impotence; I slipped them into my jersey pocket and he smiled more broadly than ever. His family followed suit, and after a festival of waving I left these wonderful people behind.

'Jesi? What the fuck?'

Silvio's reaction when I'd told him where I was intending to sleep that night suggested this town was at best unremarkable. I'd been reluctant to explain that Jesi bagged a tangential mention in my account of the 1914 race, and lay at the approximate end of my daily physical tether. In truth, now slightly beyond it: it was past four, and I still had 65km to go. No time to pause at Urbs Salvia, the Roman town whose entirely unprotected ruins Silvio had explored as a boy, and which I rattled through now. Glancing at the massive, stubby remains, I thought of the magnificent Renaissance laundry I'd passed in Ascoli that morning, six hundred years old and still in daily civic use. It is a source of bottomless wonder that Italians have led the Western world out from the grunting darkness, not once but twice. (To be fair, Silvio must have felt a similar astonishment while pondering that the island that spawned the free-swearing drinkers of Cardiff had, not so long before, built an empire even greater than Rome's.)

I might have left the Appenines' foothills behind, but their endless toehills made a terrible mess of my afternoon. Up to 250m, down to 100, back to 250: on it went for hour after shattering hour. If this was the mountains' last gasp, then they could certainly hold their breath. I tipped a sachet of Sustenium Plus Intensive into a bidon and put my head down.

The road seemed determined to prolong my exposure to this restless landscape, zigzagging distractedly between hilltop farms and the last gildings of sunset. While doing so it also fell very neatly to bits, shedding geometric hunks of surface until I felt I was riding along the Giant's Causeway. (When Silvio offered to lend me his mountain bike for the ride to Jesi, he evidently hadn't been joking.) My new-old front tyre reacted to this challenge by squirming about the rim I hadn't stuck it to, offering me peek-a-boo flashes of fabric underbelly. Speeding round a valley-bottom left-hander, a mild shimmy suddenly blossomed into a crazy, spin-cycle jolting judder. I pulled over and in the gloaming beheld a tyre twisted to buggery, more off the wheel than on.

Prickly with alarm, and perhaps the first stirrings of Sustenium Plus Intensive, I let the air out, pulled things back into some semblance of order, reinflated and rode more warily on. Then less warily, once I noticed that my AVS had dropped back to 17.1. Our lives, as I'd discovered during a hotel Google session in L'Aquila, had overlapped by precisely three months. But at this rate, Mario Marangoni really would be the death of me.

With 130km up for the day, the clustered lights of a hill town asserted themselves through the dusk. Those final kilometres passed in a light-headed, heavy-legged blur of drained infirmity. Sustenium Plus Intensive, I can now report, does not refresh the parts other performance supplements cannot reach, though after the second sachet I did try and get off with a tractor.

CHAPTER 22

In defiance of Silvio's unflattering assessment of Jesi, I mustered a weary affection for this unpretentious little town, with its brick-built churches and low-key Friday-night buzz. Rather less endearing was its low-key Saturday-morning buzz: something absolutely had to be done about that tyre, but in defiance of the hotel receptionist's promise – and indeed the opening hours posted in their windows – both of Jesi's bike shops were closed. Just to rub it in, one of them had an inner-tube vending machine on the wall outside, offering 24-7 salvation to the stricken owners of normal bicycles.

Mumbling compound swears at the sunny tarmac, I lurched and shuddered towards the coast. It was 171km from Jesi to Lugo, where the penultimate stage ended – surely within my daily compass on flat roads. Taking stock of my physique in the shower that morning – yes, we've all heard that one before – I was genuinely unnerved by the enormity of my frontal thigh muscles: when I tensed them, a whole new bulge of firm tissue popped out at their fundaments, as if I'd grown an extra pair of kneecaps. Completing a single 1914 stage in three days seemed a mere bagatelle for such mighty bollards of flesh, yet this modest objective was now being slowly pulled from my grasp with every faltering, lumpy revolution.

By the time I hit the Adriatic at Senigallia, the scarred and gashed front tyre was again working its way off the wooden rim. Weekend cyclists approached with smiles of encouraging approval, which withered into concerned and sometimes disgusted frowns as my stupid wobbling plight manifested itself. I couldn't acknowledge either response with the gesture it deserved: to raise a glove from the bucking, shimmying bars was to take my life in my hand.

'Cicli Marocchi'. The words on the shop sign were good, the open door beneath them better, and the window display best of all: several vintage Bianchi jerseys arranged behind a restored Great War military bicycle carrying a rifle, a shovel, an acetylene lamp and – slap my moobs and call me Fonso – tubular tyres.

I didn't even have to go inside: a young man in overalls who had evidently been watching me strode out, nodded approvingly at the Hirondelle and shook my hand. A shout over his shoulder summoned the man he called Papa to his side. After further pleasing exchanges – Papa, a full-figured man in his fifties, proudly confided that he was a veteran of three Eroicas – I rather superfluously waved a hand at my contorted, threadbare front tyre.

Both men rubbed their weekend stubble and wandered back inside, emerging long minutes later with a packet of glue and two very dusty tubular tyres. As I began to explain I was only after one, Papa drew my attention to the rear, his finger dwelling on a Sauron's

Eye of a gash that stretched a good four inches around its crown, spewing tufts of dirty fabric along the way. This hardly looked a recent phenomenon, which made my failure to notice it all the more appalling: I nearly retched with shame.

'*Molto, molto pericoloso,*' said his son gravely. Very, very dangerous. I paid and thanked them, then pallidly remounted. Papa clamped a farewell hand on my shoulder and cleared his throat. 'For you, mister – goad lack.'

I took up station by a weather-beaten, powder-blue beach hut, setting to work before an audience of seagulls and a dozen hardy sunbathers, squeezing the last drops out of summer. The three-hour pit stop that now ensued killed off my hopes of completing the stage in three days, and would indeed have cost Alfonso Calzolari the Giro. Still, it could – should – have been worse. 'Apply glue to tyre fabric,' began the multilingual instructions packed inside the tube, 'and leave to cure for a minimum of twenty-four hours.'

The front tyre slipped on a treat, like something out of an online video tutorial. There were issues of aesthetic authenticity: the tyre was far too thin for the era, and too black – my boys all rode on big, fat reds or off-whites. I had a dim sense that at some point I might give a shit about these shortcomings, but that point could wait. When I raised the handlebars aloft and watched the wheel below them spin round and free and true, my celebration sent a thousand gulls into the windy blue sky.

My engagement with the rear tyre elicited bird-bothering sounds from an uglier spectrum. In line with Papa's suggestion, its intended substitute was a tubular that had evidently lain in some corner of the Cicli Marocchi storeroom for many years. 'Clement Grifo NEVE' read the label, in typography that would have looked at home on those packets of interwar spokes I'd bought all those moons ago from an unscrupulous communist plumber. *Neve*, as Papa had explained via an entertaining mime, meant snow. A *snow* tyre? A snow tyre for a *bike*? Still, the knobbly tread that delayed cycling's most irresponsible lunatics from tumbling to a richly merited wintry death would also, said Papa, cope better with the weight of my saddlebag.

Everything that had gone right with the front now went wrong with the back. Most woefully, I forgot to stretch the tyre before smearing glue all over it: bad news for my hands, kit and pride; good news for the three nearest sunbathers, a group of hair-gelled young men in Speedos who had begun to take an uncharitable interest in proceedings. Pulling this ring of slippery, reluctant rubber into place involved gripping the wooden rim between my knees, and half an hour of empurpled straining in an earth-mother birthing posture, with my shorts falling down. The fitful jeers that greeted my eventual triumph were swiftly drowned out by a more strident noise: the final tug had trapped several hairs on both thighs between rim and rubber.

Blinking out tears of agonised chagrin and gasping raggedly, I set about aligning the tyre, getting it straight on the rim before the glue started to harden. Only now did I notice how very un-round the rear wheel had become of late. When I held the axle ends and span it, the rim twitched and waggled like a gyroscope entering its death throes. For days – like, dozens of them – the spoke-wrench had lain forgotten at the bottom of the tool bag; I now dug it out, squatted down and got to work. Wheelwright's Arse had barely taken hold when I encountered a spoke that wouldn't tighten, on account of no longer being in one piece: it had snapped clean through at the hub end. I frowned, tore it out and continued. Three spokes along: the same story. The leaden weight of that saddlebag over the back wheel, a million clattering potholes, my abysmal neglect of routine maintenance – a perfect spoke-buggering storm.

I sat heavily back against the beach hut, pressed a begrimed and sticky palm over my eyes and contemplated the full wretchedness of this discovery. Spokes could be replaced – I had brought four spares along – but doing so meant removing the freewheels from the hub, a task that demanded specialist tools and ugly brute force, neither of which I currently possessed. Cicli Marocchi had now been closed for two hours, and it would be two days before it or any other bike shop pulled up their shutters.

With a reedy hum quavering from my lips, I did what I could with the spoke wrench. Very little, it transpired: the two missing spokes were near neighbours, and no amount of twisting, turning or Speedo-clad cackling could correct the conspicuous buckle that annexed their share of the rim. It was gone three; I put the Hirondelle back together, wiped my hands on the beach hut and rode away up the esplanade, acknowledging a hindward ovation with a doffed cap and two fingers.

The coast was flat and straight and the road hugged it tight. For an hour I trundled cautiously through a nondescript straggle of defunct wig clubs and tripod-exchange superstores, circumnavigating potholes and drain covers and affording new respect to all other tarmac interruptions. Broken wheels were the principal cause of mechanical retirement in 1914, forcing four riders to quit in the last two stages alone.

A tailwind began to lean on me and little by little I built speed. It struck me that I had managed without those two spokes for a while, very possibly for an age, thundering carelessly down huge, twisty mountainsides: what, really, was the point in now crawling along such benign and innocuous roads as these? Plus, post-pit stop, the Hirondelle was an undeniably improved machine, smoother, straighter and more silent, its Keith Moon drum solo subdued to a 'Girl from Ipanema' *shicka-shacka* backbeat. And so quite soon I was fairly caning along, past the strip malls and petrol stations and on to the sand-scattered esplanades of the seaside proper.

Pesaro announced itself with serried ranks of empty sunloungers and a parade of blandly identical mid-rise hotels. It was gone six and the streetlights were flicking on; I pulled up by the first set of glass doors with two stars on them. A downward glance rounded off a bad day on a good note: my AVS was up to 17.3, and at some point I had built enough speed to splatter a massive bluebottle all over the frame badge. *'Faster than life itself!'* I cried, flicking it off with an exultant whoop, then looking up to find I was being watched from behind the reception desk. Handily there was an even cheaper hotel right next door.

As a resort Pesaro seemed entirely unremarkable, a grid of cereal-box holiday residences laid out behind a yawning forecourt of sand. A long weekend there would probably feel too long, but it did the job for me that night: give me a warm sea breeze and a starry sky and I can tolerate any amount of beige concrete. I dined on the boardwalk, at an outside table with a view of the silvery wavelets below: there was a *pizza ciclista* on the menu, which I'd have ordered had it sounded even slightly less austere (oil, salt and rosemary – it's a party in your mouth, with two old nuns and no booze or music). Pleasantly bloated with funner food and the joyful return of *sfuso frizzante*, I ambled back down a promenade full of yelping toddlers and Asian street vendors performing prodigious aerobatic feats with those sling-shot illuminated helicopter things. The place was impressively abustle for late September. Great swathes of the Italian coast are clotted with seaside towns like Pesaro, anonymous and indistinguishable, yet beloved of natives with a stubbornly traditional holiday agenda: breakfast, beach, bar, bed. Good old-fashioned, foreigner-free family fun.

It wasn't yet 11 p.m. when I draped my kit over the hotel balcony rail to dry. In more contemporary European resorts things would have been building to a noisy, neon climax, but the street below was emptying and lights were blinking off in windows all around. It suddenly felt like Margate in the 1950s. The event I was retracing lay a century in the past, but not for the first time I felt I'd gone back halfway to meet it.

Sunday meant fewer cars and more bikes, most of them in large and noisy club pelotons who bossed the traffic, three abreast, and threw me the odd cheer. Just past Rimini, where the road turned inland, I reeled in and passed an unsteady seventy-year-old rider wearing one of those leather-sausage helmets. 'Fantastico, fantastico!' he croaked out after me, and when I turned to give him a smile I saw his face pucker with the conflicting emotions of bitter-sweet retrospection. I caught his gaze and felt my own features tugged in strange directions: I was his past, and he was my future.

It was a day tailor-made for the easy accumulation of distance: flat, quiet roads, a following wind and tirelessly uncaptivating scenery. The very air was drab, a skimmed-milk haze that hung listlessly around all day, absorbing orderly, bland towns into the ironed-pancake fields. As shambolic, impoverished and hatefully undulating as it had largely been, I was now rather pining for the south.

I spent most of the time contemplating my front wheel – so straight and true, a pleasure for the catatonically bored cyclist to look down on – and trying to ignore the knobbly, wobbly disorder of the rear. That kink was now scuffing the rim against the brake blocks with every rotation, and as well as looking stupid and wrong and awful, the lumpy snow tread contacted the tarmac with a slappy, swooshing noise that precisely imitated a maturing slow puncture. Could I bear to devote vast chunks of Monday attempting to rectify this under-arse disaster, or would I just recklessly crack on with my father's favourite Italian word ringing through my head? *Speriamo*, let's hope for the best. Even as I asked myself the question I knew the answer.

Lunch was a twin-*panino* job in a bar full of silent old men watching the Grand Prix on a telly the size of a barn door. I necked an espresso, then another, and set out to reel in the afternoon with redoubled intensity. It was a literally straightforward challenge. After all that squiggling about on mountain roads like varicose veins, I now found myself riding across a giant Etch A Sketch portcullis: long, linear avenues bordered with trees that converged towards the milky horizon. As ever on such thoroughfares, my thoughts turned to the existentialist writer Albert Camus, who became a non-existentialist when the car he was in lost an argument with a plane tree on a

dead-straight, bone-dry road. I have to report that these sombre musings did not temper my conduct: I hit and maintained speeds that would have been physically and technically beyond me three weeks before, when I'd ridden across the other side of my map of Emilio-Romagna. With legs ablur, I hauled in and passed Fiat after dawdling Fiat, each of them home to a straight-faced couple in their Sunday best, the wife in no hurry to visit that aunt she'd always hated, the husband in a sulk at missing the Grand Prix.

The shell-shocked truce that drew the 1914 riders together on the road out of L'Aquila held throughout the stage. With allowances for hierarchy: when Calzolari snapped a rim, his rivals slowed while the Stucchi team sorted a replacement – but as an unattached *isolato*, Maggiore Albani found himself left behind after suffering the same fate. In despair he gave up, leaving Enrico Sala as the isolated *isolato*: Sala celebrated this achievement by being knocked off his bike by a large dog. At Pesaro just nine riders were left in the race: eight in the front group, with 'Tache Durando toiling distantly behind through his private alimentary hell. Those eight became seven with the exhausted abandonment of Giosuè Lombardi, who had earlier dropped all the way back to help his team leader Durando. 'What are you doing here?' muttered the whey-faced 'Tache when the two met. 'Leave me alone and get back to the front.' The effort of obeying this order finished Lombardi off.

Having rolled together through Pesaro at midday to a clamorous reception, throughout the afternoon this huddle of 'glorious survivors' was mobbed by a growing entourage of fans and well-wishers on bicycles and in cars. It was a spectacle to gladden the hard heart of race director Armando Cougnet: his field whittled to a lonely cluster of heroes by sheer gladiatorial attrition, and the public loving it. Towards the stage finish at Lugo, the crowds thickened further: this was as close as the race would come to Bologna, the leader Calzolari's home town.

A touching sense of localism is one of the sweetest things about modern professional cycling – in fact the only one, apart from the stuffed toy that stage winners are usually given to wave about. Even an event as facelessly globalised as the Tour de France will still pause to allow a rider to roll on ahead of the peloton as it enters his home town, to wave at his friends and neighbours and give the wife and kids a peck on the cheek. Cycling has always been a parochial sport, and nowhere more so than in rivalry-riven Italy. Having pledged to win the Giro for Bologna, Calzolari was now determined to put on a show for his townspeople packing the Lugo pavements. With a kilometre left, at his instruction Clemente Canepari broke to the front to lead him out for the sprint. The finish was in sight when Canepari fell foul of those exuberant idiot-encroachers who are always over-represented in any cycling crowd. Pierino Albini was first over the line; Calzolari fourth a second later; a bloody and cussing Canepari last of the bunch, forty-two seconds back. The bunting was being taken down when 'Tache Durando – what a man – walked his bike over the line an hour and a quarter later. Adding insult to digestive injury, 6km outside town he'd burst his last permitted spare.

In the ninety-eight years since elapsed, Lugo seemed to have mislaid whatever it was that persuaded Cougnet to end the Giro's penultimate stage there. Perhaps it never had anything, and just blagged its way onto the itinerary: I've just discovered that the noted swindler Charles Ponzi was born there. At any rate, every other leg of the Giro had begun and ended in a major settlement marked on my map in heavy capitals; Lugo was meekly identified in lower-case italics. Pedalling through its grid of subdued and modest streets, I found no trace of a mighty or important past, just suggestions – a slight rounding off of decorative edges, the unusual preponderance of concrete rendering – that Lugo may have found itself in the wrong place (the front line) at the wrong time (1944). (An ironic survivor was the towering Fascist memorial to a Great War flying ace – a sinister, totalitarian but undeniably impressive limestone spire that bullied the entire main piazza into submission.) What I did find, to my slight astonishment, was an extremely appealing palazzo hotel, in whose rearward car park I now dismounted.

'English?'

I smiled, hardly minding by this stage. The gracious receptionist said she'd watched me lock my bike up, presumably in a really English manner, on her CCTV. 'Could I ask what brings you to Lugo?'

From what I'd seen of the town, I imagined this to be a routine and earnest question. I provided my stock answer and her eyes widened; as I embellished it she began to emit coos and gasps and other gratifying sounds of amazement and appreciation. I don't mind admitting I was in the mood for a few slaps on the back. It had taken a long, hard week to crank my AVS up from 17.1 to 17.3; in nine breathless hours, I had just raised it by the same amount again.

'Oh, your *bici antica* is famous!' I looked over to share her view of the CCTV monitor, upon which a bald guest was fuzzily appraising the Hirondelle through the open window of his long BMW. A moment later this perma-tanned little Pablo Picasso walked past the desk and the receptionist – or rather the mana-geress, as I would later discover this demonstrably splendid woman to be – hailed him in Italian. I caught snatches of her address: wood, cork, *Milano a Milano*. His expression throughout was of studied indifference.

'*Bici francese?*' said Pablo briskly, turning to me. I nodded: a French bike; this guy clearly knew his stuff. At some length he then held forth about his own vintage bicycle, which I gathered was a very beautiful and fully restored 1937 Benotto. '*Tutto auten-tico.*' A thin smile. '*Senza pneumatici di neve.*'

Completely authentic, *without snow tyres*. You horrid little shit! I looked him up and down – it didn't take long – and saw stubby legs whose pedalling days were over, a gaudy fat watch that had never timed its owner up a mountain, and two piggy eyes begging for the robust and repeated introduction of my thumbs.

'*Signore, i pneumatici originali sono . . . sono . . .*'

My reedy explanation hit the vocab buffers; his smile broadened and he waddled off into the lift. After it took him away, the man-ageress turned to me with kind eyes. 'You are doing a very special thing,' she said, 'and I want to do something special for you.' I do believe I gulped. 'I want to wash your clothes in my machine.'

Lugo looked an awful lot better two hours later. I'd spent 1.8 of them poncing about my palatial room in a bath robe, savouring the high-end luxuries of aquatic massage, non-Italian television and not having to thrash dirty wool about in bidet-froth. It simply wasn't possible to think ill of a town graced with this splendid establishment and its god-like ruling laundress. Bolstering my reappraisal, I discovered that Lugo's arcaded and passably grand junior piazza was hosting some sort of retro festival, with enthusiastic displays of foxtrot-era ballroom dancing and a market selling vintage clothes and bric-a-brac. I spent a happy half-hour poking around in boxes of shonky old crap, experiencing a heady blurt of déjà vu before a tea chest filled with corroded bicycle parts. As I picked up a buckled and largely orange brake caliper, those distant days of citric acid and wire wool spooled through my mind. How had such a fumbling klutz as I ever managed to make a working thing out of stuff like that? It defied belief, and shall defy it ever more.

I'm not ashamed to say that I now loved my bicycle. Mine wasn't the wanky, anthropomorphic love that men of my age tend to nurture for vintage machinery, at least not quite: l hold my hand up to a bit of saddle-patting, and though I'd started talking to the Hirondelle on a regular basis had never referred to it in the feminine third-person. I had certainly developed a weighty respect for the stout mechanical integrity of the – cough – old girl's frame and forks, an assemblage of ninety-eight-year-old tubing that had uncomplainingly soaked up so much punishment: dropped onto Milanese cobbles and the rocks of Chianti, crashed at awful speed through countless crater-grade potholes, gang-banged by baggage handlers. Three thousand kilometres of juddering, heavily laden abuse without so much as a peep, still less the death-watch creak that Lance McCormack had warned me to listen for, that harbinger of imminent structural collapse. No, almost everything that had gone wrong with the bike, at least since the original saddle broke in half, involved a failure of some new or newish bit – the wheels and spokes, that woeful reproduction bidon rack, the crap-arse fucking Thompson.

So the frame was magnificent, but I didn't love the frame, nor the many less commendable components and accessories bolted on to it. No, I loved this bike because it was still going, just about, despite having been put together by me. My admiring affection for bike and self had conflated with every completed mile. This was the bike that Tim built; I loved the bike, because the bike was me. I placed the caliper carefully back and thought: Eat my bike, Pablo. Eat ME. Then I ate a pizza, clapped briefly along to the foxtrot-tango charlies, and lured by its soft, plump hugeness, hastened to bed.

GENERAL CLASSIFICATION – STAGE 7
(L'Aquila–Lugo, 429.1km)

1.   Alfonso CALZOLARI 118:17:22
2.   Pierino ALBINI +1:55:31
3.   Luigi LUCOTTI +2:04:25
      Timothy MOORE +52:17:11
      Stage starters: 12
      Stage finishers: 8

Laundered, pressed and daintily sheathed in cellophane, my kit was waiting by the room door when I came up from breakfast the next morning, pockets abulge with artisan bread. What a joyous treat! Gone now was the ear-warming shame with which I'd handed it to the manageress, balled up to conceal all those sweat-sealed blotches of oil and jam.

I unwrapped my gift with the glee of a child at Christmas, then held shorts and jersey aloft by the 10-foot windows. At once my full beam dipped. I hardly cared that the more stubborn stains lingered on, speckling my jersey's front and rear with the pale ghosts of loose chippings and Clanger blood. Nor that the rigours of mechanical cleansing had all but detached the chamois pad from my shorts. The headline deficiency, stark even before I forced it over my head and limbs: this kit was now that of a much smaller man. Shrunk tight as a wetsuit, diddy as a playsuit. Those once generous cuffs now clamped my upper forearms so firmly it was as if two doctors were checking my blood pressure at once. Even with all the neck buttons undone I felt discomforted to the point of tongue-waggling suffocation, like Bart being taken to task by Homer. Assessing the other end, I hoped that northern Italians just couldn't get enough of hairy white midriff. On the plus side, when at herniated length I got the shorts on, it was clear they wouldn't be falling down again in a hurry.

'Everyone has a limit,' said the manageress when I checked out, smiling at me like Buddha. 'You can be proud to have reached yours.'

This cryptic assessment didn't, on the face of it, augur well for the post-limit days ahead, but explaining there were still 429.1km to go required more syllables than I could currently muster.

'Hank-ooh,' I wheezed tightly. 'Hank-ooh veh mu.'

Flat, fast, grey and sultry: the morning picked up where the previous afternoon had left off. My stifling swaddles of extra-tight merino wool began, mercifully, to relax their death-grip on my neck and limbs; I settled into a high-tempo rhythm and continued the business of reacclimatising to the north. Better coffee, worse pizza. Duller scenery, busier people. The welcome return of the risible, fenced-in little yapper, after a month of free-range flyblown wolfhounds with murderous intent in their one remaining eye. Orchard fruits had ripened to maturity since I'd last been in this part of the world, and so too had my Italian. I could have gone up to a farmer and told him how much bigger his plums were since I'd last seen them. Then sprinted away at a previously unthinkable speed when he came at me with a scythe.

An on-the-go lunch of purloined breakfast was stuffed down, and off I rattled across the fresh-ploughed flatlands. Every delay was now a threat to my crowning glory: riding this final stage in three days demanded a daily average of 143km, further than I'd ever previously managed in even one.

I redoubled my efforts through the drably industrial outskirts of Ferrara, where kindred slowcoach Mario Marangoni had died three months after I was born. (It transpired that Marangoni was just twenty when he rode the 1914 Giro, and that in the same year he'd finished Milan–San Remo in the main bunch. Despite competing again after the war, it appears this was the only professional race he ever managed to complete.) Have it, Mazza! My AVS clicked up to 17.6 as I caned along past the grubby warehouses. Just 0.2 more and I'd beat him, at least in accordance with those ridiculously contrived and heavily me-weighted rules of engagement. On a more eventful morning my brain would have left it at that, but with nothing else to do it chose this moment to provide me with the crushingly dismal imperial conversion: I was busting my sweaty, woollen guts out to complete this race at an average speed of just over 11mph. *Eleven miles per hour.*

I've just Googled '11mph on a bike' and here, discounting the torturous imbecilities of Yahoo Answers – 'If I'm going 11mph on a bike, like how far can I go in two hours?' – are the top matches, from fatsecret.com and bikeforums.net:

'Bicycling (slow): burn 229 calories by riding at 11mph on a
    bike for 30 minutes.'
'11mph on a bike would be close to my average speed in
    deepish snow.'

If I'd had any pride, I'd have cast aside the entire pathetic business right there, and would never speak of it again. But I don't, so I didn't, and I will.

Re-entering the agrarian flatness outside Ferrara – it was hotter and muggier now, and with the widespread and ongoing applica-tion of fertilising ordure, enormously more pungent – I raised a hand to an approaching oldie on a road bike.

'*Salve!*'

Having gathered this to be the preferred greeting between men of my age and above, I had of late begun declaiming it to all passing cyclists in that bracket. The word had a pleasing air of archaic fraternity to it, and not just because I remembered Caecilius and chums busting it out all over my O-level Latin picture books. Its ring of gentlemanly respect seemed a bond with the era of Calzolari, of Coppi, of Gerard Lagrost and the two local cyclists I'd seen commemorated on those mountain-top plaques. In my more emotionally overblown reveries – and by this stage there were plenty – I thought of this simple salutation as more than a hello. *Salve* was a mutual acknowledgement between fellow keepers of the flame, us men of a certain age who alone grasped the bicycle's transcendental import. Only we remembered how this perfect, simple machine had liberated our parents and grand-parents, rolling back the tight horizons of their lives. Bicycle jour-neys were to us different and better than all others, because they were all your own work, but not like walking, because walking was rubbish. When my *salve* was returned, it came with a knowing, weighty glint that said all this and more.

I've no idea why I bothered you with that tripe, though, as this *salve* was not returned. Only now did I see that the old man had half his face down the front of his jersey, which was zipped tight up over his nose. He shot me a hollowed look, shook his head and rode slowly by. I shrugged – yes, it stank here, but Italy often did – then raised my head and felt something flick my right cheek. Another flick to my left, a frail hum in both ears, a twitch up a nostril . . . in an instant the world was a hell of buzzing dots.

Monotony would thereafter prove conspicuously absent from my agenda.

I emerged from that first midge cloud with my forehead on the bidons and my airways clogged. After a clumsy dismount I cleared each nostril in turn onto the roadside, then dredged up and expelled a great, stringy throatful of frog spawn. With this complete, I filled my lungs and treated the surrounding fields to a long roar of disgust.

The following three hours were spent either engulfed in midges or flicking, scooping, spitting, snotting and literally weeping them out of and off my person in their dead and dying thousands. In giant, swirling spindrifts they hovered across my path, enmeshing themselves in my leg hairs and face holes, even penetrating the tiny gaps in my goggle side-shields, crawling about on the inside of the round blue lenses like restless specimens under a microscope.

Pursed, clamped lips were incompatible with the aerobic demands of sustained high speed: I'd been trying all day not to drop below 30kmh. For some time my lungs had to get by on a 50/50 blend of atmospheric gas and winged invertebrate. My jersey was now too small to permit the old man's method of respiratory-passage protection; in desperation I tied a handkerchief round my face, cowboy dust-bandit style. Teamed with the goggles it was a hugely arrestable look.

It had felt since morning like one of those soupy, late-summer days, the air heavy with the promise of long-awaited rain. When those first wristy gouts now dashed against my goggles I whimpered in relief, willing it to bucket down and wash the midges out of my life. My wish was granted, at once and with cataclysimic watery violence. Headlights came on and the iron heavens poured forth, then fifth and sixth. 'OK, that'll do,' I shouted, or rather gargled. But it didn't, and at Legnago – a subdued and almost

submerged town 40km short of Verona, where I'd intended to stop – I sloshed to a defeated halt. It was half four but black as night: gutters swelled and churned, every drainpipe was a fire hose and sodden pedestrians huddled in shop doorways, peering glumly out through a cascade of drips.

The motel room I eventually squelched into was careworn and startlingly cheerless, brown lino scattered with wonky, mismatched furniture. To be fair, it held few real horrors for a veteran of 1980s off-campus student accommodation in Sheffield, but the evening ahead was a bit Eleanor Rigby all the same. After blocking the liver-spotted shower with sluiced insects, I did the same to the blue-veined sink. In doing so I found that the Venus Fly Trap of my front jersey pouch was home to a huge accumulation, the dead piled in drifts at the bottom, a hundred survivors still clambering clumsily through the merino forest in a quest for freedom – a quest that now ended in a froth of travel wash. Two hours later, eating a circular stonebaked food whose name I forget, I opened the map and a dozen mangled corpses fell out into my side salad.

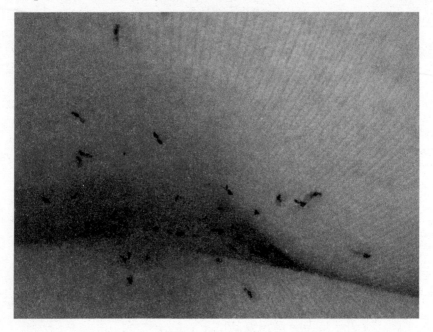

I was up and out early: breakfast played no part in the Albergo New Touring's guest experience. Having retrieved the Hirondelle from the back yard, I pushed it to a supermarket up the road. This had yet to open – we're talking *early* here – and while waiting for the shutters to clank up I considered the challenge ahead. Finishing the last stage in three days was a big ask that had just got bigger: the storm-shortened 114km I'd managed the day before meant I now faced riding 315km in forty-eight hours. As food for thought, it was a prospect that made my brain retch. And this before the more conventionally nauseating spasms I experienced half an hour later, conducting Number 7's pre-departure check with a litre of drinking yoghurt and a plastic-boxed pastry assortment sloshing around my insides. Another two rear-wheel spokes failed to respond to the wrench; both had sheared through at the hub end. I was now four spokes short of a pointy metal picnic. All were culled from the same quadrant, with two of them adjacent: an unsupported void I could have put a child's head through.

Wind-assisted flatness sped me to Verona in two bearably wobblesome hours: a decent start. It was long years since I'd last passed through the alluring backdrop of Shakespeare's best-loved double suicide, but I slalomed through the tourists and out of the city walls without even slowing down. The road beyond it was another tarmac ruler, but it wasn't quiet and by mid-afternoon nor was the bike. A painful twin scraping chafe from below – *thwickity-shickita, thwackity-shuckata* – announced that the rear wheel's ratcheting warp and weft were now causing it to scuff both sides of the frame, as well the cork brake pads, during each revolution. It sounded awful, felt bad and plainly didn't look great, either. Just past Roverbella, two riders in local-club jerseys rode up from behind, pointing urgently at my wheel and gabbling their consternation. '*Mi manca quattro raggi,*' I shouted above the racket: I'd been waiting all day to christen this rehearsed assessment of my spoke crisis. Their expressions as they rode away suggested I'd said something else, perhaps that my bidons were filled with cat's blood.

Thwickity-shickita, thwackity-shuckata-rackita-nockita. It occurred to me, watching this pair disappear into the traffic, that with a few different words I could probably have secured a full-wheel overhaul in their club workshop. But what would Fonso have done? Though his final stage was unfolding as an incident-free procession, events of the previous fortnight had proven that even a huge lead could be whittled to nought by roadside repairs. 'Clemente! Listen up, my back wheel's going a bit wonky: let's stop and get some new spokes and have it all trued up and stuff. There we go –

all done! Hey, that feels so much better. Really *round*. Right, where's everyone else? *Milan?* Bummer.'

No, Calzolari would have wobbled on, and so would I. A blue sky, a following wind, and nary a hill from here to the finish: hit it! The rationale seemed obvious now. My bike was slowly falling apart, so if I went really fast, I'd get to Milan before it did completely. And if I went really, *really* fast, I'd get there before the toiling ghost of Mario Marangoni.

The Alps poked hazily up on my right-hand horizon, and presented with hard geographical evidence that my circle was nearing completion I kicked on hard. Truly terrible things resulted down below almost at once. I stole a juddery glance: it was like an unfolding collapse on the *Generation Game* potter's wheel.

I bucked to a halt, propped the Hirondelle against a tree and dug out the spoke wrench. The rim was all over the place. No point just winding the spokes tight, as I'd been doing for the past few mornings: I needed to cajole the wheel back into shape with those judicious tweakings of yore. How did it go again? Righty-tighty, left-hand down, three and in, port out, starboard home. Bollocks. In the twenty wrist-burning minutes that now followed I somehow contorted the side-on profile into an onion dome, with an obvious flat spot and an opposing peak. Final score: Ride Quality 0, Onlooker Hilarity 4.

What would happen if the wheel collapsed? The many prece-dents of 1914 suggested a crash with a decent risk of race-ending injury, and back then they didn't have articulated lorries to slide under. But my nerve held. Indeed, I even picked up the pace after establishing that the faster I went, the more bearable it seemed – the worst jolts and shudders sort of cancelled each other out. As I barrelled through Cremona's early-evening rush hour, my AVS clicked up to 17.7.

'Italy – land of contrasts': sweeping daily shifts in mood and milieu were a defining feature of this journey, and of all those shifts, few had been sweepier. From breakfast in a puddled supermarket car park to dinner in one of the world's most glorious shadows, from a lino-floored truck-stop to a duplex awash with thick towels and flat screens. Cremona had been described to me, by an English bowmaker who once plied his trade there, as the snob capital of Italy; with a record 151km in my legs and the end so tantalisingly nigh, I felt fully entitled to snob myself silly.

I breezed into the warm night aglow with complimentary lotions and home-straight portent, and almost at once found myself stepping across the wondrous penumbra referenced above: the façade of Cremona cathedral, a soaring chevron of marble, glass and brick that paid extravagant tribute to three centuries of wealth and gifted architectural whimsy. Its adjacent campanile, a huge pillar of brick I could see from my room if I stood on the bed, is over seven hundred years old but still looks down on all but a dozen modern buildings across Italy; its western face is graced with an only slightly younger astronomical clock that remains the world's largest. I peered up at it: crab past lion already!

My stride began to falter as I hunted a restaurant in old-town Italy's classiest alleys: no wee-stink, no graffiti, the shrill ululations of a trainee soprano spilling down from some gentrified garret. It was hardly a surprise to find my feet dragging over the cobbles. The drained and vacant shuffle had been my default evening gait since that very first ride out of Milan. Indeed, it was almost a badge of honour. Reading Tyler Hamilton's autobiography, I'd been rather taken by the commitment to listlessness that characterised a professional cyclist's out-of-saddle existence: moving between sofas with elaborate, geriatric sloth, conserving every microjoule of energy for the next race. Obviously my hunched stumbling after hours was less about saving strength than the result of having just used it all up, but still: when I shambled, I did so with a certain weary pride.

There was something different about this shamble, though. I tried to establish exactly what as I trudged on, pausing now and then to gaze woodenly at some terse and exorbitant bill of fare. Exhaustion, check; malnourishment, check – pallid, day-end emptiness was present in all its usual forms. But also in another form, which opened itself up to me an hour later, as I dabbed habitual red stains from around my mouth at an outside table with cathedral views.

A successful conclusion to this endeavour – a turnout that for so long had seemed unworthy of sensible consideration – had stealthily progressed first to plausibility, and now imminence. This alone seemed grounds for slack-jawed, mind-hollowing incredulity, but there was a void within this void, a midge in the ointment. I was looking forward to going home – of course I was, and hungrily so: in recent days I had often found myself bellowing my children's silliest nicknames across the fields. But this – the vase of *sfuso frizzante* beneath a floodlit cathedral, the balmy night air, the diligent savouring of pleasure earned through pain – all this I was going to miss. I sat there shaking my head because I couldn't believe that my ancient bike and I were about to make it to the finish. And because a part of me didn't want us to.

CHAPTER 24

Gazing with flinty, eve-of-accomplishment significance through my window at an unpromising morning, I looked down and spotted the Hirondelle, resting where I'd left it against the wall of the covered courtyard two floors below. Even from this range I could see it had not slept well. The previous afternoon I'd had to pump up the rear tyre, Old Snowy, a couple of times; now it sat flaccid and utterly airless. If it was a slow puncture, it had sped up.

Throttling back the big swears, I ran through my options. I was all out of Stan's miracle sealant, and with 164km to go, sourcing a new tubular tyre seemed like a really great way of ensuring I didn't make it to Milan until the following day – thereby failing to complete a stage in three days, and sensing Mario Marangoni pull away for good as I pootled about Cremona's commercial suburbs at shopping speed. Ghastliest of all, as silly as it sounds, was the realisation that an extra day would mean a farcical, portent-sapping rerun of farewell experiences. I just couldn't bear to think this only *might* be the final time that I squeezed into my damp and shrunken jersey, that Savlon kissed my arse, that the shoes of Gerard Lagrost imprisoned my calloused toes. Nope, buttocks to all that: today was Milan or bust, a 164km blaze of death or glory. I got dressed with as much purposeful defiance as my outfit allowed, then stopped off en route to the breakfast room and pumped Old Snowy so taut that it pinged when I flicked it.

One last deserted canteen, one last buffet plunder, one last maps-across-the-table navigational briefing overseen by the breakfast-telly weather generals. This was more like it: the stuff of history, one small brioche for a man and all that. Blinking something out of my eyes, with unsteady fingers I instructed the sat-nav to direct me to the Via Giovanni da Procida, Milano. *Biddle-iddle-ip!* 'Distance to target: 91.3km.'

Come again? The stirring trumpet fanfare in my head mangled itself into tuneless flatulence. I scrabbled the map back open and riffled through Paolo. Neither turned up even one of the missing 70-odd kilometres. In his perfunctory account of the last stage, Paolo didn't mention a single town between Cremona and Milan, which the map agreed lay around 90km apart via any sensible route. I took a moment to admire the circuitous dithering contrived by the Giro organisers to join these cities in almost twice the distance. How could I make up the difference? Ride seven sides of some gigantic and spurious Lombardian hexagon? Do a few hundred laps round a hypermarket car park? The solution presented itself when I clicked through the sat-nav's various screens, and noted that my accrued distance to date stood at 3,236km. Courtesy of sundry detours and getting lost, I had already ridden 74km further than the 1914's Giro overall total. I sniffed, rubbed my nose with the palm of my hand and thought: Well, that's all right then.

The rear tyre was still firm to the touch as I prepared to leave, though it sank onto its haunches a little when the saddlebag went on, and a lot more when my bottom followed. Rain had been sprinkling the cobbles since my third brioche, and was now the wrong side of steady. A subwoofer boom of thunder rolled along the flanks of brick and marble; I pulled the brim of my cap down and weaved away through the pedestrian-zone umbrellas. If this day was to be my last, it had just got a lot shorter. But also a lot hairier, as I'd now have to thrash the crap out of my dying bike on sodden roads to have any hope of reeling in Mario Marangoni across the reduced available distance.

When at last I left Cremona's splashy, honking rush hour behind, I swiped rain off the sat-nav with the shred of oily suede that was my right glove, and noted that the AVS had dropped back down to 17.6. My shoulders hardly had time to sag in defeat before a familiar corrugated rumble told my bottom that the rear tyre was flat. I hadn't quite covered 15km; I stopped and with an air of blank, automatic duty pumped it back up.

The rain went off to someone else's parade just before eleven. By then I'd stopped twice more to reinflate Old Snowy, which now held air for less than 10km. On the plus side, I hadn't lost any more spokes, and the soundtrack of locomotion was enormously less painful after I opened up the rear calipers as far as they'd go: the warped rim now barely scuffed the cork pads, at the trifling cost of reducing the efficiency of my rear brakes from modest to zero. And so I bumped across the blotted, grey-scale plain in a state of reflect-iveness and diminishing resignation, greeting a compendium of representative challenges with something close to fondness. A demented dog pressed up to a chain-link fence, huge lorries on a tiny road, a pothole brimmed with brown water, a headwind and a gob-full of midges: everything but the heat and the hills.

'*Bici antica*, I like,' cooed the young barman, bending down by the Hirondelle. 'To where you go now?'

I told him through a mouthful of salami *panino*.

'Oh, Milano is no far, forty *chilometri*. Where you start?'

The same answer emerged with the odd bubble of Coke.

'Milano and return to Milano?' He chuckled chidingly. 'But is a so small *viaggio*!'

My grip tightened around the can tilted into my mouth, then relaxed. I drained it and placed the empty on my little round table, beside a half-drunk litre of fizzy water.

'I know,' I said, peering up at the re-darkening sky, 'but that's an old bike and I'm an old man.'

He responded with many small sounds of affable objection, and as I downed the water we shared a companionable silence, looking out past his awning as the sky unloaded again and the lunchtime citizenry of Sant'Angelo Lodigiano scurried for cover. Then I paid, pumped the rear fit to bust, put my cap on and for purely theatrical effect hooked the arms of my goggles over my ears, turning the wet world blue.

'Eh, old style!'

To give this winning response the send-off it deserved I caned away into the rain, shooting past the scabby grandeur of yet another rundown, magnificent nowhere. Stealing a glance at the sat-nav as I sent an arc of standing water against a bus shelter, I saw that my AVS had just gone back up to 17.7. Given the conditions and the state of my bicycle, my reaction to this didn't so much tempt fate, as grab fate's bottom while flicking her enormous boyfriend repeatedly on the nose. *And Moore's gone! He's got the hammer right down and he's absolutely flying along these roads! It's crazy and it's doomed, Phil, but by fuck it's tenting my pants out!*

*

Ninety-eight and a bit years before, down a road I could sadly but guess at, eight cyclists pedalled steadily towards the end of the most punishing race of their lives, or of anyone else's. The merciless attacks and chicanery were over now: it was after 4 p.m., and they'd been riding in a tight group since the midnight start in Lugo. The sky, at last, was clear and the roads, for once, were good, but still the shattered survivors would be denied a gentle run-in. From morning onwards the roadside crowds began to build in noise and numbers, and once again the little peloton found itself choking through the dust raised by a thousand bellowing idiots in cars and on bikes. Pierino Albini, on his way to second place overall, took commendably direct action: those who got in his face had their hats snatched off and flung in the ditch, and if that didn't do the trick, a forearm smash to the jaw sent the owner the same way. Leaning out of their Fiat Tipo Zeros, the race organisers eventually subdued the crowds in a manner I think we'd all like to see rolled out on the oaf-lined Alpine climbs of today: with horse whips.

The riders hit Milan just before 5 p.m., followed now by cars carrying the fêted fallen – come, in Paolo Facchinetti's words, 'to applaud the bravery of comrades who had the luck and courage to survive this deadly race'. Ganna, winner of the inaugural Giro; future *campionissimo* Girardengo; Bordin, hapless protagonist of that record breakaway on the longest stage in history; Gremo, wine-loving scourge of the excisemen. All the big-name victims but Giuseppe Azzini, understandably reluctant to see a rival claim the victory that his farm-based nap habit had once again deprived him of. (Perhaps he'd also got wind of Bianchi's petulant response to their humiliation: along with every one of his teammates, Azzini was to be sacked with immediate effect. He later rode again, but with little success. In 1925, ravaged by years of over-exertion, strychnine and crushing disappointment, Azzini succumbed to tuberculosis: aged just thirty-four, he went to sleep in that big barn in the sky.)

Roared along by huge crowds, the riders wearily wound up the pace for the showpiece final sprint, a lap of the open-air Velodromo Sempione, just a block from the boulevard they'd started out from sixteen days and 3,162km previously. Having punched his way through Lombardy, an invigorated Albini crossed the line first with the others at his wheel, all awarded the same time in the traditional manner. But cheering acclaim died in the spectators' throats as one by one, the eight riders hobbled onto the presentation stage. 'Tache Durando and his teammate Luigi Lucotti had to be held upright. Unhealed wounds from their terrible crashes on the previous stage had left Clemente Canepari and Ottavio Pratesi almost unrecognisable. The winner was a grime-etched skeleton: the hearty, boater-wearing Stucchi executives flanking Calzolari in the victory photo might have just found him crawling out of a collapsed mineshaft. Every rider was similarly emaciated, their cheeks and brows wizened, their eyes dark and deep: the faces of old men. No one could believe that Umberto Ripamonti, the local hero and solitary surviving amateur, had yet to turn twenty. Ripamonti came home a distant last, almost seventeen hours behind Calzolari's aggregate time of 135 hours 17' 56", but his achievement was perhaps the most heroic: fixing his own bike, finding his own food and lodgings, entirely self-motivated and self-sufficient from start to finish. (It took a lot out of him: Ripamonti never won a race and rode only one more Giro, retiring halfway through the 1924 edition.)

The tiny clutch of survivors and their shocking condition sparked an immediate scandal. The 1914 Giro, everyone now saw, had been in every respect a race too far: the stages too long, the

route too cruel, the conditions too relentlessly brutal. 'An event that seeks to destroy its competitors has no place in sport,' wrote one commentator. 'The organisers have no right to call this inhuman spectacle a success.' The only paper to do so was the *Gazzetta dello Sport*, which of course happened to own the Giro. Having dutifully praised the robust reliability of the bicycles and tyres supplied by the principal sponsors, and the daring genius of cheerily unrepentant race director Armando Cougnet, the *Gazzetta*'s final report built to a rousing martial climax: 'An army left Milan; only a brave patrol has returned. A handful of men who held fast against unimaginable hardship and stood undaunted in the breach.'

Hollow as it may have sounded at the time, three weeks later this paean to military attrition began to seem the very pinnacle of poor taste. On 9 June, Alfonso Calzolari was waving his way through the thronged streets of Bologna in an open car. On 28 June, Archduke Franz Ferdinand made the mistake of doing the same in Sarajevo. The four-year global conflict catalysed by his consequent assassination cut down almost a whole generation of young European men. Lucien Petit-Breton, who had abandoned the 1914 Giro with such impressive fury at the foot of Sestriere, was one of three Tour de France winners killed on the Western Front. A good number of the Italian pros from the 1914 Giro, amongst them Albini and Azzini, fought in the Alps; Carlo Oriani, one of Azzini's most faithful Bianchi lieutenants, didn't return. A hefty swathe of the amateur entrants would have shared his fate, and I'd often wondered about my Hirondelle's first owner: as a Frenchman of fighting age, he stood a 30 per cent chance of never coming home to his shiny new pride and joy.

When the Giro was resurrected in 1919, the ghastly suffering of brave young men had rather lost its appeal as a spectator sport. Never again would professional cyclists be compelled to set out at midnight on twenty-hour rides. The stages in the first post-war Giro were on average 100km shorter – seven of them won by Girardengo, in an unparalleled display of dominance. The *campionissimo* claimed victory in the colours of Stucchi, stoutly assisted by Alfonso Calzolari, who was running third when he retired on stage seven.

Fonso, who had endured a rather easier war in the catering corps ('Eggs again, boys – get 'em while they're raw!'), never raced with much distinction thereafter. Fearsome saddle sores wrote off the rest of 1919, and early in 1920 a car ran over his left hand. He failed to finish that year's Giro, and didn't bother again. In fact his *palmares*, as we professionals like to style our career achievements, show that he never won another race. The 1914 Giro wasn't just

his finest hour, it was pretty much his only hour. But what an hour
it was.

And what an hour I was having. Five kilometres of lunatic pedal
mashing, a brutal roadside workout with the pump, then five more.
My legs glowed with pain and my biceps burned: it began to feel
like some punishing new endurance sport, the pumpathlon. The
sustained violence breached my bottom bracket's final defences.
Something gave in the left-hand crank as I powered up a long
bridge across a motorway intersection, and from then on both
pedals skipped two beats each. Beneath my whirring feet swelled
the painful tones of Thompson's Final Symphony, a drawn-out
rending shriek, like the Eiffel Tower having one of its legs sawn
off. I had a sudden vision of the most nobly tragic finale in sporting
history, when Derek Redmond's hamstring snapped in the 400m
at the 1992 Olympics, and his father ran onto the track, helped
him up and walked his crippled, weeping son over the line. The
rear wheel was now bending like a bamboo Beckham: one more
broken spoke and I'd be dad to the Hirondelle's Derek. Come in,
Number 7, your time is up.

Farms gave way to the distribution centres and deckchair sex
workers of Italy's urban hinterland. The rain stopped but I kept my
high-vis jacket on: I was closing in on the world's largest concentration of Italian drivers, and getting crushed to death at this stage
would be a serious frustration. As the arterial traffic thickened I
was forced into a sliver of hard shoulder, rutted as a cattle-grid and
bestrewn with cat-sized rodent stiffs that – *bwolp!* – couldn't
always be avoided.

The ever-lairier motorists, the grating creaks and wobbles, those
breathless pump-stops and that overarching commitment to
maximum speed . . . it was difficult to conduct the pensive review
that my proximity to the finish seemed to demand. All I could

summon was a parallel with my last day at school, and the kindred feeling that a riddance long dreamed of was about to leave me numb and a little regretful, more demob-sad than happy. Where now were all the bad times? Well, there was Sestriere. Both up it and down. Choc-Vom Hill, obviously. School buses. Sickly breakfasts with a damp gusset. And with that a great shoal of endured miseries bobbed to the surface: broiled madness in Chianti, the Potenza Kidney Misfortune, Bari's death-dog, double-brandy mountain, prune-faced assassins at the wheel of a thousand Fiat Pandas. A litany of despair and bedragglement, from that first afternoon with half a saddle up my jacksie to the throat-coating Lombardian midge plague.

Buildings grew taller and the pavements filled. I stopped for a final bout of roadside hyper-inflation, snatching the chance to offload superfluous weight, like a pro hurling his bidons into the crowd before the final bunch sprint. Into the bin with that box of bicarb, four half-carved prosecco corks, the beastly Savlon and a tube of travel wash – erstwhile cornerstones of my life, all suddenly redundant. I emptied my little bottle of oil through the filler flap on the bottom bracket and ditched the two shredded, punctured old tyres I'd kept lashed to the saddlebag for some obscure emergency that wouldn't be happening now. Then I dashed into a Spar for one last lilac bar of Milka Extra Cacao, and dashed out with two plus a bottle of cheap fizz: a whimsical, weighty one-man podium kit. We were going to make it. My decrepit velocipede and I were actually going to make it. Bollocks to all those old farts in bike shops who said the Hirondelle would never get me here. Bollocks to me for secretly agreeing with them.

Cramming eight squares into a brown-ringed maw, I considered my slavish dependence on this afternoon delight. Strange to recall that in the course of normal daily life I never eat chocolate, on account of not really liking it – my mouth would henceforth be a stranger to 45 per cent cocoa solids. And with that, my coated tongue sparked off a Proustian reverie, the highlights showreel of an abnormal daily life so nearly at an end. That first refreshment stop just outside Milan, looking around at the bell-towers and waddling old widows and understanding at once that I might happily see out my days in almost every town I would pass through, particularly if a vacancy came up at the pharmacist's. The aromatic splendour of valleys wreathed in rosemary and wood-smoke. The motherly kindness of grocers and waitresses and hoteliers; the infectious party mood of so many balmy civic nights. The pizzas – oh, the pizzas, bubbling to crispy yet tender perfection in my mind's oven. The mood-enhancing Italian landscape in all its three-season majesty, those invigorating and bewildering snow-to-sand metamorphoses between dawn and dusk. The precious gratification of bridging these different worlds under my own steam, the woozy evenings spent reliving implausible daily accomplishments through a hotel window, on the screen of a digital camera, in the heavy folds of those beautifully antiquated Touring Editore maps. And all those little old men on their pampered road bikes, rolling over the plains and scuttling up the mountains. Those phantom Fonsos, those me-to-bes.

In the throes of an autumnal rush hour, Milan was unrecognisable from the roasted ghost town I'd pedalled through so nervously five weeks before, Stupid Boy Pike on a bike. Look at me now, keeping my speed up in an enmeshment of Italian motorists via manoeuvres that incited a rolling maul of horn noise. I was mean, and I was lean. If my jersey had shrunk as it had in the first week, I'd never have got it over my B-cup Cameroons; they were gone now, part of a one-and-a-half stone downsize. Those aggressively musclebound legs powering me through the traffic looked almost genetically modified, and would gladly have kicked sand in the jowly, pallid face that had greeted these streets back in August. That face was now a decent homage to the 1914 survivors: burned by wind and sun, its many new lines showing clear through the mud and road grime. (You will, I'm sure, be tearfully grateful to learn that my genitals have since come back to life – and in some style, if I may say so. By way of a more regrettable physiological update, I've put back on a proportion of that lost weight. This proportion currently stands at 103 per cent.)

Biddle-ip! 'Turn right.' *Biddle-ip!* 'Third exit at roundabout.' I hit a long boulevard and with a juddering thumb clicked back to the sat-nav's data screen. There it was, in two words and three beautiful, liquid-crystal digits: *Avg. Speed 17.8*. Mario Marangoni reeled in and passed on the home straight.

On to the downtown flagstones and tram-lines. It was all getting a little too much. My eyes prickled behind the blue glass, and my heart battered the walls of its cramped merino prison. Over 3,000km on a gearless, brakeless ninety-eight-year-old barn find, built with my hands and powered by my legs. No time now to take account of any achievement-tarnishing mitigations, the thirty-two days it had taken me to ride what they rode in eight, and the unflattering light this cast on my almost literally pedestrian rate of median progress. There was a party in my soul and Mr Rational Perspective wasn't invited. Alfonso Calzolari got in as my plus-one.

Victory in history's hardest race would bring Fonso fame and a small fortune. A genuinely small one: the 3,000 lire first prize was hardly enough to retire on, even when supplemented with his Stucchi salary of 500 lire a month plus a curious bonus of 7 lire per competitive kilometre. All told, Fonso earned the inflation-adjusted equivalent of around €18,000 for his glorious fortnight in hell. Still, that was enough for him and his wife to settle down:

they bought a house and raised two sons. And you couldn't put a price on that mantle of greatness. Fonso would never have to pay for another drink in Bologna, and no Italian would undervalue the life-long adulation of his parents. 'I always believed in him,' said his carpenter dad, coining the default expression of long-haul parental pride.

Alfonso Calzolari's last recorded achievement as a cyclist came in the 1924 Italian National Championships, in which he finished forty-fourth. By then he was thirty-seven and had been racing as an independent *isolato* for three years; after another fruitless two, he called it a day. He made a comfortable living thereafter on the back of his celebrity, putting his name to track events across northern Italy. Fonso's fame had a long tail: in July 1975, sixty years after his epic feat, President Giovanni Leone personally appointed him to the Order of Merit of the Italian Republic. He was then eighty-eight, and peaceably ensconced at the Villa Serena nursing home in Ceriale – a town on the Ligurian coast that he'd swept along the day he took the Giro lead. Fonso eventually checked out in 1983 at the suitably long-distance age of ninety-six, a tremendous advertisement for spending one's young adulthood riding up mountains on raw eggs and rat poison.

Biddle-ip! 'Turn left.' *Biddle-iddle-iddle-ip!* 'Arriving at destination.' To a chorus of glass-muffled protest I pulled blindly across several lanes of traffic and bumped the Hirondelle up onto the pavement. Via Giovanni da Procida, I saw, would be ending my journey in the understated manner of its start. Five weeks before I'd snapped myself outside the drab apartment block that had replaced the Grand Ristorante Sempioncino; ranks of the same inconsequential structures trudged off down the street that had once been home to the Velodromo Sempione. The open-air stadium was demolished in the 1920s, and I'd been unable to pinpoint its former location more precisely than somewhere along this road. In truth, I hadn't tried very hard: as betrayed by my slap-dash research of the route beyond Cremona, I'd never convincingly imagined myself getting this far.

Sighing in eight ways at once, I pushed the Hirondelle up Via Giovanni da Procida, scanning its dreary walls in search of a plaque or some other evidence of the velodrome's site. Failing that, an even modestly photogenic backdrop for the ceremonial self-portraits I'd begun to envision, dousing myself and my bike in alcoholic foam.

Two mishaps now blighted this search. As I heaved Number 7 beneath one of the sickly trees that lined the pavement, the bottle of fizz I'd semi-wedged under a saddlebag strap threw itself to the ground. A percussive tonk stood in for a liner-launching shatter: miraculously, it hadn't broken. The act of leaning the bike against the tree while I retrieved this enchanted flagon begat a second and more profound adversity. An odious pulping sound introduced a catalogue of multi-sensory dismay: I had marched the Hirondelle's front wheel straight through a fresh and very generous dog turd. In half a revolution this had somehow applied itself to most of the tyre and a goodly stretch of wooden rim. An unfortunate reflex yank of the brakes had left claggy, retch-inducing lumps hanging from the front calipers and blocks. Even the forks hadn't escaped and nor – Jesus God no – had the underside of my bidons. In the absence of an undressed Silvio Berlusconi, it was impossible to imagine a more repulsive and dispiriting denouement.

Jersey over nose and heart in boots, I stooped down, picked up a twig and conducted that grim street symphony, flicking bits of foul catastrophe into the gutter. Then I took my soiled and stinking steed by the handlebars and shuffled blankly up what was left of Via Giovanni da Procida.

At its final junction the apartment blocks parted to make way for a large, low-slung oval structure. There was no identifying signage, but approaching its curved grey walls I spotted a banner thanking sponsors for their assistance in restoring 'la pista di legno del Velodromo Vigorelli'. The wooden track of the Vigorelli Velodrome. I cracked a pale smile: this, of course, must be the velodrome that replaced the old Sempione. And not just any velodrome: I'd encountered the Vigorelli while studying the cyclists of old Italy, and one in particular. It was here, on this very pista di legno, that Fausto Coppi set his world hour record in 1942. And here, fourteen years later, that Jacques Anquetil finally beat it.

It was a little poignant to behold the mothballed decline evident during my circuit of its shuttered outer walls – I later learned that almost two decades had elapsed since a competitive wheel was last turned in anger on the Vigorelli boards, and that these days the stadium is primarily employed as the home of Milan's American football team, the Legacy Desecrators.

All the same I began to feel much less distraught as I paced the perimeter. Come on: I'd made it over the line, and the line was a historic velodrome, bonded to one of my greatest cycling heroes. And how about that 17.8? This little victory and the outrageous perfection of its timing was surely worth a solo toast. Increasingly upbeat, I clicked through the sat-nav's final data screens, choosing not to dwell on the one that said Alfonso Calzolari had beaten me to Milan by 635km. Here we go: 3,336 total kilometres, average speed 17.8kmh, 32,328 accumulated metres of ascent. This last figure had an especially awesome ring to it. Thirty-two vertical kilometres – whooooosh! See you in the stratosphere, kids.

I checked the camera battery and quickened my stride. There would surely be some appropriate monument to stage my photo-call

before, a statue of Fausto or a giant brass bidon or something. Yes, I could work with this: my bike was covered in shit, but success tasted sweet and photos don't smell.

Right round the back I found something better than any sculpture: a jet-nozzle hose, coiling out from the side door of a lock-up unit set into the Vigorelli concrete. I put my head round the door and told the darkness inside that I had dog shit on my bike. The echoing male reply made no sense to me, but its tone was cheerfully obliging; I picked the hose up and pressed the nozzle trigger. In the light of the events that were to follow, let's not dwell on the instant aftermath of this action, which for the record blasted particles of faecal matter over every part of the Hirondelle and my entire body. God love those goggles.

'*Eh, bici antica!*'

I wiped a glove across the unprotected parts of my face and

looked round. The owner of the voice, an oily-handed smiler of about my own age, had come out to see what all that English swearing was about. Angelo, as he would soon introduce himself, seemed instantly captivated by the Hirondelle, and waved away my warnings of its toxic new coating to pay intimate, crouched tribute. 'Cerchi di legno,' he cooed wonderingly, rubbing his thumb over the front rim, then the malodorous hand-crafted wine corks that crowned it. 'E freni di sughero – eh, Alberto! Alberto!'

Thus summoned, an elderly bespectacled man in a blue shop-coat emerged from the lock-up shadows. He appraised the Hirondelle with a curt nod, then whipped a set of engineering calipers from his front pocket, bent down and began to measure its tubing in forensic detail. As Alberto went about this strange and silent work, Angelo beckoned me into the lock-up, unveiling a competent grasp of English to ask why I come with such old shirt and hat and bike.

He threw the lights on and my reply died on my lips. The large workshop now revealed was a shrine to the road-racing bicycle of a certain age: gleaming examples of its traditional form in various states of assembly, tools and machinery pertaining to its bespoke manufacture and, most compellingly, a photographic history of its golden era that filled the back wall.

'Is father of Alberto, Signore Masi,' said Angelo, noting my distraction and pointing at a bushy-eyebrowed face in one of the larger black-and-white prints. More familiar was the beaky chap standing beside him.

'Piss and biscuits, Fausto Coppi!'

My blurt seemed to disappoint Angelo. 'But of course, Masi make bike frame for all great campioni.'

I didn't dare confess that the name still meant nothing to me, though the faces of those happy customers posing with their

Masi-framed bikes most certainly did. There on the wall was Eddy Merckx, Jacques Anquetil, and Fiorenzo Magni, riding to the finish of that second-worst-ever 1956 Giro with four broken bones. All those machines had been built right here. This Masi fellow was the Stradivarius of cycling's most fabled epoch.

'Please,' said Angelo, interrupting my unworthy gawping. 'I like to ask again – what it is you do here?' We walked back outside and I dusted off my explanatory spiel. It would be the last time I ever did so.

Alberto had completed his tubular examination, and was now surveying the Hirondelle's headline deficiency: he waved at us with his arm through the rear wheel's largest spokeless area. The tyre around it was already entirely flat. Angelo had been struggling with my story, and this spectacle seemed to bolster his bemuse-ment. 'I understand, is correct, you ride this bike with such wheel from Cremona.'

'The tyre went flat in Cremona. The wheel's been like that for days.'

He frowned. 'So this *giro antico* you do, where he start?'

'In Milano.'

'No, no, where he *start*?'

It seemed easier to let Paolo Facchinetti explain: I rooted his little book out of the saddlebag and handed it over. Alberto got to his feet and they both peered at the victorious Stucchi team on the cover photo. 'Alfonso Calzolari,' I said, indicating the slightly worried little cyclist on the left, with the bouquet on his handlebars. Their cautious hums indicated they knew as much about my notorious race and its winner as I did about their legendary bike frames.

I stumbled through some of the 1914's more infamous records – the longest ever stages, the fewest ever finishers – but they weren't listening. Angelo had thumbed his way to the Giro's stage itinerary in Paolo's index, and he and his boss were both staring hard at the enclosed data.

'*Prima tappa, 24 maggio, Milano–Cuneo, 420 chilometri,*' read Angelo. 'You do this *tappa*?'

I nodded.

'Is mountain, yes?'

'Sestriere.'

He turned the page. '*Lucca–Roma – 430,3km! Incredibile.* You do also this *tappa*?'

'I do every *tappa*.'

As he flicked onwards, the two of them shook their heads and mumbled ever more incredulously.

'Every *tappa*,' summarised Angelo when they had reached the eighth and final stage, Lugo–Milano, 429.1km. 'Every *tappa*, three thousand something *chilometri*, on such bike.'

I would like to take this opportunity to thank that Milanese dog and its owner, because without their repulsive negligence all this would have been denied to me. I would not have needed the hose that led me to this hallowed birthplace of bicycles. And so I would never have met the son of the man who built them, and the actual man – as I've since discovered – who as a sixteen-year-old served as Fausto Coppi's mechanic on his final Giro d'Italia. I would have walked on by and toasted my accomplishment unacclaimed and alone, instead of pulling this man close to my side and coating him, myself and my very old bicycle with booze froth.

Most vitally, I would never have heard the words that his colleague, having kindly photographed the above scene, now delivered, one hand clamped to my shoulder and the other on the saddle of my flat-tyred, crap-spattered, wobbly, wonderful 1914 Hirondelle No 7 Course sur Route. Words that at my stage of flaccid middle age I had given up on ever hearing. Words I would dearly love to build up to with ratcheting, tremulous import, but my wife is shouting up the stairs about the shonky old wooden bike wheel I've left in bits all over the kitchen table, so, well, here they are.

'My friend, you are really a hero.'

GENERAL CLASSIFICATION RESULTS

1. Alfonso CALZOLARI 135:17:56
2. Pierino ALBINI +1:57:26
3. Luigi LUCOTTI +2:04:23
   Timothy MOORE +52:20:12
   Race starters: 81
   Race finishers: 8

LIST OF ILLUSTRATIONS

174. The white roads of Chianti plotting my downfall.
195. Paul thoughtfully captures my grovelling distress up Monte Bibico.
199. Pushing hard into Umbria. Must emphasise that my vast rearward bulge is a rear pocket full of travel essentials rather than weird flesh.
204. Bye, Paul. Off you go then. Don't worry about me.
216. Yes, this man is 48 years old.
224. Another road-closure defied. I don't play by the book but I get results.
230. The Snails of Dehydrated Madness.
241. On 11 September 2012, Timothy Moore Cried Here.
247. Lunch of champions.
254. Alfonso Calzolari: a five-foot man with watermelon bollocks.
263. Topless family breakfast at Matera.
280. The double-brandy descent after Roccaraso.
301. Dr Stan's Sticky White Fluid squirts into my valve once more.
309. My three-hour beach-hut pit stop at Senigallia.
315. The default Tim's-eye view of Italy.
326, 327. The bastard plague of midges: up my nose and down my jersey.
338. A filth-slathered Alfonso Calzolari (left) and his faithful wingman Clemente Canepari held upright by their Stucchi team bosses at the finish.
347. The final analysis: slow and steady loses the race by 635km.
351. Celebrating with a slightly bemused Alberto Masi outside his workshop at the Vigorelli velodrome in Milan.
352. Alfonso Calzolari at 90. What a man.

The Riders
ATALA
(grey and blue jersey, Dunlop tyres)
1 CONTESINI Giuseppe
2 DUBOQ Paul (FRA)
3 GRUBB Frederick Henry (GBR)
4 PETIT-BRETON Lucien (FRA)
5 ROSSIGNOLI Giovanni
7 BRIZZI Gino

GLOBO
(yellow-gold jersey, Dunlop tyres)
8 ALBINI Pierino
10 GARAVAGLIA Gaetano
11 SPINELLI Rinaldo

GANNA
(white and blue jersey, Dunlop tyres)
12 CORLAITA Ezio
13 FASOLI Pietro
14 GANNA Luigi
15 GREMO Angelo
16 SANTHIA Giuseppe

STUCCHI
(white and red jersey, Dunlop tyres)
17 BENI Dario

18 CALZOLARI Alfonso
19 CANEPARI Clemente
20 PETIVA Emilio

MAINO
(grey jersey, Dunlop tyres)
21 DURANDO Carlo
22 GIRARDENGO Costante
23 LOMBARDI Giosue
24 LUCOTTI Luigi
25 TORRICELLI Leopoldo

BIANCHI
(white and turquoise jersey, Pirelli tyres)
26 AGOSTONI Ugo
27 AZZINI Giuseppe
28 BORDIN Lauro
29 CERVI Giovanni
30 GALETTI Carlo
31 ORIANI Carlo
32 PAVESI Eberardo
33 SIVOCCI Alfredo

GERBI
(red jersey, Dunlop tyres)
34 GERBI Giovanni

ALCYON
(sky-blue jersey, Wolber tyres)
35 PRATESI Ottavio

Isolati

(privateer professionals, white jersey)

37 ARATO Ettore
38 ROBOTTI Michele
39 MOLON Luigi
40 BARSIZIA Giovanni
41 COLELLA Giovanni (SUI)
43 GOI Sante
44 MARANGONI Mario
45 ALLASIA Domenico
46 ARESO Giovanni
47 FASSI Giovanni
49 PIFFERI Giuseppe
50 BIANCO Eligio
51 VERDE Romildo
52 SUSSIO Marcello
53 BERTARELLI Camillo
55 GHEZZI Giuseppe
56 FERRARIO Arturo
57 SAVINI Nerino
58 GOFFIN Georges (BEL)
59 RONCON Giovanni
60 BASSI Gaetano
61 ERBA Angelo
63 SALA Enrico
64 ANNONI Luigi
65 BENAGLIA Telesforo

66 REDAELLI Lorenzo
67 CASETTA Giovanni
68 MARCHESE Giovanni
69 ALBANI Maggiore
70 CHIRONI Emilio
71 CITTERA Domenico
73 DILDA Giuseppe
74 VERCELLINO Guido

Aspiranti

(unsupported amateurs, white jersey)

77 DELLA VALLE Mario
81 BONFANTI Giuseppe
82 PRADA Giuseppe
84 DORATI Alessandro
86 RIPAMONTI Umberto
87 MAGGIORI Floriano
88 RICCI Ciro
89 PALEA Riccardo
90 SANTAGOSTINI Mario
91 PAVESI Angelo
93 SANTAMARIA Luigi
94 MAGRI Luigi
95 GARAVAGLIA
   Gaudenzo
98 MENOZZI Luigi
99 CABRINO Giovanni

1914 Giro D'Italia: Stage Results and Classification

STAGE 1 May 24 MILAN-CUNEO 420km

1. Angelo GREMO in 17h 13'55" (24,373 km/h); 2. Durando at 13'55"; 3. Calzolari s.t.; 4. Girardengo at 44' 20"; 5. Ganna at 44'21"; 6. Sala at 1h04'22"; 7. Oriani at 1h07'15"; 8. Cervi s.t.; 9. Bordin at 1h15'30"; 10. Beni at 1h16'31"; 11. Canepari s.t.; 12. Pratesi at 1h31'07"; 13. Corlaita a2 1h42'42"; 14. Azzini at 1h47'19"; 15. Lucotti s.t.; 16. Casetta at 2h02'50"; 17. Albini at 2h16'31"; 18. Garavaglia s.t.; 19. Lombardi at 2h24'17"; 20. Spinelli at 2h55'40"; 21. Sussio at 2h55'44"; 22. Bertarelli at 3h08'41"; 23. Albani at 3h18'16"; 24. Goi s.r.; 25. Roncon at 4h18'16"; 26. Vercellino s.t.; 27. Ripamonti s.t.; 28. Gerbi at 4h24'27"; 29. Sivocci s.t.; 30. Pavesi s.t.; 31. Robotti at 5h08'05"; 32. Aresu s.t.; 33. Molon s.t.; 34. Bassi s.t.; 35. Fassi s.t.; 36. Palea at 6h53'55"; 37. Marangoni at 6h54'20". *Fasoli, Prada and Santagostino all disqualified for taking a tow from at vehicle.*

STAGE 2 May 26 CUNEO-LUCCA 340km

1. Alfonso CALZOLARI in 14h26'15" (23,584 km/h); 2. Azzini at 23'45"; 3. Girardengo at 34'42"; 4. Albini s.t.; 5. Spinelli at 35'22"; 6. Sala at 39'33"; 7. Pratesi at 44'i3"; 8. Canepari at 44'35"; 9. Goi at 57'28"; 10. Gerbi at 59'38"; 11. Casetta s.t.; 12. Sivocci at 1h05'05"; 13. Bordin at 1h16'0l"; 14. Lombardi at 1h39'06"; 15. Sussio at 1h43'56"; 16. Lucotti at 1h48'13"; 17. Durando at 1h48'58"; 18. Robotti at 1h51'51"; 19. Oriani at 2h01'46"; 20. Pavesi s.t.; 21. Ripamonti at 2h33'50"; 22. Bassi at 3h23'24"; 23. Beni at 3h24'25"; 24. Bertarelli at 4h48'35"; 25. Palea at 6h55'45"; 26. Albani s.t.; 27. Marangoni at 6h59'45"

General Classification:
1. Calzolari in 31h54'15" (with 10-minute penalty for unauthorised assistance); 2. Girardengo at 1h05'07"; 3. Sala at 1h30'0l"; 4. Canepari at 1h47'12";5. Durando at 1h48'58"; 6. Azzini at 1h57'08"; 7. Pratesi at 2h01'44", 8. Bordin at 2h17'36"; 9. Albini at 2h37'18"; 10. Casetta at 2h48'32"; 11. Oriani at 2h55'06"; 12. Spinelli at 3h16'06"; 13. Lucotti at 3h21'36"; 14. Lombardi at 3h49'27"; 15. Goi at 4h11'48"; 16. Sussio at 4h24'45";

17.Beni at 4h34'00"; 18. Gerbi at 5h09'l0"; 19. Sivocci at 5h14'37"; 20. Pavesi at 6h10'18"; 21. Ripamonti at 6h23'55";22. Robotti at 6h46'00"; 23. Bertarelli at 7h39'26"; 24. Bassi at 8h17'41"; 25. Albani at 9h56'11"; 26. Palea at 13h20'50"; 27. Marangoni at 13h25'15"

STAGE 3 May 28 LUCCA-ROME 430,3km
1. Costante GIRARDENGO in 17h28'55" (26,202 km/h); 2. Durando s.t.; 3. Oriani s.t.; 4. Albini s.t.; 5. Azzini s.t.; 6. Lucotti s.t.; 7. Calzolari s.t.; 8. Canepari s.t.; 9. Sala at 14'53"; 10. Bordin at 16'50"; 11. Gerbi at 17'25"; 12. Pavesi s.t.; 13. Sussio at 28'32"; 14. Lombardi at 32'18"; 15. Sivocci at 36'41"; 16. Pratesi at 1h12'05"; 17. Beni at 1h26'44"; 18. Goi at 1h37'22"; 19. Spinelli at 2h11'42"; 20. Bassi at 2h28'57"; 21. Albani at 2h32'05"; 22. Casetta at 2h53'30"; 23. Ripamonti at 4h11'05"; 24. Palea s.t.; 25. Robotti s.t.; 26. Marangoni s.t.

General Classification
1. Calzolari in 49h33'0l"; 2. Girardengo at 55'07"; 3. Sala at 1h34'49"; 4. Canepari at 1h37'12"; 5. Durando at 1h38'57"; 6. Azzini

at 1h47'09"; 7. Bordin at 2h24'25"; 8. Albini at 2h27'19"; 9. Oriani at 2h45'06"; 10. Pratesi at 3h03'59"; 11. Lucotti at 3h11'37"; 12. Gerbi at 3h26'34"; 13. Lombardi at 4h11'46"; 14. Sussio at 4h43'18"; 15. Spinelli at 5h17'46"; 16. Casetta at 5h32'03"; 17. Goi at 5h39'08"; 18. Sivocci at 5h41'17"; 19. Beni at 5h50'43"; 20.Pavesi at 6h18'41"; 21.Ripamonti at 10h25'04"; 22.Robotti at 10h28'36"; 23 Bassi at 10h47'05"; 24.Albani at 12h29'l0"; 25. Palea at 15h32'49"; 26. Marangoni at 17h10'14".

STAGE 4 May 30 ROME-AVELLINO 385,4km
1. Giuseppe AZZINI in 13h18'23" (28,940 km/h); 2. Albini at 35'18"; 3. Pavesi at 42'54"; 4. Calzolari s.t.; 5. Gerbi at 45'18"; 6. Oriani at 48'27"; 7. Canepari at 1h02'50"; 8. Bordin at 1h19'0l"; 9. Sala at 1h20'06" (with 15-minute penalty); 10.Robotti at 1h35'47"; 11. Spinelli at 1h40'30"; 12. Durando at 1h44'32"; 13. Albani at 2h40'32"; 14. Girardengo at 2h45'28"; 15. Sivocci s.t.; 16. Lucotti s.t.; 17. Lombardi s.t.; 18. Palea s.t.; 19. Pratesi s.t.; 20. Goi at 3h10'38"; 21. Ripamonti

at 4h13'19"; 22. Bassi s.t.; 23. Marangoni at 5h13'37"

General Classification:
1. Calzolari in 63h35'18"; 2. Azzini at 1h03'15"; 3. Canepari at 1h57'07"; 4. Sala at 2h12'00"; 5. Albini at 2h19'42"; 6. Durando at 2h36'34"; 7. Oriani at 2h50'37"; 8. Girardengo at 2h57'40"; 9. Bordin at 3h00'32"; 10. Pratesi at 5h09 26 ; 11. Lucotti at 5h14'10"; 12. Gerbi at 5h28'39"; 13. Lombardi at 6h14'18"; 14. Pavesi at 6h18'12"; 15. Spinelli at 7h12'21"; 16. Sivocci at 7h43'50"; 17. Goi at 9h06'52"; 18. Robotti at 11h37'08"; 19.Albani at 13h26'47"; 20. Palea at 13h31'32"; 21 Bassi at 14h06'20"; 22. Ripamonti at 14h11'26"; 23. Marangoni at 22h16'56".

STAGE 5 June 1 AVELLINO-BARI 328,7km
1. Giuseppe AZZINI in 12h50'27" (25,598 km/h); 2. Calzolari at 1h03'21"; 3. Lucotti at 1h32'21"; 4. Durando at 1h49'13"; 5. Canepari at 1h53'38"; 6. Spinelli at 2h04'07"; 7. Albini at 2h05'03"; 8. Sivocci at 2h23'58"; 9. Bordin at 2h32'28";10. Lombardi at 2h32'52"; 11. Robotti at 2h42'45"; 12. Sala at 3h08'42"; 13. Goi s.t.; 14. Oriani at 4h13'42"; 15.

Ripamonti s.t.; 16. Pratesi at 5h39'33"; 17. Bassi s.t.; 18. Gerbi at 7h00'00"; 19. Pavesi s.t.; 20. Albani; 21. Marangoni. *Finish-line staff departed at 22.45 before arrival of last four riders – these riders awarded approximate times.*

General Classification:
1. Azzini in 77h22'00"; 2. Calzolari at 6"; 3. Canepari at 2h47'30"; 4. Albini at 3h31'29"; 5. Durando at 3h22'32"; 6. Bordin at 4h29'45"; 7. Sala at 4h32'28"; 8. Lucotti at 5h13'17"; 9. Oriani at 6h01'05"; 10. Spinelli at 7h13'13"; 11. Lombardi at 7h48'53"; 12. Sivocci at 9h04'35"; 13. Pratesi at 9h45'44"; 14. Goi at 11h12'19"; 15. Robotti at 13h16'47"; 16. Ripamonti at 17h05'59"; 17. Bassi at 18h42'33". *With undefined times: Gerbi, Pavesi, Albani, Marangoni*

STAGE 6 June 3 BARI-L'AQUILA 428km
1. Luigi LUCOTTI in 19h20'47" (22.123 km/h); 2. Durando* at 18'59"; 3. Calzolari* at 34'22"; 4. Canepari* at 43'30"; 5. Pratesi at 1h12'04"; 6. Albini at 2h11'53"; 7. Albani at 2h14'21"; 8. Lombardi at 3h05'34"; 9. Sala at 3h06'03"; 10. Pavesi at 3h08'15"; 1]. Sivocci

at 3h10'00"; 12. Ripamonti at
3h22'29"

*Durando, Calzolari and
Canepari later penalised for taking
a lift in a vehicle: overnight
awarded finishing time of final
rider plus one minute.*

General Classification:
1. Calzolari in 100h28'39"; 2.
Albini at 1h55'31"; 3. Lucotti at
2h04'26"; 4. Canepari at
2h56'40"; 5. Durando at
3h07'17"; 6. Sala at 7h04'l0"; 7.
Lombardi at l0h20'09"; 8. Sivocci
at 11h40'15"; 9. Pratesi at
12h25'28"; 10.Pavesi at
14h34'54"; 11. Ripamonti at
16h54'09"; 12. Albani at
21h50'42"

STAGE 7 June 5 L'AQUILA-
LUGO 429,1km
1. Pierino ALBINI in 17h45'47"
(24,090 km/h); 2. Lucotti s.t.; 3.
Pratesi s.r.; 4. Calzolari at 1"; 5.
Ripamonti s.t.; 6. Sala at 3"; 7.
Canepari at 41"; 8. Durando at
1h14'15"

General Classification:
1. Calzolari in 118h17'22"; 2.
Albini at 1h55'31"; 3. Lucotti at
2h04'25"; 4. Canepari at
2h57'19"; 5. Sala at 3h59'41"; 6.
Durando at 5h11'25"; 7. Pratesi

at 9h20'57"; 8. Ripamonti at
16h54'09"

STAGE 8 June 7 LUGO-
MILANO 429,1 km
1. Pierino ALBINI in 17h03'29"
(24,621 km/h); 2. Canepari at 1";
3. Durando at 2"; 4. Lucotti s.t;
5. Pratesi s.t.; 6. Calzolari s.t.; 7.
Sala at 4"; 8. Ripamonti at 6"

FINAL CLASSIFICATION:
1. Alfonso Calzolari (Stucchi),
   3,162 km in 135h17'56"
   (23.374 km/h)
2. Pierino Albini (Globo) at
   1h57'26"
3. Luigi Lucotti (Maino) at
   2h04'23"
4. Clemente Canepari (Stucchi)
   at 2h57'16"
5. Enrico Sala (Atala - Isolato) at
   3h59'45"
6. Carlo Durando (Maino) at
   5h11'22"
7. Ottavio Pratesi (Alcyon) at
   7h20'58"
8. Umberto Ripamonti
   (Aspiranti) at 16h54'11"

Winner in isolato category:
Enrico Sala

Winner in aspiranto category:
Umberto Ripamonti

Winning team: Stucchi